# THE HOME EDUCATION HANDBOOK

A Comprehensive and Practical Guide
to Educating Children at Home

## GILL HINES and
## ALISON BAVERSTOCK

piatkus

PIATKUS

First published in Great Britain in 2019 by Piatkus

1 3 5 7 9 10 8 6 4 2

Copyright © 2019 Gill Hines and Alison Baverstock

The moral right of the authors has been asserted.

A CIP catalogue record for this book
is available from the British Library.

ISBN 978-0-349-41936-7

Typeset in Sabon by M Rules
Printed and bound in Great Britain by
CPI Group (UK) Ltd, Croydon, CR0 4YY

Papers used by Piatkus are from well-managed forests
and other responsible sources.

Piatkus
An imprint of
Little, Brown Book Group
Carmelite House
50 Victoria Embankment
London EC4Y 0DZ

An Hachette UK Company
www.hachette.co.uk

www.improvementzone.co.uk

*To Leonard Hines and Edna Scott,*
*who sadly did not live to see this completed*
*but whose contribution was significant.*

**Gill Hines** has worked in education for over 40 years, starting out as an infant teacher before going on to work with children and young people with English as an additional language. In the 1980s she began training in her spare time with a national charity for people living with HIV/Aids to lead workshops on living powerfully and creatively in the face of a terminal diagnosis, eventually leading workshops throughout Britain and in Paris. After a period of travel she began working in West London, bringing together her two passions, education and well-being. Originally working with pupils, students, staff and youth workers, she began extending her work at the request of schools to include parents, and today runs dozens of parent workshops in schools and local venues on an ever expanding range of subjects. She also has a growing list of clients for her parent and family consultation work.

**Alison Baverstock** began her working life as a publisher, before establishing a consultancy for authors and the broader creative economy. She has researched and written widely about publishing, writing, art and parenting (with Gill Hines) and is currently Associate Professor of Publishing at Kingston University. A strong believer in the power of the book to connect communities, she is the founder of the award-winning Kingston University Big Read (now operating across four UK universities and influential internationally) and Reading Force, an initiative to encourage Forces families to remain in touch through share reading. She and her husband have four children, and their many postings and house moves required flexibility and brought a great deal of experience of different styles of teaching and schools. She met Gill through attending one of her workshops and this is their fourth book together.

# Contents

## Section 3: Social Skills

# List of Figures

# Foreword by Dr Adam Boddison

Throughout my professional career working with children, home education has been a recurring theme. I have met families where the decision to home educate has been related to the complex learning difficulties of the child, and I have met families where the decision has been related to the high learning potential or the academic giftedness of the child. The reasons given for making the decision to home educate are broad ranging and often related to specific contextual circumstances. The truth is that home-educated children do not have a particular set of characteristics that are distinct from children taught in schools. Both groups span the full range of needs, abilities and cultures, and both deserve a high-quality education. It is important to remember that all learners are unique individuals who will thrive in different contexts, so home education has a crucial role to play as part of a fully inclusive education system.

The decision about whether or not to home educate a child can be complex, and there are often many competing factors to consider. Families can find themselves in situations where they are trying to optimise educational outcomes, happiness and social development for their child alongside a whole host of other considerations. As if this task were not challenging enough, the potential costs and benefits are not well understood by society at large, so parents and carers may have to tackle misconceptions about home education from their wider circle of family and friends.

There are, of course, many success stories, such as those of Emma Watson, Taylor Swift and Serena Williams, all of whom were home educated and have achieved excellence in their chosen careers; however, home education is not an easy option, and if it is poorly delivered, it could cause more problems than it solves. Conversely, if it is in place for the right reasons and properly delivered, home education has the potential to deliver an unparalleled level of personalised provision, and it could certainly be the making of a child.

Reflecting on my own time as a schoolteacher, I am acutely aware that children can spend a significant proportion of their time at school and away from their families. For some children, this delicate balance between home life and school life works well, but for others school education can come at the expense of stronger family relationships, so I am delighted to see that Gill Hines and Alison Baverstock have emphasised the importance of the family relationships within this handbook.

The handbook comes at a time when the school system is in the midst of major change and at a time when the number of children being home educated is accelerating. Regardless of whether the rationale is dissatisfaction with the school system or a desire for fully personalised provision, it is widely acknowledged that home educators want to provide a high-quality learning experience for their children, and this handbook is an excellent resource for making this aspiration a reality. Reading the handbook in its entirety will be valuable for both current and prospective home educators, but the handbook is arguably an excellent resource as a day-to-day reference guide, too. The format is accessible, using a question-and-answer format where appropriate and drawing on personal experience through case studies to provide context. The tone is non-judgemental and explores options from different perspectives rather than seeking to prescribe a particular right or wrong approach.

Ultimately, parents and carers are looking to make decisions that will be right for their children's education and will prepare them well for the future. For those opting for home education, *The Home Education Handbook* is a useful companion containing a wealth of knowledge, experience and expertise that could transform a good home education into a great one.

*Dr Adam Boddison, Chief Executive of National Association of Special Educational Needs*

# Acknowledgements

We would like to thank our commissioning editor at Piatkus, Jillian Young, who suggested we write this book, and then our editor Anna Steadman, who inherited the title and has been such a source of support and encouragement. Thanks also to copyeditor Jan Cutler and publicist Jess Gulliver for their work on the book.

We would also like to thank Alison and Oliver Allmand-Smith, John Baker, Bridget Blankley, Mary Blankley, Adam Boddison, Jane Braithwaite, Andrew Brown, Izzy Byers, Tracey Gaggiotti, Stacia Garland, Ebony and Aariyah Hope, Sue Leney, Suzanne Marchment, Janette Simpson, Charlotte Phillips, Andrew McAleer, Kim Murray, Lemn Sissay, Priscilla Smith, Annette Williams, and the many people who helped us without wishing to be named. Finally, thanks to our family and friends for support throughout.

# Introduction

If you are thinking of home educating your child, your initial surprise might be at how easy it is to turn intention into reality. Taking your child out of school (or 'deregistering' as it's officially termed) requires giving formal notice to the proprietor of their current (or enrolled) school, usually the head teacher, informing them of your intention to take personal responsibility for their education in future and asking that they be removed from the school's register of enrolled pupils. Thereafter, there may be visits or inspections to check that all is going well, depending on your child's needs and your local council policy, but if there are no concerns, you may find that you are left to get on with delivering education from your home as you see best. You will find that there are lots of resources and support groups to help you do just that. From good-value educational materials to communities of parents willing to share their experience, there is no shortage of advice. Why therefore is this book needed?

**Clarification of the objectives of the home-school experience** for the parent and child. In an exam-driven world, opting for a different kind of educational experience can allow a gifted child to shine, a creative child to develop their skills and interests, and a child in need of extra care and attention to get just what they need to thrive and achieve. Being clear of your aims and intentions in relation to the decision to home educate is vital in developing the right learning environment for your child.

**Objective guidance**, based on our long experience of working with children and young people, and of providing advice and support to parents, teachers and schools. Our strong empathy with those seeking to deliver home educating, for whatever reason, enables us to offer considered advice in seeking to identify the broad characteristics of a 'well-educated' young person as a guiding principle, and supporting parents who have taken the decision to home educate to identify and exploit development opportunities and plan creative ways to fill the potential gaps in provision that might arise from not being part of a large institution.

**Full consideration of the socialisation of home-educated children** is an issue that is widely mentioned (often as the 's' word) but not always fully engaged with. We consider how socialisation means more than having nice manners or an ability to converse with adults, and we explore how to support the home educated child in the development of age-appropriate social skills, promoting their ability to make and maintain friendships and to build relationships with their peers.

**Exploration of both why and how best to ensure you and your child** remain up-to-date and engaged with the world. Whatever your reasons for thinking about home educating, and there can be many, both those seeking this solution and the wider society need to think about the longer term and how to integrate all within the community. Home educating does not have to mean isolation, and we will offer top tips for developing rounded adults who are comfortable with the world.

**Consideration of emotional resilience** and how to build it within home educated children. Resilience is now widely identified as the key characteristic of engaged effective citizens. It's needed in the workplace and at home, and it correlates with an individual's ability to self-sustain and develop a positive attitude to life. Emotional resilience is the ability to get along with others without feeling hurt or diminished by their behaviour. With extensive experience of running workshops on how to encourage resilience, Gill is particularly well placed to offer advice. Many children are home educated because they are unable to manage in mainstream schools for a number of reasons, most of which are beyond their control. For these children the development of self-belief and emotional resilience are imperative if they are to integrate later in life.

**Advice on motivation,** for all involved. Parents managing home educating for their children need to think about how they can motivate them to learn, how to ensure the learning is both fun and interactive, and how they can maintain their own stamina in delivering and maintaining an experience of benefit to all.

Throughout the process of writing this book we have interviewed and shared thoughts with many home-educating parents and with young people who have experienced home education. You will find these interviews boxed for easy access.

## A FATHER'S EXPERIENCE OF EDUCATING
## HIS DAUGHTER AT HOME

**How did the decision to educate your child yourself come about?**

Our daughter had been in primary school for two and a half years, but was having anxiety and friendship problems that were affecting her sleep, her mental health and her overall happiness. She is naturally bright and responsive to learning, but did not react at all well to the formal structure of a school day, the slow pace of learning to make sure others can keep up and the inability to focus on subjects that interested her more than others.

She was very sensitive to perceived injustices or to moments of unkindness from her friends – the kinds of things you could help her address quickly as a parent if present at the time, but which she instead would dwell on all day and often not tell us until bedtime, when her worries and fears would prevent her getting to bed at a reasonable hour. It was unhealthy and damaging to her overall well-being, and while her school did introduce some measures to help her address her worries, and to give her a small amount of more personal attention, it was causing us great heartache to see her so unhappy. But when a relative who is also home educating talked to us about the benefits, we looked into it further, and realised just what a good fit it could be for us. My wife comes from an informal education background and was able to commit herself to being available for our daughter 100 per cent of the time, so we felt that this would be a much healthier way for her to develop. Deregistering from the school was an instantaneous thing when it came to it, and after a period of adjusting and just getting school out of her system (known as 'de-schooling'), we have settled into a regular routine where we let her determine how a day progresses for the most part, and she finds the ways in which she wants to learn.

**At what stage did you start to home educate?**
She had experienced reception and year 1 of school and was just over halfway through year 2, so she left school at the age of seven. She's eight as I write this, so we're approaching a year out of the school environment.

**How do you manage your daughter's time?**
There are numerous ways to approach home education, and some styles can be more timetabled and based around having certain subjects studied on particular days – without the negative connotations of a formal 'school' day. Our personal approach is very much to 'un-school' our daughter, and let her find her own learning style. There are no timetables, rigid lesson plans or examinations.

**What are the advantages of home educating for your family?**
The advantages of home educating are endless. Our daughter is able to find her own learning style, is able to feel comfortable in her surroundings, her activities and her friendships, without being forced to do certain things at certain times, and to keep pace with 30 other children. She is able to mix with and learn from people of all ages, rather than just a select group of people of exactly her age group, which seems much more natural. She is able to pursue a subject

or a project fully and in many different ways, and learning becomes an all-day thing, no longer stuck in a 9am to 3pm structure. There is much more time and opportunity to take advantage of activities and travel because we are no longer limited just to weekends and school holidays to do things with her. Local home education groups have provided lots of chances to try things out that she would rarely get a chance to do in a school environment, and ensure she doesn't miss out on chances to socialise and make close friends.

**What are the challenges?**
It's not practical for everyone. We are lucky that we were able to have one parent available full-time to be there for her, but for families with two working parents, the option to do this would be much more limited – not impossible, but certainly much more complicated to arrange. Dealing with the local authorities is also fraught with worry. We've not had a bad experience of that ourselves yet, but we have heard of others who have, and we have tailored our responses to the local authority very carefully as a result. It's not uncommon to have requests for samples of work or for home visits. Neither is a legal requirement, though, and it's important to get involved with local and national home education groups for advice from your peers, and to have a clear grounding on what is reasonable to share with the local authority. Of course, they need to ensure that you aren't neglecting or abusing your child, but there's a balance to be struck between ensuring that isn't the case and interfering to the degree that the parent is basically enduring an Ofsted inspection. So often the stance is combative, and home educators can seem secretive or prickly as a result,

but that shouldn't be the case, and it's largely driven by a lack of public awareness. This is still treated as a weird and wacky way of letting your kids be 'feral', instead of a caring, informed and evidence-based way of raising a child in the best possible style. Similarly, a key disadvantage can be the frowns and disapproval of friends or family members who simply don't understand this, as it wasn't what they did. Books like this are needed as much for sceptical grandparents as they are for parents considering home education.

**How do you manage the education process?**
We deliver it ourselves, my wife all day round, and me outside work hours. We don't have tutors, although we know other people who do go down that route for particular subjects. Informally, all kinds of friends, family and others are involved in nurturing and educating our daughter, of course.

**Has anything taken you by surprise?**
There has been something surprising every day. The overall improvement in her level of happiness and confidence has been remarkable; she's unrecognisable from the anxious, shy person she was a year ago. But what hasn't changed is how kind, sensitive and loving she is – it's been a delight to see how much she thinks of others when given more opportunity to make her own choices. There have been many moments when I've been impressed by her willingness and ability to learn something specific, without the pressure of 'you must learn this now'. She's currently learning to code, and within just a couple of weeks of teaching herself, she seems to understand all the mechanics and is making customised games to order.

**Would you recommend home education?**
Wholeheartedly. Technology means it's a very different world from the one I grew up in, and one where learning is available to all in ways that were inconceivable even 20 years ago. The traditional school structure seems ridiculously anti-quated as a result. I can see no logic in imposing a system of schooling upon a child that makes them unhappy, when they can build their skills and knowledge in a way that better suits them and end up a much more confident, able and rounded person ready to enter the workplace. There's no obstacle to them taking exams or entering university if they wish, further down the line, but even if they don't, I suspect that the CV of the future will be less about formal qualifications and more a portfolio of what you have done with your life.

**Do you think it would be a different experience for just one child/more children?**
Probably, but no more so than it's a different experience simply parenting one child or more than one child. We only have one child, but we know many people with more than one child being home educated, and it seems to work very well, sharing activities, but also pursuing individual interests as much as possible. Sharing your time between a small number of children is still going to lead to a better learning outcome and more personalised attention than a teacher sharing their time with 30 children in a rigid way.

**How do you maintain your daughter's contacts with other children/people?**
There are numerous home education groups you can join for regular contact or for one-off activities. There are networks

on Facebook that are invaluable. There are lots of opportunities for socialising, and just being freed up from the routine of school runs and school terms makes this much more likely, in fact. Our daughter is far more confident around other people, and is developing much healthier relationships than she did in a fixed school environment.

# Section 1

# Home Educating a Child:
# Why, When, What and How?

# 1

# The Benefits of Home Educating

There are currently no accurate figures available for the number of children being home educated in the UK, but most estimates vary between 35,000 and 50,000. Sources agree that these are rising dramatically year on year. Between 2011 and 2017, the numbers of home-educated children almost doubled, with a rise of 141 per cent of pupils in year 6 being deregistered over the same period. Speaking on Radio 4's *Weekend Woman's Hour* on 3 March 2018, Dr Helen Lees, Reader in Alternative Education Studies at Newman University in Birmingham, again confirmed uncertainty about how many children are involved but thought it likely to be 1–2 per cent of the relevant UK population.

The reasons why parents choose to withdraw their child from formal education are varied, but there are common threads running through the motivation of those involved. Our first chapter, therefore, provides background: on how the schooling on offer to our children might not be what's needed for the future, and how many parents are viewing home educating as part of seeking more flexible solutions for the education of their child. There are some inspiring success stories to draw upon.

Those home educating often talk about the environment it

offers for the development of the individual and the growth of entrepreneurialism, and it's interesting to note that home education has produced a variety of people who have strongly influenced wider society. The former US Secretary of State Condoleezza Rice and the first US president George Washington were both home educated. Home education has been the pathway for many children (or parents) with specific talents for whom attendance at regular school might have been difficult. Examples include prominent and influential sports stars (e.g. Serena and Venus Williams, Maria Sharapova), entertainers (Taylor Swift and Justin Timberlake) and actors. The British actors Emma Watson and Millie Bobbie Brown were both home educated; Emma Watson is now a UN Goodwill Ambassador, and Millie Bobbie Brown was named as one of *Time* magazine's most influential people in the world at the age of just 13. Both the actress Nadia Sawalha and the singer/television presenter Jamelia are home-educating parents.

Let's also not forget that home educating was originally the norm. Whereas in the UK the 1870 Education Act established state provision for schooling for all children from five until 12 years, even after that date those with sufficient funds might continue to educate at home, either because they preferred it or due to the child's inclination (for example, the Queen and her sister Princess Margaret were both home educated).

Let's begin by exploring the benefits sought by those both considering and delivering home educating.

## An alternative to the 'sausage factory' of modern schools

The education system, as well as individual schools, is exerting unprecedented pressure that many parents find counter-productive to the experience they want to secure for their child. School league tables, fixed developmental targets, larger class sizes with lower adult-to-child ratios, new educational initiatives that require changes in the way children are taught and which stress the teachers trying to deliver them, financial stringencies over budgets – all are leading to unparalleled pressures that affect everyone involved: school management, teachers, parents, carers, children – and wider society.

With increased concentration on English and maths, the broader curriculum is curtailed, and wider learning is made more difficult in the time available within the school day. Many parents feel schools provide an overly competitive and unhelpful atmosphere, with children acutely aware of where they sit within class achievement levels. They worry that 'winning', grades and SAT scores are being emphasised, which, although it might suit some children, does not suit all – and that in the process a delight in learning is being squeezed out. Schools are not moulding themselves to the needs of pupils and the wider community; children are being made to fit the system.

## A HOME-EDUCATING MOTHER COMMENTS

Home education means you have more freedom to teach what you want to teach and when you want to. Looking back, I think I might have put them into secondary school slightly earlier, in order to access expertise around areas of the curriculum with which I was not familiar, but it was an enjoyable period that brought us very close as a family.

## A better response to the fast-paced momentum of society

Modern society needs entrepreneurs who can motivate themselves rather than simply to prove that they are good at exams. The current education system, which requires young people to follow the rules and each syllabus, is not necessarily creating young people fit for the modern workplace. More and more often we are seeing successful individuals who have a portfolio of skills that can be adapted to a range of settings. Although there will always be a need for experts in all fields of knowledge, those predicting the worker of the future describe the kind of individuals that will be needed in an increasingly fast-moving world in terms of broad skills and open thinking.[1] They talk of the need for individual resilience, self-motivation, flexibility, self-reliance, entrepreneurialism and a capacity for free thinking – characteristics that are likely to develop more from individuals recognising and developing their own aptitudes, abilities and interests rather than through an overwhelming emphasis on obedience and meeting prescribed goals.

## Working at a child's own pace

Parents often seek ways of using methods suited to their child's individual learning style. Children undoubtedly learn in different ways, not all in the same way, and in recent years we have become used to discussions about those who are 'visual', 'auditory' or 'experiential' learners or 'collaborative', 'competitive' or 'avoidant' learners. But for all the effort put into identifying learning style and applying these to teaching methods, no beneficial results have really emerged. It is almost impossible to provide differentiated learning to each individual pupil. Although there might be common factors in learning, each individual will learn differently simply because each person, of any age, is different. Not only do their styles of learning and interest in learning vary but, just as with all of us, their learning will also fluctuate according to mood, family upsets or events, health issues, personal interest in the subject and energy levels. Whereas some children like rules, others do not; some children like to be told what to do, others to create 'what ifs?' and then to work out what happens next. Home educating can enable the matching of empathetic learning methods that suit the individual day by day, prioritising the child's abilities, interests, passions and skills – something that is simply not possible within the existing school system with its time constraints, curriculum pressures and pupil numbers.

While considering the particular needs of individual children, it is important also to consider the best way of supporting very able children, who can appear disengaged from what is going on in the formal classroom for their year group, and hence irritate the teacher, simply because they are bored (in the same way that adults who are familiar with the issues in a meeting, and hence do not find it stimulating, might switch off). Such children may have a capacity to learn, and an intellectual potential that outstrips those of their classmates, but they might find social interaction much more difficult. One mother of such a child particularly recommended PPUK (Potential Plus UK, formerly the National Association for Gifted Children),[2] especially the workshops and activities they organise for both children and their parents.

## Prioritising experiential and self-directed learning

Children also develop by learning how to do things rather than simply being told or memorising, creating conceptual understanding through experiential and hands-on learning, working things out through trial and error and then reflecting afterwards. Learning through direct experience can be managed in schools up to a point, but in the time- and money-conscious modern school, experiential learning that can't be done at a table or desk is unlikely to happen. The days of nature walks, field trips and community involvement are over for many children, as red tape and admin make anything in the real world outside the classroom so much more complicated to access. For the home-educated child, learning can be a 24-hour-a-day, seven-day-a-week exploration of the world around them, the people they interact with and the experiences they have, just by being alive.

Schools might want to offer children a range of opportunities and encourage children to choose which they want to pursue, but with the current stressed curriculum, and pressure on targets, there is less time to do this. In many secondary schools it is simply impossible for children to choose to study exactly which subjects they wish because of timetabling issues. If the economics lessons are taking place at the same time as the geography lessons, students will need to choose one or the other. Home educating, although it might not be able to meet every child's requirements in situ, does offer time to develop, encourage and enable self-directed learning, thereby opening the door to a lifetime of new learning opportunities.

## More individual attention

Children learn best in small groups or in one-to-one settings with others – impossible in the average-size class seen particularly in state schools. Private schooling is growing in popularity, with parents often attracted by smaller class sizes and pupil-to-adult ratios that give more time to individuals. Home educating offers the potential for working in one-to-one settings or small groups most of the time. There may be drawbacks to this, some solutions for which we will discuss later in this book, but there are also many advantages, particularly for children with needs or abilities that require a level of special help and attention that mainstream classes struggle to provide.

Schools spend a great deal of time managing pupil behaviour, with many pupils under-achieving because of their own behaviour or the behaviour of others that diverts their attention. The home educated child might achieve far more learning in a shorter space of time then their traditionally schooled peers, simply because the need for constant behaviour management is not redirecting the available adult attention.

Evidence is clear that boys tend to receive more of a teacher's time than girls, which may reinforce the widely projected stereotype that girls are less important than boys to both groups. In 2017, UK newspapers reported new evidence from the US, showing that at the age of five, children did not see any great difference between the sexes, but by the age of six girls were more likely to consider boys cleverer than girls and to steer clear of activities they deemed difficult.[3]

## The flexibility to maximise family interaction and personal body clocks

The modern workplace increasingly requires versatility, with many people moving to flexible contracts that no longer depend on a nine-to-five working day or full-time attendance at a particular base, and which can be fitted around both employer and employee preferences. Along similar lines, the freelance economy is growing.

At the same time, childcare is expensive, and there are parents who seek to match their working hours to their children's routines, both to coordinate childcare and to ensure they have quality time at home and with their children. Home educating fits well into this pattern and is at its best when home-educating parents form networks with others nearby to provide variety for their children in terms of venues and input as well as opportunities to work, explore and study with others.

Home educating can make good use of the time available. Within formal school environments, a lot of time is taken up on administration: learning routines and roles, register taking, disciplinary issues, and repetition to cater for different abilities within the classroom. Home educating offers possibilities for creating a learning environment more centred on the individual child's particular circumstances, with more parental-child interaction and more quality time – that fits with the body clocks of those involved.

In summary, those attracted by home educating are drawn by the possibilities it offers for exciting and engaging their children in learning, for fostering a love of learning that fits with the preferences of their child, which enables sufficient time to develop and pursue ideas and to nurture and develop the whole individual. Later chapters will concentrate on how to deliver and support this experience, how to encourage the children's effective social interaction and understanding of others, and how to maintain the motivation and capabilities of those managing the experience of all involved.

## The disadvantages of home educating

Having explored the benefits, it's only fair to put the other side of the situation, and here are common issues that have been raised as we have researched our book.

### The multi-tasking required

**A HOME-EDUCATING MOTHER COMMENTS**

One difficulty was that as a parent who was home educating I had to be everything to them – mother, counsellor, classroom teacher, PE teacher and school nurse – at times this did not permit enough distance and could feel overwhelming.

### The associated costs

Employing tutors and buying courses for your home educated children can be expensive, as can the cost of entering examinations (paid for by the local authority if they are being taken through schools), so many parents do not realise that there is an associated cost. For information on how to develop a curriculum and manage external tutors, and for options for sharing the process, see Chapters 5 and 6.

## A MOTHER WHO REGULARLY COUNSELS PARENTS WHO HOME EDUCATE COMMENTS

A parent who decides to home educate ideally needs another parent who is both working full-time and fully (and particularly emotionally) supportive. If you decide to home educate, although you are saving the local authorities a lot of money by not taking up any of the state provision to which your child is legally entitled, there is no additional funding for your child's specific or general needs.

A particular difficulty, if you are home educating, is trying to get an EHPC (Education, Health and Care Plan – what used to be referred to as a 'statement'), partly because they are complex documents to fill in, but also because some of the information you need to provide comes from the local authority, and that is much easier to obtain if you are established within local authority educational provision. Yet without an EHPC the various treatments that would really benefit your child (such as speech and language provision, and holistic treatments) become impossibly expensive.

## A loss of income

If a parent gives up their job to manage their child's education at home, they will lose their income, and this can also result in missing the workplace and experiencing social isolation.

Although a parent who gives up their work to educate their child at home can protect their government pension rights by ensuring state child benefits are paid to them, they will probably not continue to build up their personal or company pension, which can lead to significantly reduced income once pension age is reached.

## Limited access to their peer group

Children need to learn to get along with each other, to manage conflict, cooperate, collaborate and compromise – the four Cs that are just as important as the three Rs. Schools have never really fully allowed children to learn social behavioural skills, as rules and behavioural restrictions are designed to keep the peace and maintain it rather than to encourage free socialisation. There are lessons in many schools, mostly under the heading of Personal Social and Health Education (PSHE), which help children develop their knowledge and understanding of behaviour, although it has been known for many years that children learn social behaviour from other children by interacting and observing, not through adults 'teaching' them or instructing them. While learning to interact and share needs to be happening long before school starts, changes in family and wider social structures may result in fewer opportunities for truly free play without constant adult supervision. The 'helicopter parent' is a modern phenomenon: the parent who hovers above children's interaction seeking to sort out difficulties and ensure that children get along, thus blocking the natural learning in managing relationships and asserting the wants and needs within groups that children need. Too often home becomes more like school rather than school becoming more like home.

A recent 20-year study conducted through Princeton University[4] has shown a clear link between young children with good social skills and future success in education and employment as well as a reduction in addiction and abuse problems.

At the same time, there is increased peer pressure on parents to be over-protective – to feel that they are responsible for everything their child says and does. In the process we have lost sight of how children interact with each other, with a growing view that children are inexperienced adults rather than children.

Children need to develop as children first, and enabling them to do this is an important part of encouraging them to develop as rounded individuals. Those pursuing home educating may feel this is best done within a less pressurised and time-rich environment. But home educators need to keep in mind that in a traditional school there may be children of all backgrounds with all kinds of unusual ways of behaving. Although this can obviously have problems for one's child, those home educating need to think about how to ensure a diversity of experience for their children as a preparation for meeting all kinds of people in later life, not just those who have come from families with similar ideas.

## Potential physical and social isolation

If you are home educating because of geographical isolation, the effect can be increased. For guidance on how to build a community, see Chapter 9.

For those home educating children with special needs, it can be difficult to share teaching/responsibilities with other parents in a similar position, and feelings of isolation can be particularly profound. What is more, those taking this route might not initially have chosen it but rather felt pressurised into doing so through the increasing unsuitability of provision offered.

## A HOME-EDUCATING MOTHER COMMENTS

My seven-year-old son, my third child (who has two much older siblings) has attention deficit disorder and a range of other special needs, all of which were discussed with, and I thought understood by, his local state primary school before he started as a 'rising five'. He is not aggressive, rather over-enthusiastic, so, for example, when story time happened at the end of the day he wanted to be part of the action, to make the noises of the animals, rather than sit quietly on the mat and listen. I found increasingly that he was being excluded – from school trips (on the grounds that they were not educational so he would not benefit) and from wider class activities (so during story time he had to sit in a corner of the classroom with a key worker and do something else rather than be part of the group activity). Of course, this impacted on his relationships with his class-mates and their parents. I raised this with the teachers, and as it kept happening I found I had to do so again and again, but it reached a point where I was just fed up with battling on his behalf and decided to educate him at home myself. Before I made the decision to do so I looked up to see what provision there was locally for him to attend groups and meet other children, and for us both to meet other parents in the same position. Luckily, I found several groups that we could join.

For his education, which I now manage myself, I use materials that are suited to his particular needs and learning style, and we get along reasonably well. The groups we come to, so we get out of the house, are very important.

Parenting a child with special educational needs can be a very lonely and draining experience, and in the process the parents might neglect themselves, their own needs and their relationships. It's widely acknowledged that at least half of those parenting a child with special educational needs are themselves single parents, as the strains of parenting impact very significantly on most relationships.

## Feeling criticised

Many home educators report stress from friends and family who feel free to criticise a decision to home educate without investigating either the needs that led them to take such a decision, or the associated processes and outcomes. News coverage of occasional tragedies that feature home-educated children (for example the Turpin Family in California, 2017)[5] can lead to all home-educating parents feeling generally criticised, with an implied, and evidently wrong, assumption that all home educated children may be abused and there are no abused children attending mainstream schools. For guidance on how to promote your child's social skills, see Chapters 9 and 11.

## Attracting attention from social services

This might be perceived as hostile to your endeavours and overall philosophy, and hence experienced as stressful. For guidance on how to manage a productive relationship with your local authority, see Chapters 3 and 4.

## CASE STUDY: JESSICA

Jessica, aged 22, is the eldest of three children and was home schooled for the last two years of primary school, missing years 5 and 6. Gill asked Jessica what were the best things about being home educated:

- Being able to follow her own interests – she was into geology at the time.
- Having lots of creative outlets and drama – she remembers putting on plays with other children from her home education network.
- The flexibility – she loved being outside all summer.
- More time – she appreciated being able to take more time to settle into a task. She was diagnosed as being dyslexic three weeks before her finals and, looking back, she thinks this also affected her performance at school.

When asked about the not-so-good aspects of the time, she commented that the relationship with her mother was not so good, intensified through home education when they were together all the time. She also commented that when she started secondary school there were lots of social conventions that she didn't understand. She remembered someone from the local education authority coming to visit and being scared of the process.

In terms of how she was taught, it was entirely flexible. She attended dance classes from the age of five until she was 15, so that provided a stable group in her life. She went on visits to museums with her mother, they had lots of science equipment at home because of Mum's role and at some point she remembers someone from her network having a touring science bus (for experiments on board, as used in rural communities or to go to schools that are likely to benefit)[6] to their home and enjoying that.

Jessica and her mother regularly met up with other parents and children from a local home-school network, and she made some friends from that group. They often did visits to places of interest or worked together in a small group.

Jessica's experience highlights a couple of important factors about home educating that we will address throughout this book:

1. Whilst many parents and children experience closer relationships through home education, if the relationship between educating parent and child is troubled or conflicted, these issues can be exacerbated by increased contact.

2. Removing a child from school because they are experiencing difficulties with peer interaction may only defer problems if the child is to be later reintegrated into school. Social skills don't simply 'grow' as a child matures but are developed by a process of experience and reflection. Taking a child away from free peer interaction to an environment where peer contact is tightly controlled by adults – in this case deciding when and where interactions take place – and having parents present throughout will not help a child develop coping strategies or normative behaviour with peers, though it may well result in a young person who is extremely confident

and socially adept with adults. We have devoted a
lot of time in this book to helping home-educated
children develop the skills they need to interact
equally well with others of their own age.

Interestingly the years 4, 5 and 6 in UK schools (from approx-
imately 8 to 11 years) are the years in which there is a marked
increase in independent social experimentation, and they are
therefore important years for developing peer group interaction skills. Gill reports that these are the ages at which most
of the individual clients she works with begin having problems
with being part of groups.

---

### CASE STUDY: PRISCILLA

Priscilla is a trained secondary school teacher (RE) and
the former housemistress of a girls' boarding school. She
and her husband home educated their four daughters
(now ranging in age from 18 to 25).

We asked her about the advantages of home educating:
'An early advantage is children not having to leave the
home environment before they are ready and not having
to suffer separation anxiety. Home-educated children
generally know where they belong.

'In the process of home educating you get to know your
child really well, their learning habits, preferences and interests, and hence can match the educational experience and
intended outcomes to the individual, developing a curriculum and wider educational experience that really suits them.

'In the process, the relationship between parent and
child changes. I had been a teacher, so was used to

classroom management, but I found my style had to develop into encouraging my daughters to participate in their learning and keeping them on task, without maintaining classroom discipline in an overly formal manner.

'For parents who are home educating, all the additional learning they acquire is a big advantage; they are constantly learning themselves.'

In talking about the downsides, Priscilla said that home education can be isolating. 'Discussions of home education always home in on the need to socialise the children, and this was a particular priority for us. Our girls went away on drama courses and camps, and interacted with as many people as possible. As a family we also spent several months in France, so we could all develop our French, and all the children went to a local school during that time. I liked the way every child in the village went to the same school, which I felt boosted connectivity and a sense of community. The girls became very used to mixing and getting on with all sorts of people, so much so that when they did go to a formal educational setting, at 16, people were often surprised how many people they knew – whereas a child in a formal school all the way through might only know others in the same class, not even the same year group.

'Home educating is a very immersive experience, and it can be stressful on the parental relationship if one partner is completely absorbed in the children. The best experiences of home educating that we have seen have been when both parents are involved. Whereas I managed most of the teaching, my husband would regularly take the girls out on day trips.'

If the reason for home educating is the social anxiety

of the parent, home educating can be an experience that further isolates the child, and having children shut away at home is not a good idea.

'Home educating can be an anxious process, and certainly in the early days I worried that I would not be able to do it, or that inspectors would come along and tell me that I was doing a bad job. My husband's siblings were pretty dismissive of home education, and my own parents were initially very worried by the course that we were taking. They accepted that I was a qualified secondary teacher, but they were concerned about my competencies in teaching small children. Others helpfully volunteered further feedback. I once sat next to a judge at a dinner who had recently adjudicated in a case of a child who was home educated, isolated and neglected – and as a result gave me a lecture on the folly of what we were doing. But I'm resilient by nature and was able to point out that one bad example does not invalidate the principle.'

Would they do it again? 'Definitely, but this time I would do it better. We started home educating 20 years ago, when hardly anyone else did it, but since then we have seen it work really well in a variety of situations – because people home educate for a variety of different reasons.

'Since we began, so many resources have become available to home educators, whereas all the materials I initially used were from my own head. I would also change my expectations: as a teacher myself I initially expected my children to behave in our home classroom as they would have done in a school, and I had to learn to change my approach from one that relied on management to one that built a relationship.

'As time went on, I realised that home educating is not just about academic learning, it's also about relationships and family cohesion, developing the whole person in life-long learning. I learnt that education takes place not just in the school room but also around the dining table, where we would often extend the conversation we had been having within school time into long discussions. I learnt that no subject was isolated and everything related to everything else; the learning environment was fully integrated into home life – so the learning went on over weekends, indeed within whatever we were doing. Conversations were very important – although sometimes I would read to them at mealtimes.

'I feel, too, that home educating them means that they have been fully involved at home, and seen the day-to-day experiences that are part of everyday life. When I nursed my sister through the final stages of her illness, they were involved and aware. Having not been excluded, they were not frightened of what was going on.

'Looking back, over the years there have been some big highs; for example, a local music student, who formed three choirs in the area for her practical dissertation, decided to unite them all to sing in public, and two of my girls were chosen to be soloists. It was interesting that they were entirely unafraid to get up and perform, and yet their inner confidence was in no way affected – they were not showing off. Similarly, I remember my eldest daughter going off to attend a drama course and being given the lead narrating role, with the producer commenting that "this is the child who can hold the whole thing together".'

## Questions and answers

**Q:** *How bad does it have to get before you consider home educating?*
**A:** The first response to this is, bad for whom? The decision to home educate is not just about your child, but also about you and your life – and the lives of your wider family.

It's important to say from the very start that home educating is not an easy option for parent or child, just a different one. Great benefits can come from home educating – such as bringing the parent-child relationship much closer through the learning and exploring that is shared, and working together in a hands-on approach to education. But home educating can also be the source of great stress, because in order to make it work, the parent may have to make significant sacrifices in their own working or personal life. If your work or career delivers particular satisfaction to you, then the compromises required by the decision to home educate can be significant, not to mention the cost of tutors (if you decide to employ them) and the loss of income. Home educating your child may simply require more resources than you have either to give or are able to access.

The decision to home educate also requires some real honesty about why your child is not doing as well at school as they might be, or is just not as happy there as you would like them to be. If your child has particular support needs, although the school may not be able to deliver them, you might find that you are similarly challenged.

Many parents say what they want above all is for their child to be happy. If they are not happy, and it's school that is making them unhappy, home educating may indeed be a solution. But bear in mind that this will mean a complete change in the way that you and your wider family live your lives.

Making a decision to home educate will almost certainly be one of the hardest things you have ever done. Whether it also turns out to be one of the best may be down to the thinking you put into why you are taking this big step and how your aims are going to be turned into reality.

**Q:** *My teenage son doesn't want to go to school any more. He keeps taking time off, and although he may leave to go to school, I regularly get reports that he does not turn up or is sighted in town. Should I come down heavy on him and insist he goes, or is now the time to let him stay at home and arrange for tutors to teach him?*

**A:** Teenagers not attending school involves an everyday battle for most secondary schools, and for parents faced with this situation every day it can feel like a battle too. Some young people are unhappy and just don't go, refusing to get up in time, others leave the house but never arrive, others check in for registration but then absent themselves on school property. Thinking about home educating might offer an obvious solution to the problem.

Before taking such a big step, don't give up on formal schooling altogether. Do talk to the school, as many have a flexible attitude, with special programmes available and will go to significant lengths to ensure young people stay in the system, particularly as key examinations approach. Taking a young person out of school before they take key examinations, and away from the momentum of the rest of the class, could be very difficult in the long run. If they subsequently decide that they do need the qualifications they have missed, studying on their own can be much harder. Bear in mind, too, that young people who don't want to go to school may not be that keen on being home educated either. If it is the whole area of education or of being expected to fit in with a system of restriction and discipline that bothers them, they may be happy to do nothing. For a teenager to be home educated successfully they need a high level of self-motivation, to have something that they really enjoy on which to build a wider basis for involvement. That something need not be an academic subject – it might be art or music, but it could as easily be skateboarding or running – but there needs to be a central passion to the learning experience around which to build their wider involvement in study outside the classroom.

Another option before proceeding to home educate is to encourage your young person to talk to someone other than you or their existing school. If they are able to articulate their hopes and dreams to a third party, along with information on what it is they find so difficult about school, you might find a way forward. Similarly, you should try to find people to talk to who are organising home educating for their teenagers and find out how the experience works for them.

In conclusion, our advice would be to hold off doing anything on the spur of the moment, and to be aware of the significant task of organising and planning or of employing home tutors for their education at home. Unless all parties concerned feel an excitement about the idea of home educating your young person, and that excitement has outlasted a realistic discussion of the alternatives and processes involved, then this may not be the right way to go. Teachers should be particularly wary of how difficult it is to home educate their own young people: teaching others might not necessarily equip you well to teach your own child.

**Q:** *Our family have the opportunity to live abroad for six months, due to a work placement, and as our children are* *only in primary school I am tempted to take them out of school and go too. It's the opportunity of a lifetime, and the chance for us to all go and have an adventure together. Their school has warned us that this will be disruptive for their education and that having taken them out, we might not get back into the system when we return. I don't want to send them to board as they are so young, but to be honest I don't want to miss out on the chance of six months away in a country I might otherwise never see. What should we do?*

**A:** Go for it. The experience of being in a school system in a different country (and climate and season) will be educative, and even if you are not able to get your children into a school you can always use the curricula that are available online and home school for the six months. You could get each child to complete a log of their experiences and provide interesting material for them to look back on one day. Most daily experiences on the road can be turned into educative ones, from reading timetables to analysing menus for anticipated overall costs.

When you get back to the UK there may be some catching up to be done, but this will not compare with the experience they will have had of a shared adventure. Although school provides a sound routine for many children, your home-life foundation will be sufficient, and richly developed, by so much shared learning experience while you are away. Their enquiring minds will have been developed and the knowledge they missed out on (which is not the same thing as learning, of which they will have had lots) can be rapidly built up. As for getting back in the UK system, this will depend on your residential location and the flexibility of school admissions. You could always offer to keep the rest of their current class informed about your progress while you are away – and turn your adventure into a learning experience for everyone.

# 2

## What Are Your Reasons for Home Educating? Finding Your Style

Every child – and every family – is different, so the decision to home educate can be a complex one with its own set of challenges, outcomes and rewards. Most families involved seem to share a common experience that the decision was not made lightly, and in some cases involved a complete reorganisation of family life – or even a change of home.

'The problem with the school system is that it is built with everyone else in mind. If children find life at school difficult, and issues such as bullying can be significant for autistic pupils, then home education may be the right solution – but it may not be. It all depends on the individual.' (Chris Bonnello, autism advocate, http://autisticnotweird.com.)

Some of the most frequently stated reasons parents have expressed for making a decision to home educate include:

- Believing standard education to be insufficiently stimulating for their child.
- Having specific objections to particular parts of the curriculum.

- Poor class control, impeding access to learning within the current provision.
- Special needs – ASD (autistic spectrum disorder), ADHD (attention deficit hyperactivity disorder), ADD (attention deficit disorder), dyslexia, and so on – as well as physical, emotional or developmental needs that may be insufficiently supported in a school environment.
- No suitable local provision within the state system. For example, a special-need provider is available but at such a distance that it would require the child to stay overnight during the week.
- Social challenges: anxiety, shyness, bullying, separation anxiety and so on.
- Geographical/transport access to schools being difficult.
- No place available at a preferred school.
- Preparation for a particular exam or entry to a specialist school; for example, a highly specialist grammar school or music/arts college.
- Children excluded from mainstream education.
- Gap in education; for example, Forces children who can't find a school on arrival.

Anyone considering home education might hear a lot of reasons why they shouldn't take responsibility for their child's education themselves, as it is a subject that arouses passionate responses from either side. Some of these are due to a lack of understanding about the whole home education process, believing that home-educated children, having been allowed to run free, will struggle to find a place in society, or make any valuable contribution to it. This is clearly nonsense, as the experience of being home educated can be highly rewarding for child and parents alike, but it is important to note that there are some potential disadvantages that a wise home educator can easily overcome. Some of these include:

**The child(ren) becoming alienated from their peer group culture.** Schools are a major place for sharing information and making alliances, such as what trainers are the most desirable, what the current term for expressing like or dislike is, and how young people currently greet each other. This gap in communication may be particularly apparent in children who have been home educated from a young age, even though they may have plenty of friends from within home education networks. The problems may not be apparent until the young person re-enters their peer group at college or university level.

**Lack of resources and equipment.** For example, science lessons require equipment such as biological samples and glassware; art lessons might involve clay and a kiln.

**Lack of exposure to cultural, religious and ethnic diversity.** Although home-educating families cover a huge range of ethnicities and beliefs like any other group of people, networks frequently consist of families with a shared ethos. This can limit a child's exposure to families very different from their own.

**Reduction in resources.** Home educating may require one or both partners to give up their professional role or reduce their hours, while creating an additional need to pay for provision (tutors, learning materials, cost of trips) to support the child's learning experience. This can have both short- and long-term consequences (for example, an immediate reduction in income and a long-term reduction in pension provision).

Networking is important for so many reasons and should include not only an excellent home education network but also opportunities for children of all ages who are being home educated to spend time with others who are still in the school system. It has never been so easy for young people to stay in touch with each other and to share their thoughts and experiences as it is today with modern technology. Used wisely, and under supervision, social media can offer a virtual peer group to everyone.

One of the best things about a good network for the home educators themselves is the facility it provides for sharing ideas, resources and materials as well as providing opportunities for those with particular skills or interests to share them.

There are many different styles of home education, and the style you choose will probably reflect your reasons and intentions for home educating in the first place. In order to provide a stimulus for thinking about what it is you want and how you might achieve it, we have created a simple questionnaire. It is intended to be thought provoking rather than diagnostic, so take your time and think about your answers. It might be that you agree with several of the possible answers to each question, but see if you choose just one that best represents your thinking. Marking your answer with a tick is a good way to record your thoughts.

## Questionnaire: choosing your style

1. When I think about education as a whole, I consider academic achievement and good exam results to be:

☐ (a) Extremely important in the modern world. Without good grades and qualifications success in life is hard to achieve.

☐ (b) Unimportant. Too much emphasis is placed on exams and academic achievement. I want my child to learn all about the world they live in and the people and creatures they share that world with.

☐ (c) I think exams matter, but schools operate too much on a one-size-fits-all approach that doesn't sufficiently recognise or accommodate individuality.

☐ (d) Not as important as the system likes to claim. More than ever before, these days it is who you are, not what grades you get that determine your path in life. My priority is for my child to be happy and confident.

2. Today's job market is extremely competitive, and getting ahead often depends on:

☐ (a) Choosing a career that has the potential for advancement and growth – and one for which there will always be demand, such as law, medicine, education or a role in the media.

☐ (b) Seeing the opportunities to make a good living. I want my child to grow up seeing life as full of options and choices.

☐ (c) Following your dreams and passions, and becoming the best you can be at the things that inspire you. Using your gifts and talents is the route to personal fulfilment, far greater than making money.

☐ (d) Keeping an open mind. I don't feel children should be encouraged to think about their future career options or choices too early. When thinking about work, so many adults I meet would have preferred a different path in life from the one they are on. I want my child to be open to everything and not forced to think about her/his choices too soon.

3. When I think about my child in a large modern school with a complete mix of people and working in a class of up to 30, I feel:

☐ (a) They cannot possibly reach their full potential when resources are so thinly spread.

☐ (b) It's easy to get lost in such a lot of people and in so many rules. Childhood and youth should be about expansion, not containment.

☐ (c) I like the idea that my child is meeting and mixing with lots of others, but I feel there is sometimes a conflict between social and peer-group interactions and meeting one's goals.

☐ (d) Horrified to think that my child will be processed to be just like everybody else. Schools operate on a system of rules and expectations designed for the masses, but they don't suit everyone.

4. I think the responsibility for a child or young person's learning falls to:

☐ (a) Parents. I consider it my job to ensure
that my child has the very best education I
can provide, and I will work hard to make
that happen.

☐ (b) The family and society at large. I'm a great
believer in the old adage that 'it takes a village
to raise a child'.

☐ (c) A range of people and life experiences, but
parents overall; only they know what is best for
their child.

☐ (d) The child or young person themselves.
But it is the duty of every adult to help that
learning take place.

5. When I think about educating my child at home in
our flat/house I think:

☐ (a) It shouldn't be a problem. It will be
relatively easy to set up a system and storage
for their books and other materials.

☐ (b) I will only use home as a base, the
rest of the time we will be out and about
in the world, mixing with other people
at museums, galleries, libraries, the park
and other local open spaces – or even
further afield.

☐ (c) There will need to be compromises, but I
see no real obstacles to achieving our goals.

☐ (d) I'm rather looking forward to creating a
stimulating environment, not just for my child
but for all of us.

6. Some people think that home education should only be undertaken by those with a high level of educational attainment – a university degree at the very least. I believe:

☐ (a) Everyone should know and understand their limitations when it comes to providing education for their child at home. Ensuring the best possible education may mean providing the best teachers available.

☐ (b) The most important lessons in life can be learnt in the simplest of ways. A conversation with a homeless person on the street can change a child's viewpoint or understanding forever in a way that the very best teacher cannot compete with.

☐ (c) It depends on the subject being taught. I certainly believe that being an expert in a given area means you have the potential to inspire and educate others, but for most day-to-day education, good planning and researching means anyone can be a good teacher.

☐ (d) That's rubbish. With a library full of books nearby and the Internet at your fingertips, all knowledge is available to all of us if we want it. Good education is not about knowledge, it's about understanding, having a point of view of your own and keeping an open mind. Learning should be a life-long experience.

7. Some people worry about the cost of home education. I feel:

☐ (a) That my child's education is a priority, so I'm prepared to work hard to ensure we have money to provide the best possible experience.

☐ (b) Money is fairly irrelevant. Of course, we all need enough to live on, but beyond that having a child educated at home is no more expensive than sending them to school.

☐ (c) I consider any costs incurred to be an investment in their future.

☐ (d) I don't think you can put a price on the experience of home educating your child or children. As a family we will have had to make some sacrifices, but we all consider it worth it.

8. When I think about spending a lot more time with my child or children, I feel:

☐ (a) That as long as we maintain good boundaries and rules we will all get along very well.

☐ (b) Excited – there are so many great things we can explore together.

☐ (c) Deeply committed – I am sure we can accomplish their dreams by working hard at them together.

☐ (d) A little anxious at taking on such a big step, but in the long run I feel that our family will get stronger and stronger.

9. When I think of myself as a home educator, I believe the most important quality that I bring to the role is:

☐ (a) Organisation and structure both in how I manage things and in how I think about things.

☐ (b) An open mind and love of new experiences.

☐ (c) Dedication. I don't stop until I have achieved my goals.

☐ (d) Flexibility and creative thinking. I love to find new ways of doing things to engage my child(ren).

10. When I think about the increased workload that comes with home educating my child(ren), such as record keeping, planning and assessment, I feel:

☐ (a) Good habits and good organisation should keep it all manageable.

☐ (b) Most of it is unnecessary. Lots of photographs of work completed, combined with blogging and journal keeping, will provide everything we need.

☐ (c) Having clear goals and outcomes is the secret here. When you know what you are trying to achieve and what is involved in reaching your desired goals, it is relatively easy to plan for and assess progress towards that achievement.

☐ (d) My fear is that this can take over and remove the joy from the experience, but listening to others within my network and keeping lots of examples/samples of our work along with photographs and other creative ways of recording, I've learnt that we can build assessment into every task in a natural and reflective way.

## Reflecting on your answers

This quiz was written with four distinct styles of home education in mind, so it might help you decide how you wish to manage your child's experience – although, of course, you might want to have a range of styles or, if you are new to home education, to start with what seems most manageable and allow for change as time goes on.

### Mostly (a)'s

If you selected answer (a) most frequently, you are possibly someone who feels you can do a better job of educating your child at home than any school can. The kind of environment that an (a) parent would want might be one in which the educating of their child is done primarily, though probably not exclusively, by tutors or other experienced educators. They see exams and standardised testing such as SATs to be important milestones towards a successful future career and may well have the goal of getting their child or children into the very best university possible – even if they are only aged ten at the moment. Providing tutors to deliver a carefully developed programme is a perfectly valid form of home education and many home educators working with their teenagers will provide at least some support from tutors for part of the learning experience.

Obviously this can be quite an expensive way of educating

a child, but sharing costs with other parents through a home education network might be an excellent way of providing both expert tuition and opportunities for collaborative working. One of the major benefits of this way of working is that it can provide a high standard of academic education, or of carefully tailored education for a child with specific learning needs, while allowing parents to continue their own careers with minimal disruption. Individual tutoring at home provides a level of education that schools simply cannot compete with, so if academic success is your priority this may well be, at least in part, the way to go.

## Mostly (b)'s

If you selected answer (b) most frequently, you are possibly someone who believes that the whole world should be a child's classroom and that you can provide an immersive and experiential learning environment that no school could possibly manage. The kind of home education a (b) parent might want to provide is a freewheeling series of adventures and explorations, possibly travelling abroad for extended periods of time or, if staying in the UK is required, the parent will provide day trips, weekend trips or extended periods away as part of the excitement and novelty of learning. Meeting new people from diverse backgrounds, and varying ages and life experiences provides learning in a way that expands a child's understanding of what it means to be human in the modern world. For those travelling extensively, networks are virtual rather than physical, and the use of blogging and photography/video are integral elements of selection and reflection of the learning taking place.

This way of educating a child might not provide the best academic results, but it can certainly build very strong relationships between parent(s) and offspring, as they learn to depend on each other in unique ways. They say that travel broadens the mind, and even if you have limited funds, a trip to a local market, an airport, an all-night supermarket at two in the morning, a homeless shelter, a retirement village or a sewage works, combined with interviewing the people found there, will certainly broaden everybody's mind. If this matters to you, then this might well be something you want to integrate into your home education programme to some degree or for a given period of time.

## Mostly (c)'s

If you selected answer (c) most frequently, you are possibly someone who has a child with a very specific need or talent that you wish to support or extend to its fullest with the intention of getting them back into mainstream education at a later date. There are many parents who choose to home school their child or children for a limited period of time before reintegrating them back into the system, and many of these will have picked (c). Perhaps you are helping your child pass a particular exam or extending their abilities in a way that mainstream school cannot, with the intention of helping them excel at their chosen subject, such as music, art, dance, football or another sport, or maths, and so on. Perhaps you have a child with a specific learning difficulty and are trying to prepare them for mainstream integration and coping with an often bewildering environment.

Parents providing this form of home education often rely heavily on downloadable resources or curriculum outlines, which they can follow to bring their child to the required level. Many children with exceptional gifts are home educated this way so that they may spend a lot of time pursuing their passions while maintaining their academic progress in relation to peers, so that reintegration can happen at any time.

Sometimes parents remove their child from school in order to prepare them for the entrance examinations of other establishments, and again they rely heavily on a list of requirements as the basis for their education programme. In some instances this is referred to as 'hot-housing' or 'cramming'.

Providing an opportunity for a child to pursue their passion or talent is one of the most popular reasons for parents to choose home education for their child.

## Mostly (d)'s

If you selected answer (d) most frequently, you are probably someone who puts family at the head of your priorities and who considers developing your child as the unique individual they were born to be as a guiding principle for your style of home education. This is the type of learning in which the child's experience is absolutely central and, rather than following a given curriculum, the developmental needs, interests and skills of the child determine the programme. As the child grows older, they begin to take more and more responsibility for their own learning and contribute to a greater degree in designing the programme to be followed. This approach is generally very hands-on so it can be quite messy at times; it can quickly take over the living environment if allowed to, especially with young children.

Children educated this way are often very confident and decisive, both of which are excellent qualities, but these traits have the potential to develop into arrogance or control if there is insufficient socialisation. The child-centred approach is a wonderful opportunity for the adults and children to have a complete wrap-around education experience: the day is unstructured and the learning moves in the direction and at a speed determined by the child. Planning can be a complicated business, but the use of mind maps and learning logs/journals helps to record the evolving programme and is helpful, and as children grow older, a slightly more formalised method of planning on a day-by-day or week-by-week basis is achievable.

Making sure that children have plenty of opportunities to mix with and play/interact freely with others is essential in helping them become well-rounded individuals, able to effortlessly reintegrate at university or college level (if not before) with peers. This is the type of home education that is probably most likely to produce free-thinkers and entrepreneurs, so incorporating some periods of time where your child or children can self-determine their learning will always be beneficial even if you prefer a more formalised approach the rest of the time.

Many people completing the above questionnaire will find that they have quite a mix of answers rather than an obvious preference, so perhaps for you a mix of styles is called for. Organising your week to provide both formal and informal learning opportunities, perhaps a tutor session or two, regular visits and experiences, and lots of time mixing and working with others will provide a home education designed to bring out the very best in your child(ren).

## Questions and answers

Q: *My partner and I are home educating our eight-year-old twins because they were not doing well in school and were forever getting into trouble. We share the time spent with the boys between us and have both managed to adapt our work lives to give us time at home. We do, however, have a problem in that we have very different views on how we should be educating the children. I want to give them more responsibility to direct their work, to review and assess it, and am quite excited by the things I have read about how enabling them to participate in directing their learning can stimulate them to become more creative individuals. My partner, on the other hand, wants to create an extremely formal environment with heavy discipline and rules as a way of making the boys concentrate. Bearing in mind their age and their education history to date, what would you recommend is the best way forward?*

**A:** As you and your partner are both providing the home education, there is no apparent reason why you can't have both styles existing side by side. There are benefits to both ways of working: the very disciplined approach will undoubtedly be good for academic achievement, whereas the more self-directed approach will, as you rightly say, encourage responsibility and self-determination. Children in schools are well aware that teachers have different styles, so having two approaches won't confuse or disorient them. You don't mention the gender of you or your partner and my only concern would be that they don't see one gender as strict and forceful and the other as open-ended and easy-going. The best approach would be for both of you to deliver both kinds of format. Perhaps you could save some of your education sessions for weekends or the evening so that you can observe each other working with the boys. This will help you both to hone your style into the most effective it can be and will also help you both mix-and-match to avoid stereotyping or playing one of you off against the other!

**Q:** *I was home educated myself and generally found the experience very fulfilling. Academically, I did well and was able* *to go to university, eventually achieving a master's degree in economics. I am now home educating my two children aged four and seven, and while I passionately believe that home education is the best I can give them, I found university life very difficult at first because I was very used to adults and not good with peers. Eventually, of course, I became an adult – and so did my peers – and mixing with others became easier as time went by. I would really like my children to be easy and comfortable around all ages.*

*We have a wonderful network here, and several times a week children come over or my children visit others, but how do I make sure they learn to manage social relationships easily without the angst I experienced?*

**A:** Firstly, congratulations on being a home education success story yourself.

Your children are growing up in a different world from the one you experienced, not only in terms of their education but also in terms of how social relationships between children have changed. They are very young at the moment, so it's vital to maintain plenty of opportunities for free play, not just learning experiences. Enabling them to run around outside with others to play with, ideally in the park or the garden, will help a great deal. Allowing children to play out of your sight and without direct adult supervision is also an excellent way of building their emotional resilience and social learning, as they manage difficult situations that arise by trial and error rather than by being told how to do it.

Of course, learning alongside others is also excellent practice, as they learn to cooperate, take turns, share and collaborate through carefully planned activities where success depends on those skills. Something simple like a team obstacle race (even with only two in a team) or a more complex activity like a cafe simulation with roles, menus, money and jobs to do, will encourage the children to work together successfully. Make sure that when you carry out reflections or assessments with the children after an activity you let them know that working together is one of the criteria you value; you can do this by asking them how well it went and what part they played.

**Q:** *My 13-year-old daughter has been permanently excluded from school for assaulting a teacher. There had been a catalogue of other incidents, none particularly serious, ever since she started at secondary school. My wife and I have had some difficulty with her behaviour, but nothing like this. Our local authority wants to send her to a special unit, but we are horrified at the thought and are considering home educating her instead. The local authority has told us that if we do this we will need to show that she is working full-time and learning appropriately. We are obviously concerned that we give our daughter the very best help and support we can. Would you recommend finding one tutor for everything or several with different responsibilities? What do you think works best?*

**A:** Without knowing more about your daughter's history it is hard to give any specific advice on what will work for her; however, it would probably be remiss to ignore the potential in the placement she has been offered by the local authority. Although you might feel horrified at your daughter attending a specialist unit alongside other young people with emotional and behavioural problems, it would probably be a good idea to visit the unit before you dismiss it entirely. Many such units offer extremely good programmes designed to help young people reflect on the reasons why they have not been successful in mainstream school and to learn or develop the skills they need, tailored to their requirements. Not all units are equally good, however, so have a look at the Ofsted report for the unit in your local area.

Providing her with specialist help in developing her learning skills, while supporting her at home to maintain her academic levels, seems to me the very best combination to get her back into mainstream schooling at a later date, which includes college or higher education should she so wish. Many units will take in young people on a part-time basis or have a smaller number of hours per week than schools, allowing you the opportunity to home educate her at the same time. Many units will also be very enthusiastic about such an arrangement and will assist in every way they can, even recommending tutors with experience of working with challenging or permanently excluded pupils.

It appears that your daughter probably has some emotional and or behavioural needs that traditional home education is unlikely to change or meet; however, if you do decide to go down the wholly home-educated route after considering the options, we recommend that you find someone to be a learning mentor or even a life coach for your daughter, to provide her with some of the same opportunities to reflect and learn new ways of managing.

Her home education should probably start with the basics of English and maths as well as the emotional and behavioural support that a councillor/therapist/life coach/learning mentor can provide. Add new subjects as and when she is ready to move forward. It would be in the best interests of most young people in a similar situation to aim for reintegration into secondary school once the tools to cope and learn have been established.

# 3

# Home Education Options

Once you have considered the feelings you have around your child's education and what kind of home education you want to provide, it's time to consider how you will deliver in a way that is most appropriate for you and your family. There are many choices, many resources and many voices claiming one way is better than another. The essential things to think about are what suits your child best, what best fits in with your family arrangements, and what changes you are prepared to make for it to work.

## The choices available

There are no limits to how you should educate your child at home, except those you identify or impose yourself. The age of your child, how much available time you have or can have, your income, your flexibility of employment, whether you are educating your child alone, with a partner or within a wider family setting, any specific needs your child might have, such as being particularly gifted in one or more area or needing additional support for one or more area, may all impact on the choice you make. But as there is no requirement to submit any detailed documentation about your intentions, you can change and adapt how you deliver your child's education at home as your confidence grows or as you learn about what's available.

The following are intended to offer some guidance for those starting out or considering educating at home:

## 1. Home educated fully by parents and others

This is the way of delivering home education that most people think of when they hear the term. This is the model whereby a parent or parents takes full responsibility for educating their child or children within a home setting – although what constitutes 'home' may vary. Frequently, both parents are able to adjust their work commitments to enable them to spend time with their children during the day and early evening.

For many people, this is a semi-formal set up with a timetable, curriculum and range of topics being delivered along with plenty of opportunities for learning by play, and visiting places of interest, such as museums, galleries, castles, bird sanctuaries, mountains – the list is endless.

For others it is about a 24-hour wrap-around learning environment where opportunities are exploited whenever they occur to learn more about whatever presents or grabs the child's attention. This style of home education tends to be with younger children, though not exclusively.

*What works best?*
This model works best when:

- The whole family is equally involved and committed (including any other children).

- The family makes contact with other home-educating families to create a network for support and shared working.
- Parents are prepared to change their routines and working habits to accommodate a different lifestyle.
- Children are well motivated to set their own learning challenges and targets.
- Families have a broad range of interests, or are prepared to develop them.
- Children are young (under 11) or exams are not a primary consideration; most home-educated young people are unlikely to achieve the same number of exam passes without specific tutoring (see below).
- Parents and children have a loving, boundaried and respectful relationship with each other, or are prepared and committed to develop these qualities
- The family has sufficient income to allow one adult to be with the family at all times and to cover potential costs in materials, additional heating, food during the day, visits and trips, and so on.

### Advantages and disadvantages

The advantages of this model of home education are:

- It can take place anywhere, so is ideal for families who have to travel for periods of time (or would like to).
- It can strengthen family relationships and parent–child bonds.
- It allows for a great deal of freedom both in content and structure.
- It allows the child to establish and follow their own interests.

- Networking is facilitated easily with a potential for a great deal of social interaction for child and parent.

The disadvantages of this model of home education are:

- Parents alone may not be able to extend a child or young person's knowledge and skills sufficiently for every interest they display, although this can be rectified fairly easily if parents choose to seek help from specialists or members of their network.
- The home-educated child might feel that they don't have enough downtime when home and 'school' are the same place – particularly when a more formal set-up is used.
- Children, and particularly teenagers, need to learn how to communicate with their peer group in order to fit in easily at a later date. Some time spent in clubs or groups with the wider peer group, including those in school, can help ease this.

## 2. Home education for a fixed period

This form of home education would be used before re-integrating into (or starting) mainstream school. Many children are home educated for a period of time with the intention that they will eventually reintegrate into mainstream school, often, where possible, the school they have left. Some are home educated before joining school at all, with the intention of taking up a place at a later time. Most commonly, this model is used either with young children who have yet to join school to give them more time at home to grow in confidence and skills before entering schools, or where a child has experienced difficulty in mainstream school, possibly through social anxiety, experiencing bullying, displaying behavioural difficulties or having problems integrating into a large group of others. If intending to reintegrate a child, there are several issues to take into consideration, and wherever possible maintaining or creating a contact with the school the child will be going to at a later date is helpful.

*What works best?*

With a young child who has yet to start formal schooling, the following is helpful:

- A wide range of play activities, including simple tasks such as sorting, sequencing, counting, using pencils, crayons, chalk, brushes and pens, are helpful for developing the skills they'll need when they are back at school
- Having some structure to the day: some busy times, some quiet times.
- Learning to follow instructions (playing Simon Says-type games, which require careful listening to instructions, or telling them how to complete a task step by step).
- Teaching them to dress and undress themselves – including coats, hats, gloves, scarves and shoes.
- Lots of reading books together.
- Telling and retelling stories and rhymes.
- Opportunities to free play with other children of similar ages as often as possible.
- Exploring the environment using senses – making sounds with leaves, collecting mini beasts, feeling the bark of trees with your eyes closed, and so on, splashing in puddles!

With an older child who has been removed from school with the intention of reintegrating later, the following are appropriate:

- Maintaining numeracy and literacy at their current level or developing them further if possible.
- Being aware of the curriculum for any subject they will be continuing on their return. Depending how long they will be out of school, it might be advantageous for them to follow some elements of the curriculum. If they will be re-entering school at a different key stage, it will usually be sufficient to support their numeracy and literacy.
- Creating a contract with the child around how much work they will complete/how much time they will spend on self-identified projects.
- Ensuring adequate socialisation with children of their own age as well as direct teaching of social skills (such as assertiveness, conflict management, cooperation, collaboration and taking turns).
- Ensuring plenty of physical activity, such as cycling, swimming, running and sports.
- Encouraging lots of reading.
- Teaching them independent study skills – how to structure their work time.
- Making clear to them when they will be returning to school (even if it is in three years' time) and continuing to remind them that they will be returning.

For both younger and older children, the following are effective:

- Working to some kind of plan or with a clear intention in mind.
- Maintaining/creating some structure to the learning day.
- Encouraging autonomy and self-direction: clear target setting, review and reflection.
- Plenty of networking with others of similar ages including opportunities for free play.
- Maintaining any links or relationships formed during their time at school.
- Spending supervised time with peers from the school they will later attend, such as a school club or playgroup.

*Advantages and disadvantages*

For the young child who has yet to start school, this model of home education allows the child:

- To learn at their own speed without undue pressure or feeling compared to others.
- To explore the world with a parent, which increases their confidence.
- To mature at their own pace.
- To follow their own bodily rhythms, to rest when tired, to play when full of energy and to snuggle when they need reassurance, none of which they can do in school.

With an older child who has been removed from school with the intention of reintegrating later, this will provide:

- A safe and supportive environment in which to build confidence.
- An opportunity to self-direct learning – to

concentrate on those things they are most interested in or fascinated by.

- Time to develop a particular skill or talent (football, the piano, creating video, sound-mixing, painting).
- Connecting/reconnecting with family and learning to cooperate and trust them.
- Lowering stress and boosting well-being.

The disadvantages of this model of home education are:

- Lack of sufficient peer interaction. Social competences are learnt by interactions with others of a similar age or slightly older, not from adults whose brains work in different ways.
- Your child(ren) might become lazy or disorganised if *in*sufficient stimulation or structure is provided.
- Young children might become used to always doing things their own way and in their own time (which can make integration into school challenging).
- Those who find relationships with others difficult may not find them any easier after a gap.

## 3. Home education delivered all, or in part, by tutors

For some families, home education is very much about greater effort and learning than the average school provides. Having some or all of the desired curriculum delivered by tutors ensures that children have the very best teacher-led learning experience possible. This model of home education is often provided for children with specific learning challenges, physical, behavioural or neurological, or a mixture of these. It is also often provided for young people with exceptional talents or skills, whom mainstream schools cannot support sufficiently. Sometimes parents will remove their child from school for a period of time and provide tutor-led education in order to boost performance in entrance exams for specific schools or for scholarships and bursaries.

## What works best?

When employing a tutor or tutors to provide part of the educational experience for your child or children the following help maximise the child's learning:

- If tutors and parents regularly talk to each other to ensure the child is learning in ways suited to them – and that they are enjoying it.
- The child has some say in which tutors are employed – perhaps being present and asking their own questions at interviews.
- Children are able to learn in small groups with others from their home education network (this helps to share costs too).
- Tutors are not only experienced in their own subject areas but also expert in developing the whole child: they understand the importance of target setting and self-reviewing in the learning process, as well as how to give constructive and affirming feedback.
- Tutors set tasks to be completed between sessions so that the child has to manage their own time and work independently too.

## Advantages and disadvantages

The advantages of this model of home education are:

- One-to-one or small-group tuition helps a child learn at their own pace in a highly structured way – ideal for children who struggle in one or more area of traditional learning or those who find concentration difficult.

- Performance is generally boosted.
- The child can follow the same curriculum as their peers in schools at their own level.
- Behaviour and discipline issues are minimised.
- Achievement and success are easily quantified and compared to national figures.
- Parents can continue to work while home educating their child.

The disadvantages of this model of home education are:

- The child might have little say in determining their own learning, which can be a disadvantage if they are eventually to attend college or university where working independently and managing choices and schedules for themselves will be expected.
- It is now well known that being physically active encourages and enhances well-being and that well-being enhances academic learning. The tutor-led model might encourage children to be sitting for long periods throughout the day.
- If providing all education through tutors, it can be costly.

## 4. Home educating using online or virtual schooling

This is a new option for children, as it provides a full learning programme complete with 'marking' and performance feedback from anywhere with a computer. It allows for continuity while travelling and is particularly useful for those unable to attend school due to health, proximity or mobility issues or for those children who simply cannot cope with school (or schools cannot cope with them).

As time goes on, this style of schooling is bound to increase and improve, although there are already virtual schools that students must apply to and be interviewed for, where they sit exams and even have the opportunity to attend graduation ceremonies. Some of these do not require any particular supervision from parents, although for primary-age children these are usually programmes that will require some adult supervision and support.

## What works best?

When building online or virtual learning into your home education programme the following points may help to maximise the learning for the child:

- Mixing online programmes with other delivery methods so that the child or young person gets the best of both worlds
- Ensuring adequate development of social competences and social interaction with peers, not adults.
- Making sure that any programme is suitable for the age and ability of the child before purchasing. Most sources provide 'free samples', so shop around before making a financial commitment.
- Using your learning network to create small groups that can work together online – even if working on individualised programmes – to reduce social isolation.
- These programmes can make an excellent resource to reinforce or practise key skills with younger children. If used in small doses with an adult, and

ideally other children present, they can provide an
excellent stimulus for home education.

- The online secondary schools (an example is
given in the Resources section) can provide exam
syllabus-based lessons at home in a limited number
of subjects, which makes them ideal for 'school-
refusing' young people or others unable to attend
school who wish to learn. The addition of some tutor
supervision might improve their success.

## Advantages and disadvantages

The advantages of this model of home education are:

- It offers the child unable or unwilling to attend
school an opportunity to follow the national
curriculum.
- Programmes of study have been developed already,
so they require minimal preparation by parents.
- By utilising technology, lessons are presented in
highly engaging ways; in some cases far better than
schools could provide.
- By working on computers, young people may engage
more readily with learning.

The disadvantages of this model of home education are:

- The child is isolated from others and is spending a
great deal of time at a computer.
- Some of these programmes, and in particular
the virtual schools, are expensive; some
virtual secondary schools cost as much as a
private school.
- The children who most enjoy this kind of learning

are often those who need to learn social interactions and social competences most.

- These types of learning programme are not suitable for young children, despite the claims made in the advertising. Young children should not be spending extended periods of time using gadgets of any kind but should be relating to the real world and learning to use all their senses.

## 5. Flexi-schooling

Flexi-schooling is an arrangement between a child's parents and a school that enables the child to remain on the school roll as a full member of the school, but attend only part-time and be home educated on the days when not in school. Flexi-schooling is growing in popularity, although it can only be approved if both the school and the local authority agree, and agreement can be difficult to obtain unless a strong case is made that such an arrangement is in the child's best interests.

Parents might decide to flexi-school for various reasons; for example, it might be a solution for a child who is very young for their school year and for whom parents may consider a whole week in full-time school would initially be too tiring. With today's more flexible working environment, flexi-schooling might appeal to parents who want to play a more active part in their child's education, so perhaps formal schooling for part of the week and a more tailored and individual approach for other days would be attractive.

Flexi-schooling is also emerging as a way of offering some individual attention in a school environment where numbers are rising and adequate provision is arguably not. In a *Guardian* report on the rise of flexi-schooling in 2011,[7] Jeevan

Vasager reported that 'By the end of this decade, there will be 21% more primary-age children than there were in 2010. The mounting demographic squeeze on schools comes at a time when many more very young children are already being taught in supersized schools.' The same article quoted parent Ally Scott:

Ally Scott, who accepted that the school's social and racial mix is one factor in the decision to educate their child at home on a Friday. 'We have found flexi-schooling enormously valuable in our local school where particularly diverse demographics offer up a challenging spectrum of needs and abilities within one large class ... how can one teacher service the needs of the individual when each child is one of 30 very different – linguistically, culturally, emotionally – other children?'

Flexi-schooling might also be a way of easing a previously irregular (perhaps through illness) or reluctant (often due to bullying) school attendee back into full-time school, or provide a means of gaining access to particular parts of the formal curriculum that are difficult to teach at home (such as competitive sport).

Schools might decide to accept flexi-schooling as those approved count as any other pupil/student on roll, which is significant when they receive the associated 'per place' funding. In some rural areas, flexi-schooling might enable a school whose school role is threatened to remain open. The *Guardian* article highlighted:

Hollinsclough is a Church of England primary school in a pretty Peak District village of the same name, about four miles south of Buxton. A few years ago, it had just five pupils on its roll. Then, at the start of the last school year, it introduced flexi-schooling and witnessed a surge of pent-up demand from parents who were educating their children at home but wanted to bolster this with one or two days of school.

The school now features flexi-schooling, and its rationale, on its website.[8]

The head teacher, Janette Mountford-Lees, argues that all schools should be harnessing the talents and knowledge of parents. 'I've got free one-to-one teachers for the children, which I couldn't have afforded ... the education system we have is based on the Industrial Revolution, when parents themselves weren't educated.' The school now has 30 children on its roll, of which only 12 are full-time. The rest attend between one day and three days a week. The school gains financially because each of its flexi-schooled children is funded as if they were full-time.

Although flexi-schooling can enable a valuable blend of individual attention and educational activities outside the home – at a time when school trips are reducing in number due to cost and all the form filling required – there are reasons why a school might not agree. There is no consensus about how to record the children's absence, although Hollinsclough puts the missing days down as 'educated offsite', so that it does not affect their absence rate. Pupils registered for flexi-schooling are still part of the school's official entry for SATs and GCSEs, and there are issues over flexi-schooled children and young people either potentially scoring poorly or their parents not wanting their children to take the tests, which means the school scores a zero for all the untaken tests with resulting potential damage to league-table positions. Schools where a significant number of pupils score a zero, or the school otherwise has a marginal score, can be placed in special measures.

Schools may similarly be reluctant to offer special conditions to one child on the grounds that other children might follow suit. Head teachers may decide that the local authority (which is their employer) would not approve, and therefore decline. Some schools raise the issue of insurance as a reason for not allowing a flexi-schooling arrangement, so parents pursuing this route need to make it clear that as a home-educating parent they assume full responsibility for their child on the days when they are not in the care of the school. A school that has not tried flexi-schooling before might be willing to try it as a temporary experiment, with a potential longer-term intention to return to full-time schooling.

## What works best?

If you are considering flexi-schooling the following may be important considerations if you are to make it the best experience possible for you and your child:

- A school may offer flexi-schooling when a pupil/ student is experiencing difficulties or is not attending as they should, as it maintains that child's place at school while allowing for them to have help and support for the issues preventing attendance. If such an offer is suggested take time to look at everyone's needs before deciding.
- Children with specific learning difficulties are frequently flexi-schooled so that their learning needs can be fully supported at home or elsewhere.

- Flexi schooling is most effective when what is provided during time spent at school is fully integrated into the programme of home education.
- All parties equally value home and school learning.
- There are several other flexi-schooled pupils/students within the institution so that no individual is made to feel different.
- Schools are willing to support home education by recommending or providing learning materials, and recording and reflection from home is shared with the school.

### Advantages and disadvantages

The advantages of this model of education are:

- It is a flexible alternative for families who wish to have more say in their child's education or to provide specific learning opportunities that schools cannot meet.
- It provides increased options for socialisation or for optimal study; for example, attending only PE and drama or only classes for maths A level can help a mainly home-educated child get the best of both worlds.
- It offers an effective way of helping a child re-integrate into school after a period of absence or when they have been home educated for a period of time; it makes access to exams easier and reintegration simpler.
- It can allow a child starting school a much slower and supported transition, so it is ideal for the parent who feels their child is too young for full-time school.

- It makes partial home education possible and can enable a parent to continue working.
- It may suit the needs of a particularly gifted student who wishes to pursue music/sport/science at a level that the school is unable to provide.

The disadvantages of this model of home education are:

- A child can feel neither one thing nor the other.
- Enrolment at a school is entirely at the discretion of the head teacher, who may fear that allowing individual children to flexi-school might then become a general trend. Schools are still assessed on all the children on the roll, and this includes those being flexi-schooled. If the head teacher fears flexi-schooled children are missing out on key parts of the curriculum, they may be concerned that assessed standards of the whole school would fall if flexi-schooled children were widely allowed.
- Schools still have the final say over timing, content and other formalities while the child is in school.
- It can be disruptive and require careful planning to integrate fully into a home education programme.

---

### CASE STUDY: JANET AND AMY

Janet and her husband met at university. They have two daughters, the eldest of whom, Amy, had a breakdown during her first year in the sixth form and consequently spent six months being home educated.

Amy is clearly a child with a high academic performance. She passed the eleven-plus exam with a sufficiently high mark to gain a place at a highly selective single-sex state grammar school, for which competition was intense. Once there, all went reasonably well until the sixth form loomed on the horizon and she found the prospect very unappealing. She had always liked the structure of time at school – Janet remembers the young Amy asking if she could go to school on Saturdays – and she found the prospect of the unstructured sixth form terrifying.

Diagnosed with social anxiety at 15, the closer the sixth form came, the more Amy did not want to continue at school. After persuasion, and having done very well in her GCSEs, she did return for A levels, but found it an extremely anxiety-producing situation from the start. The long periods of free time were difficult, as was the pressure from the other girls who were talking endlessly about going to university – she knew this was a firm expectation on all pupils. She was confident, however, that she did not want to go on to higher education and so felt even more left out. She found social situations really difficult, had no small talk and did not know how to develop relationships with her peers. Janet saw her increasingly 'folding in on herself' with increasingly common complaints that 'she just could not do it any more'.

Janet was called in for meetings to discuss the situation, but she found them one sided and rather critical. It was a problem for her that whenever she was asked to go in and talk about Amy's difficulties, she was consistently outnumbered; faced by at least two members of staff (usually the head of special needs and the year head) at the same time and always with the pre-meeting consensus still in the air. The language used made her feel that the school saw Amy's problems as family generated: Janet was repeatedly told that she was 'over-protective', 'had to let her daughter go', that her family was 'too soft on her' and had 'made her too comfortable at home'. Things did improve when Janet took along to a meeting a therapist who had been working with her daughter, and she was able to explain that Amy, suffering from extreme social anxiety, felt 'permanently under the spotlight at school', 'very self-conscious', 'was always wanting to hide' and 'entirely unable to volunteer in class'. It was clear, however, that both the head of special needs and the year head had little understanding of what her condition meant or how best to work with Amy in practice. The feedback at parents' evenings was always similarly uninvolved: that Amy was barely noticed because she said so little in class.

The situation got worse and worse and, in the end, Amy stayed at home for two terms.

During her time at home she worked on her art projects (for art A level). Her psychology teacher offered to record his lessons for her, and although this happened for a while the recordings eventually dried up – and she taught herself through textbooks.

Amy eventually decided she was ready to return, and to the school's credit they put several measures in place to both ease her comeback and to support her once there. From then on they:

- Allowed her to go home during free periods and for lunch, as it was these unstructured times, with a requirement to be in the company of others, that she found the most difficult.

- Enabled her to sit by the door in class so that she could leave during lessons if she felt anxious – although in practice her mother says she would have found walking out very difficult, as this would have drawn attention to her.
- Allowed her to register her arrival at the school reception area rather than requiring her to go to formal class registration.
- Allowed her to take only three AS levels instead of the usual four required by the school.
- Before Amy's return to school they asked the other girls in her class not to ask her why she had been absent – which they stuck to.
- The period of home education involved no external tutors – just her educating herself at her own pace. But given that she had missed over a third of the taught syllabus, her achievement in the end of school exams was extremely good – she achieved two A*s and one B for her A levels.

Looking back, while the period of home education clearly restored her equilibrium and enabled her to return to complete her education in a mainstream school, Janet feels that the profound anxiety experienced by her daughter could have been spotted, empathised with and worked around earlier, through a more engaged and understanding response from the school. It was only after she had left school, at the age of 19 – and spurred by Janet reading a newspaper article about autism – that she was formally diagnosed as autistic.

The case study of Amy and Janet illustrates the power of flexi-schooling. Had the school been more open to Amy's needs, a carefully constructed flexi-agreement could have been made early on for this highly motivated young woman that would have reduced the enormous stress felt by her and her family. Eventually, her school realised that there were ways in which it could support Amy to learn and achieve in flexible ways, and it was happy to do so.

## Questions and Answers

**Q:** *Do I need to decide on the model I am going to adopt before I begin educating my daughter myself? Will I need to let the school know before I de-roll her?*
**A:** The model you use is entirely your business, the only time it is relevant to discuss this with your daughter's school is if you are considering or wishing to negotiate flexi-schooling. Most home-educating parents find that they don't stick with one model completely but rather pick and choose as their familiarity with timetabling, curriculum designing and target-setting increase. Some people choose tutoring alongside flexi-schooling because that best meets their needs; others choose a child-determined curriculum alongside online schooling to create the best experience possible. The beauty of home educating your child is that you get to choose.

**Q:** *My home-educated seven-year-old really doesn't like any formal learning at all. He will listen to a story at bedtime, but during the day all he wants to do is play. Which model will help him develop?*
**A:** That is hard to answer because it is not the model that helps the child develop, rather it is the way in which development is

carried out. It would appear that your son has yet to start his learning journey in any formal sense, so try lots of stimuli to spark his curiosity followed by questions to open his thinking.

A trip to the park to see the ducks can include a few well-timed questions such as, 'Why do sticks and leaves float but little stones don't?' Then you could set him the challenge of seeing if he can get some small stones to float by resting them on a leaf.

Bring the leaves or flowers home and stick them onto a chart together. Simple sticky tape may work well – or using sticky labels. Now that he has created a wall chart of flowers or leaves you can try to find out their names together in the library or online, and you can write these under the specimens. Then you can get a bucket of water and ask him to find three objects that will float and test them to see if he guessed correctly – splashy fun and learning all at once.

Learning isn't about what we do sitting at a table with a pencil in our hand; rather it is about how we make sense of the world about us. Some children are very curious and constantly ask 'why?' or 'how?' questions; others need to have questions posed to them to spark their imagination, observation and thinking skills.

**Q:** *When I started out home educating my sons I intended to let them determine their own learning. I wanted to help them find things they were interested in, and for this to be the vehicle for their education – before eventually getting them into secondary education at 11; however, it hasn't turned out the way I wanted at all, and after a couple of years of nothing but cars and football, I finally cracked and hired a couple of excellent tutors to teach maths and literacy. They still have a couple of years to go until they are due to start secondary school but I really wonder if it might not be a good* *idea to get them into a primary school and keep on with the tutoring until they are at the same level as their peers. What do you think?*

**A:** Only you can make such a decision, but having committed to home education perhaps the thing that could turn it around is to get yourself into a good local network. Perhaps you have already done this, but it sounds as if your sons' interests are very limited, and spending time with other home-educated children could raise their horizons a little. Home-educated children tend to have wide and far-reaching interests as a group, so spending time together would help them develop new interests as well as increasing their social competencies, which will stand them in good stead however you choose to proceed. You might find that being part of a busy and stimulating network will reinvigorate your own interest, too.

# 4

# Home Education and the Law

Home education might be considered a continuation of the teaching that parents and carers give to their pre-school children at home. But after the age of five, education is a legal requirement, and so if you are going to continue to home educate, careful planning is needed.

In the UK home education is legal. The Education Act of 1996 states that: 'The parent of every child of compulsory school age shall cause him to receive efficient full time education suitable a) to his age ability and aptitude, and b) any special educational needs he may have, either by attendance at a school or otherwise.' 'Otherwise' refers to the right to educate your child at home.

As a parent, you must make sure that your child receives a full-time education between the school term after their fifth birthday and the last Friday in June in the school year in which they turn 16 (in England and Wales. Dates vary for Scotland and Northern Ireland). Young people living in England (but not Wales, Northern Ireland or Scotland) must then be in full-time education, enrolled in an apprentice scheme or in education part-time while spending a minimum of 20 hours a week volunteering until they are 18. You do, however, have the right to educate them at home, either full-time or part-time, and you might be surprised how easy it is to do this. Full information can be found on the Home Office website: https://www.gov.uk/home education.

As a parent you do not have to be a qualified teacher or have any other special qualifications in order to educate your child at home, nor do you have to give a particular reason for deciding to do so (although you will almost certainly be asked, so we cover what you might consider saying later on in this chapter).

## How do I start home educating?

If your child is already attending school, you can 'deregister' (this is the key term you need to know) them by writing to the head teacher or equivalent and informing them of your intention to deregister and the date you plan to start (be sure to date your letter and keep a copy). You also need to deregister your child if you have applied and been offered a place in a school, even if your child has not yet attended. Deregistration is the process whereby your child is permanently removed from the current register of that school, and hence the 'return' (list of enrolled pupils) made by the school to the local authority. It does not mean that they cannot rejoin that or another school at a later date.

Although the school must accept your decision if you are taking your child out of school completely, they can refuse if you want to send your child to school for some of the time, say for certain days of the week (this is often referred to as 'flexi-schooling' – see Chapter 3 from page 56).

If your child has never attended school and you have never applied for a school place, you are not legally required to inform your local authority if you decide to home edu-cate your child, but it is helpful if you do so – as it is to inform it of any relevant changes, such as a change of address. Many local authorities can identify children who are 'rising five', and so you may be contacted to find out what educational provision you have made for your child. If you have already let them know, it saves the follow up. The details of your local authority and a link to its website can be found by inserting your postcode where required on this page on the Home Office website: www.gov.uk/home-schooling-information-council.

## What about children with special educational needs?

If you are removing your child from a special school (for a child with particular educational needs) you will need to notify your local authority. If your child has special educational needs and you want to educate them at home, your council may be able to help. When you contact it, you need to tell it if your child has an Education, Health and Care (EHC) plan and, should the local authority enquire, you will need to be able to show that you can provide for their needs.

## Having taken responsibility for educating your child at home, what then?

Once you have deregistered your child, and taken respon-sibility for educating them at home, there is considerable freedom. You do not need to stick to school timings, particu-lar days of the week or the standard school terms/half-terms/

holidays. You do not need to have a fixed timetable or be a qualified teacher. You are not obliged to follow the National Curriculum or take standard attainment tests (such as SATS).

What you are required to do as a parent who decides to home educate is ensure that your child receives a full-time education that is suitable for their age, ability and aptitude, and if your child has particular educational needs, these must be recognised too. You should also note that you are assuming full financial responsibility for your decision, and, whereas the funding for state schools is paid for by the Treasury, you are not eligible for any funding from central government towards the cost of home education, even though you are effectively saving the government money by not taking up the school place to which they are entitled. You are, however, entitled to claim Child Benefit, and some local authorities do provide support to parents, including free access to National Curriculum materials. You can find out more about what is available in your local area through the website mentioned above, which gives access to the local authority information for where you live.

Details of the National Curriculum for all different ages and subjects, both attainment targets and programmes of study as well as curriculum requirements for GCSE exams, can be found on the Gov.UK website.

## What about exams? Does my child still need to take SATs and GCSEs?

Testing for SATs is only required at state schools and so not for home educators. Nor can the local authority insist your child(ren) take SATs.

Formal examinations (GCSEs, A levels and IB) can be taken

as external candidates at various local centres, perhaps a local college of further education (FE) or a private school, which gains tax concessions in return for acting as a community service. You will, however, have to pay close attention to the registration dates – which tend to be a long time in advance – and to pay the examination fees, and there are no grants available to cover this cost.

## Further education after the age of 16

If you are already home educating, you can decide to continue from 16 to 18 years (although if you start home educating at this stage you cannot claim Child Benefit). From 2015 all young people up to the age of 18 have to attend some form of training or education, to be provided by the local authority, and to have time off for appropriate training by their employer if they are in work. The same principle applies to home-educated children.

### A HOME EDUCATING PARENT COMMENTS:

We had the long-term plan of our children returning to formal education for the sixth-form years, so we needed to find out how many GCSEs they would each need to take if they were to get into firstly a sixth form and then a university. In a school where there is a range of different subject specialists, a wide range of additional options can be offered. If you are mainly relying on yourself, this smorgasbord is probably not going to be possible, so I rang a few universities and asked how many GCSEs a home-educated child would need in order for their application to be considered. The answer was that the core science subjects were essential only if they were going to go on to do a science course for which a foundational understanding was necessary, such as medicine or applied chemistry. Other subjects could be covered through ongoing familiarity rather than GCSEs. Each of them took three to six GCSEs, matched to their particular interests, and this combined with subsequent A levels was an acceptable basis for all of them to get into higher education.

They studied for the GCSEs at home but took the exams in a local private day school, which acted for them as an examination centre. It was possible to ask them to let us do this because private schools have a charitable status in return for serving the local community. The eldest did find taking her exams there a bit strange, as she ran into girls she knew outside school who turned out to be pupils; but this prepared her sisters for the same experience.

## A HOME EDUCATING PARENT COMMENTS

Our four girls all attended a sixth form at a local school or college at 16. We considered which institution would suit each one best: between the four of them they attended three different institutions. In the case of every child, I was amused to find that after a few weeks the teachers would seek me out and tell me that they were amazed at how quickly our daughter had settled, that they could not believe she had not always been there given how quickly she had adjusted to her new environment.

## Attendance issues

We acknowledge that some families embark on home education because the children have been very reluctant school attendees – or the parents have sought a more flexible structure to their child's education, wanting to take them out for educational experiences. The following information is therefore offered regarding the responsibilities and potential penalties for not attending school.

### In what circumstances can a child miss school?

You have to get permission from the head teacher if you want to take your child out of school during term time. Your child can only be allowed to miss school if:

- They are too ill to attend (although you should note that most local authorities make additional support available if a child can't attend school for a long period of time due to poor health).
- You have advance permission from the school for their absence. To secure permission you need to apply to the head teacher in advance as the parent with whom the child usually lives.
- Permission will usually only be given in exceptional circumstances. If the head teacher decides to grant leave of absence, it is up to them how many days your child can be away from school. You can be fined for taking your child on holiday during the term without permission from their school.
- If you decide your child is not to attend a school trip, they still have to go to school during the time

when it is scheduled, when other activities will be
organised. Your child's school can ask you for a
voluntary contribution to the cost of school trips.
If you don't pay, they cannot stop your child from
attending but can cancel the planned activity if there
is insufficient money to cover its cost.

## What help is available for getting a child to go to school?

If you are having trouble getting your child to go to school,
both the school and the local authority might be able to help.
The school will discuss attendance problems with you, and
your local council might be able to offer support to help get
your child to school. They may agree a plan to help, and the
types of support on offer could include:

- The provision of transport.
- Additional help if the family has particular
  difficulties (for example, if the child is a carer).
- Help to deal with particular problems such as
  bullying in school.
- The drawing up of a parenting contract. This is
  a voluntary agreement between you and the local
  council or you and the school's governing body
  enabling an agreement on how, between you,
  you will find ways to improve your child's school
  attendance. Refusing to establish a parenting
  contract, or not sticking to what has been agreed,
  can be used in evidence against you if a prosecution
  is decided upon.

### What is the role of the local authority in the life of a home-educated child?

Local authorities have a duty to make arrangements to identify children outside school who aren't receiving education, but there is currently no statutory duty to monitor home education on a routine basis.

In order to establish whether a suitable education is being provided for a home-educated child, your local authority can make an 'informal enquiry' of the parents – this is usually managed by the council's education welfare officer. It might be helpful to think about the kind of evidence you could provide. You could offer:

1. Samples of your child's work.
2. A copy of their home school journal, which records their activities and progress (see page 127).
3. A report you write about the nature of their education and progress.
4. To meet someone from the local authority outside your home, either with without your child (note that local authority representatives have no right of access to your home).
5. To invite someone from the local authority to visit you at home, to meet either you or your child.

Parents can be prosecuted if they don't give their child an education, although there would usually be warnings and offers of help from the local authority before this was put in process. If the local authority concludes that a child is not receiving a suitable education at home and that a child needs to be taught in school, it can serve a school attendance order.

## What legal action can be taken to force a child to attend school?

It should be noted that as a parent you do not have to give reasons for deciding to home educate. The law does not distinguish between a parent's various reasons for deciding to educate at home.

There are various legal powers that local councils and schools can use if a child regularly misses the school for which they are enrolled, however. You might be contacted by your local education authority to help assess your needs. They can give you:

**A Parenting Order.** This is a court order that is designed to offer support and guidance in the parenting of your child. There is an associated requirement to attend parenting classes for up to three months and follow the court's instructions to improve your child's school attendance.

**An Education Supervision Order.** This is an 'order granted in the Family Proceedings Court requiring you and your child to follow directions made in the Order and work alongside the County Attendance Officer, as the Supervising Officer, to improve your child's school attendance.'[9] These orders are generally served if the council thinks you need help in getting your child to school, but you are not cooperating in the process. A supervisor will be appointed to get your child into education, and this can be instead of prosecuting you or in addition.

**A School Attendance Order.** 'If it appears to a local education authority that a child of compulsory school age in their area is not receiving suitable education, either by regular attendance at school or otherwise, they shall serve a notice in writing on the parent requiring him to satisfy them within the period specified in the notice that the child is receiving such education.'[10] This might be issued if the local council thinks your child is not getting an education, and you have to either register your child with a school or confirm that you are home educating. If you do not do either within a specified period, you could be prosecuted or fined.

A fine (sometimes known as a 'penalty notice') generally rises if not paid within a certain period of time.

Although all the above are options, the council does not have to issue these before making a decision to prosecute, which can result in a fine, community order or jail sentence of up to three months. Home education is legal in all of the UK, but the specific provisions are different in Scotland, Wales and Northern Ireland.

## Can a school decide to deregister (or off-roll) a child?

The decision to home educate is always the decision of the parent. Sometimes a school might deregister a child against the wishes of a parent, or advise a family to choose to home educate a child to avoid them being permanently excluded. Schools have occasionally used deregistration to remove children who are likely to score poorly in formal examinations and tests and thus impact on a school's league table position. If this applies to you, try to resolve the problem through discussion, but keep all the associated correspondence in case you decide to take legal advice.

Where a child loses their right to attend a school, the local authority must offer alternative provision, as the European Convention on Human Rights (part 1, A2) says that no one may be denied an education. If a child is not able to attend school, there are three usual options in such cases: finding a place for your child at another school; sending your child to a Pupil Referral Unit; or embarking on Education Other Than at School (EOTAS).

**Finding an alternative school.** Where a child has significant special needs, an alternative school might be a special school, although such places are usually in high demand. Where a child has significant challenging behaviour, and alternative local schools feel unable to meet their needs or keep other pupils and staff safe, finding another school might be impossible.

**A place at a Pupil Referral Unit.** might be offered if a child's behaviour is such that specialist care and attention are required. But places at such institutions are in heavy demand and, although needed, a place might not necessarily be available.

**Education Other Than at School.** (EOTAS) is normally intended for children who are either long-term sick or have severe behavioural difficulties. Here the local authority employs tutors who go regularly to the home of the child and tutor them, setting other homework to complete in between visits. Although the education takes place at the young person's home, this is not the same thing as home education. With EOTAS the parents are expected to cooperate with the tutors, who are paid for by the local authority, which remains responsible for the day-to-day education of the child.

Although these options exist in theory, in practice they may not be available. Parents who have turned down all the local authority's offers will be regarded as having deregistered their child and henceforth responsible for their home education. Pressure from a school to deregister a child is, however, not acceptable and should be reported to the local authority (and all correspondence, notes of meetings and phone calls kept).

## Other specific issues for those considering home education

Families are all different as are the needs of individual children within them. There may be circumstances or issues that arise for you and your family that need specific advice, tailored to your needs. The following points are intended as guidance but The Law Centres Network (www.lawcentres. org.uk) or Citizen's Advice (www.citizensadvice.org.uk) may provide additional support or advice.

### Divorced and separated couples who have shared parental responsibility

Even if you no longer live with your child, if your name is on their birth certificate, since 2003 you have shared parental responsibility (provided there are no court orders in place precluding this). This means that either parent can deregister a child without needing permission from the other parent, in the same way that both can independently consent to medical treatment for their child. The decision to deregister can, however, be challenged by either parent, and if no agreement between you is possible, the courts will make a decision that both parents have to follow. If you are separated from your child's other parent, it therefore makes sense for both parents to discuss this before making any decision or taking any associated action. A failure to discuss a decision to deregister with the child's other parent could be considered negatively by the courts.

## Access to the special needs delivered via the NHS.

Special medical care, such as speech therapy, dental checks and hearing tests, are linked to the child rather than their school, and so continue to be available to the home-educated child. You can contact the service and find out how they can continue to provide a service, and if you encounter difficulty you can ask your GP.

## How does the home-educated child fare in the employment market?

Most home educated children gain fewer GCSEs, due to the challenges of covering the broad curriculum available in schools and the costs of taking exams, but this does not necessarily disadvantage them in the market for higher education or employment. Home education can permit the management of small businesses within the curriculum and access to part-time employment when it is not available to others, during the traditional school week. GCSE maths and English are sensible ambitions, and for a young person with a particular career ambition, it's sensible to find out minimum requirements and to ensure that these are covered (such as a science or language GCSE). For a home educated child wanting to go into higher education, many consider formal education via a local sixth-form college for the last two years of full-time education.

**A HOME-EDUCATING PARENT COMMENTS**

Home-educating parents have the flexibility to do really interesting things as and when they want to do them. We would have an outings day each week when we went off to explore a gallery, museum, historical site or place of interest that related to their current theme of study. The freedom of not having a school day to stick to meant we could pursue interesting themes – so learning about the life cycle and benefits of animals led us to visit firstly a milking parlour and later on a wool factory. One of the girls wanted to be a vet at an early stage, so for three years she joined a farmer in the village for the annual day of shearing. And because there was no permission required, or associated form filling for these activities, we could simply get in the car and go; nothing needed to be planned ahead – if it was a lovely day, we could just go out.

There are also many additional activities that can be developed at the same time as home education; for example, I have seen small businesses flourish alongside home educating, offering practical learning opportunities such as children learning maths within the context of book-keeping and accounts. At the age of 14 one of our children started a small business which was very successful and made quite a lot of money.

## CASE STUDY: OLIVER AND ALISON

We take issue with the assumption that education belongs to the state, as though we have an obligation as parents to hand our children over to the state-appointed authorities at the required age. Rather, as still enshrined in British law, it is the responsibility of parents to educate their children, and the tendency in recent times for more and more influence to be ceded to the state in how we bring up our children is not in the best interests of our children. We were heartened by the upsurge of opposition to the Scottish government's recent attempt to provide every child with a nominated and state-approved representative (the so-called Named Persons Scheme) without parental involvement or knowledge. The judgment contained this devastating critique: 'The first thing that a totalitarian regime tries to do is to get at the children, to distance them from the subversive, varied influences of their families, and indoctrinate them in their rulers' view of the world.' [Paragraph 73].

Home educating is a correction to the widely held perception that it's the state's job to educate our children on our behalf, as though we as parents are not sufficiently equipped for the task! If truth be told, given the option, many children would prefer to be taught by those who know them best and love them most, and many parents are far more competent for the task than they give themselves credit for. At the end of the day, all parents are constantly teaching their children thousands of attitudes, perspectives, skills and facts every day – in fact, we have more influence in our children's lives than anyone else. In thinking carefully about what we are teaching our children we are only holding ourselves accountable for probably the single most important responsibility of our lives. By considering the option of home educating, parents are at least facing up to this.

In our present culture, however, many parents do not give this sufficient thought and actually have no idea what their children are learning at school, having little or no involvement in their children's education unless a problem arises. Home educating offers a positive alternative, the chance for parents to think about how they are going to raise and teach their children and to think about and really examine the options available – in the same way that you would if you were considering any significant investment such as a home or a car. Home educating is an important option that should be taken seriously rather than dismissed.

In our rather varied experience of educating our six children, the only constant factor has been our intimate involvement at every point! They did not all begin their 'formal' schooling at the age of four (recognising, of course, that they start 'learning' from the moment they are born). Our eldest son began formally at the age of six and it has served him well (he is now in his third year studying mechanical engineering at university). Initially, he went to a small local school three days a week and had two at home – a form of flexi-schooling that the institution in question was sufficiently enlightened and flexible to work with.

At one point, for a period of two whole years, we had all six of our children being educated at home full-time, bringing in a series of tutors to support the areas of the curriculum where we did not feel able to offer the entire teaching ourselves, especially mathematics and languages. We supported the academic curriculum with a variety of different activities outside the home: dance, cricket, fencing, swimming and church-based activities such as Sunday school and the very popular Friday Club (a mixture of games and Bible stories for groups of up to 25 children).

We did whole-family projects to which everyone contributed, at whatever level they were able, and these we have kept – they are a really precious keepsake of a period we look back on with great happiness. Their mum kept detailed journals and photo books of what we were doing and what the children were learning, and these too are a great source of pleasure. We also found that the experience of home educating developed us as well. When you are teaching something, from time to time you realise that you are not as up to date as you might be, and you go back to the books. The educational experience was good for everyone.

Alongside the academic learning there was a great sense that we were educating the whole child, not just tutoring them in specific subjects. We were able to really engage with them, meet their needs and deal with problems as and when they arose. We were able to calm them, support them and mould their world, helping them see themselves in relation to the world, which is very important. We feel that they know who they are and what they stand for, and can stand up for values that are very important to us as a family.

All our children integrated into institutional schooling

when the time was right, at various stages (from age 4 to age 15), and had no difficulty in making the transition. Indeed, in several cases, teachers commented with some surprise that children who had been home educated could adapt so successfully to a very dramatic change.

Of course, we were very particular about the kind of school they would join, and we felt it especially important that the values which had become so significant for our children were treated with respect. We are convinced that the process of home educating has not only enabled us to shape their thinking and develop life-long character, but also sharpened their ability to stand up for themselves – equipping them to put forward their own ideas with cogency and respect, rather than feeling that they have to be defensive or combative as they seek to live out their world view. This is especially important if your views are no longer considered mainstream – the last thing we want is for our children to feel that they have to 'explain themselves'. By all means, let them be challenged positively and helped to value the perspectives and outlooks of others, but they should never be made to feel excluded or marginalised.

Overall, we found that there was a freshness and a creativity to home educating; it was a lot of work, but it felt like an adventure that offered us the chance to get to know each other as a family very well and really know our children. We were able to develop each child's potential through a measured progression, avoiding pressure points, and supporting their development through instilling a real love of learning – with lots and lots of reading. It's a period of our lives that we look back on with great fondness.

## Questions and answers

**Q:** *We have been thinking of home educating our youngest child, as he was born prematurely. Although he is now five, he is still way behind other children developmentally. We have been assured he will eventually catch up, or at least be closer in ability to his peers, but right now his self-esteem is being battered by seeing what all the other children can do when he still needs naps in the afternoon. Our fear is that if we tell the head teacher that we are considering home educating him she will be annoyed with us and not let us re-enrol him in a couple of years when he is ready to be with his peers again.*
**A:** Most head teachers will be sympathetic to your son's needs and fully support your choices; however, the school will not be able to hold a place open for him for two years, and that does mean that when you want to get him back into school he may have to wait for a place. With a popular school that can be a long wait.

Another option would be to discuss flexi-schooling. Your child could stay on the roll of the school but he would receive part of his education at home. Perhaps he could attend school in the morning only and be at home with you in the afternoon? Of course, this will not necessarily help his 'I can't do it' feelings, although it might be possible for him to spend his school time in the nursery class if space allows. This can be a good solution for some children, but if he is aware that he is older than the other children, it might create new problems.

You have a choice that no one can make for you, but rest assured that the head teacher will try to help you find the right solution for your son's well-being and education, so book a meeting and talk it through.

**Q:** *I've been home educating my child since she started school. I take it very seriously, and with a master's degree I feel eminently qualified to do this. I've been on relevant courses, read books and talked to others in a variety of home-educating networks that I belong to.*

*The education department of the local council evidently sees things differently. I have been asked over and over again if someone can come and visit me, to inspect my premises and records and ensure that I am doing a good job. I feel this infringes my rights as a home educator and parent, and I have told them on several occasions that there is no way that I am going to provide what they ask for and they have no right to ask. I have involved my solicitor and sent official letters, and now they are threatening to take me to court. How do I ensure my council leaves us alone?*

**A:** Although you are clearly doing a fantastic job, this is not necessarily universally true of home educators. There are children who are officially home educated but who are receiving no education at all, and the council is required by law to ensure that every child of the relevant age is receiving an education. You don't have to let an inspector into your home if you don't want to, but bear in mind that the individual contacting you will be following a procedure established by the management system. Given some evidence, or the opportunity to discuss what you are doing over the telephone, they would probably be relieved to see how well you are doing, and to have one less case to worry about. Perhaps just providing them with a brief outline of how you work, what you are doing and a willingness to speak on the phone would get them off your back for good.

Right now, seeking to exclude them seems to be taking a lot of mental energy that could be better directed into the home education you are offering your child. In the longer term, being ready to provide some evidence of how well home education can work might make your local council reconsider how they regard home education.

**Q:** *My wife and I divorced two years ago. There was a lot of bad feeling, in particular relating to access to the children, and this has continued. I now find out from my son that she has de-rolled them both from their primary school and is intending to home educate them in future. I am very much against this, but what are my rights? Can I force her to send them back to school?*

**A:** Legally your ex-wife is able, as their mother, to de-roll them without your consent. If you have concerns about her suitability as an educator, and you feel your children are not receiving a good education – perhaps that they are just hanging out and watching television – you could contact the local council's education department and talk the situation through with them. There will be a designated person with responsibility in this area, although the job title might vary from local authority to local authority. Alternatively, look online to find out the name of the role and the named individual. Talk to them about your concerns, as they are the only people who can issue an order to return the children to school, and they will only do this if they feel the children are not receiving an identifiable education.

A more consensual strategy might be to contact your ex-wife, even though she did not consult you before removing the children from school, and find out if you can contribute to and help with their home education. Being home educated by two parents would be a more varied and probably richer experience for everyone concerned.

**Section 2**

# How to Teach a Child at Home

# 5

# Creating an Appropriate Learning Environment for Your Child

The home-educating parent faces the same problems of space and time management as everyone else, and good organisation takes time and effort.

Most of us have been programmed by our own experiences into believing that education needs to take place in a classroom of some sort. Actually, education takes place in the brain, and the brain takes up very little space. Learning is all about experience, and experience can come from sorting objects in the bath according to how well they float or from a careful description in a book about the life of a slave in Roman times followed by a piece of writing in the first person.

In this chapter we'll be looking at some of the key things to consider when setting up or managing home education for your child or children. There is some clear advice on what is and what is not important when accommodating education at home, as well as some top tips for organising and managing home education without turning the home and your life upside down.

## Creating a good place to work

A special room to function as the education base would be
ideal, but few of us can manage this. Good advice is to site the
main activities in a space that can be easily made into a workspace so that everything is to hand but is completely cleared
away at the end of the learning day. That way the family
doesn't have to sweep books out of way when they want to
eat. Anywhere with a table is fine, ideally with a bookshelf
or side table on which the materials can be kept and stowed
at the end of the day, perhaps in box files or folders so that
everything can be tidy. If your child or children have access to
a laptop or computer on a trolley, this can be wheeled in and
out. We would not generally be in favour of them working in
their bedrooms, which should be private spaces for relaxation
and to hang out in during free time. There should be a rule
that everything is put away at end of the learning day. Bear
in mind that that might be 7pm at night, in which case, if the
table is needed for eating, work might have to be cleared away
and then put back again, which involves some blurring of how
time is organised.

It's a good idea to have lots of books and reading material
in the home so that reading is seen as part of everyday life.
Remember that if you want to inspire children to love books,
they need to see you reading too, and reading aloud can be
a very formative and comforting experience long after they
are able to read for themselves. If you do not feel comfortable
doing this, audio books can be a great resource: great care is
taken with the choice of voices, and the resulting experience
can be enjoyed by everyone – not just those of the 'official' age
that it says on the box.

**A PARENT COMMENTS**

I recently made the decision to stop reading books on a device and buy physical copies. The reason is my 18-month-old daughter. I want her to see the pleasure that books give me, so it's important that she understands that I am reading books – and not always on my phone.

## Dividing up activities during the day

Although the timings can suit the individual learner and the home circumstances, it's probably best to establish two to three regular sessions in the day, especially when you are new to home education, and for each to be between one and one-and-a-half hours long, with breaks in between. For younger children, build in some play breaks. Have a snack. Do something completely different so that no one is at a table for too long. For a child under the age of eight, their concentration level is never more than 15–20 minutes on a single task, and it may be more like 10 minutes. Design lessons, or learning periods, using a range of different tasks and different media; for example, writing, drawing and reading.

Older learners (ages 10–16) might prefer to get stuck into something, and while all children are different, and home educating enables you to accommodate their different learning styles and personalities, by this age they won't necessarily appreciate a lot of chopping or changing between subjects. What you are aiming to do is encourage independent learning and study, building from the initial goal of a child being able to self-motivate for an hour at a time – which they should be able to do by the age of 12. You might, therefore, choose to start each learning period with a discussion about aims and objectives, talking through with them what they should be doing, where they hope to get to and within what time frame. You should then let them organise themselves as much as possible, coming in to check on them every 20–40 minutes or so – or letting them come and find you when they have finished.

You don't necessarily need to stand over them, but regular checking and coming in, sitting with them for a while, ensuring that they are clear about what they should be doing, or offering them the chance to show you what they are doing and how they are doing it, are all important. If your regular visits show that they are inclined to go 'off task' and start messing about, you need to come back more often. Your goal is to have children functioning as independent learners, able to self-motivate as much as possible. This can work very well, and by the age of 14 some home-educated young people are designing their own curriculum and have the ability to divide up tasks and work out what they are going to be doing each day.

If you are employing tutors at home, bear in mind that you need to make sure that either you have plenty of time to talk to them about what's going on and how it fits with their wider learning or that the support they offer includes regular reports and feedback so that you can keep track of everything. It is important that someone takes responsibility for the overall learning of the child; this might be you and/or your partner, another family member or a paid tutor. Depending on the age of the child, you can't expect one person to be a specialist in everything, so it may be necessary to have more than one tutor, but they might take responsibility for one area of the child's experience. One person needs to be in touch with all the tutors and others working with a child, or it could be one of the tutors themselves who has this coordinating role and who keeps an eye on the child's overall learning experience and how it fits with stated objectives, their progress and likely future development.

For older children who are working with a tutor who comes to your home on a regular basis, it might be a good idea for the tutor to set a programme for the week ahead on a Monday and then check back on the Friday to see how it has worked out and fitted together. If you have only one additional tutor, you might be able to manage this role yourself, but if the majority of your child's education is being delivered by others, someone needs to have an overview.

## Organising input from tutors with work between visits

Balancing input from tutors with the need to do coursework/ homework between visits can become a big role if you are dealing with several tutors. Depending on the age of the child you may need more than one tutor, and even with a young child you might find it a better experience for them to have variety. Do consider, though, whether the variety you are seeking is for you or them? And you will also have to think through associated routines and make your expectations clear:

- How long does each lesson last and will that include some kind of wrap-up activity? Note down agreed activities and feedback in the child's planner.
- Do you offer them a hot drink on arrival or should they go straight to the child?
- Should you discuss the child while they are in the same room – and even include them in the discussion

or do it separately? If so, what are you going to get the child to do while you discuss their progress?

- Would it be better to schedule a progress-checking phone call every now and again instead?

However you manage the above, it is probably a good idea to decide what needs to be done before the next time.

You will also need to consider how much you tell the tutor about child's specific needs, or whether that creates expectations on their part.

---

**A MOTHER EXPLAINS**

When we eventually got a tutor for our son we were concerned about his very regular need to use the bathroom, which drew frequent comment from his siblings at home. I had wondered whether to warn his tutor about how often he needed to nip out to the bathroom, but in the end decided not to, and left him to negotiate the situation himself. It was not an issue I wanted to draw attention to and he managed it well himself.

---

## Choosing the right tutor for your child

Many home educators will employ a tutor at some stage of their child's education. Being clear about what you want from the tutor is a good starting point in the selection process as all tutors, like any teachers, are different. Some are strict, some inspirational, some fun and playful and some rare people manage to provide all of the above when needed.

Employing a tutor can represent a considerable financial commitment for some families and for all families it means entrusting your child to the care of another person for a period of time. Getting the right person for the job is important for everyone.

Most parents would like their child to have some input into their choice of a tutor. Enabling them to have some input compares with the role of a school council, which gives children a voice in their education and the general way in which Ofsted inspections seek children's opinions in school, such as in appointment processes where their feedback counts. Asking a young child what kind of person they want will help them to think about what makes a good tutor. By asking them questions to help them think, they can create a question or several questions to ask the potential tutor. For a five-year-old these might be as simple as 'are you kind?' or 'do you like playing?' Any tutor who can't give a five-year-old a good answer to such questions isn't worth hiring!

All potential tutors will expect parents to be interested in issues of safeguarding and for any potential tutor to be DBS (Disclosure and Barring Service) checked (therefore, they are not included on a list of those considered unsuitable to work with children). You can find out more about safeguarding issues on the Home Office website (see Resources). (See also How to find a tutor for your home-educated child on page 139.)

## A SECONDARY SCHOOL TEACHER COMMENTS

When we looked for a tutor to teach our daughter history, it was a positive experience. We moved house between years 10 and 11 and, amazingly, managed to match up most of the GCSE syllabuses. History was the problem, so I recruited a young post-doctoral student from Cambridge University (now a well-known historian and full fellow) to teach my daughter the rest of the history syllabus. In the event, we discovered that although the set books for English were the same they had studied them in a different order at the two schools, with the result that my daughter did the novel twice and missed 'poets from other cultures'. The history tutor offered to teach this as well. The best aspect of this arrangement was the fact that my daughter really liked and respected the tutor – and enjoyed being treated as a grown-up. She taught my daughter how to revise effectively – learning that carried her through GCSE, A levels and five years of medical exams.

I was perfectly capable of teaching her revision strategies but had the disadvantage of being Mum! It was lovely listening to her explaining what she had been taught, and even better watching her implement the ideas, very effectively, but it did cause me some quiet amusement.

The tutoring experience provided something that was not available at school and gave access to a very impressive young woman, who left a lasting impact.

## Gadgets

When asked to research or explore something, today most children assume that online access is required. Understanding how to access information online is appropriate because we want to teach them these skills, but we also need to promote effective research habits through all sources, and this might not be best begun with open online access. For a child under ten, for example, sit with them, encourage them to explore offline first by organising their thoughts and asking some good questions to research answers to before they explore online, then teach them how to find information online, to make the best use of search engines and then to bookmark relevant pages.

Every parent with computers in the house needs good parental controls on the computer so that the children can't access sensitive sites unless you are there with them. In the same way that most of us older people, when given free access to a physical dictionary, looked up definitions of words not in general usage at home, most young people know that information on sex, drugs and other sensitive topics is available online if they want to find it. Exploring the Internet needs to be a supported experience. Help them find information on the things they want to know, even those that are in the sensitive category, that are age appropriate, and demonstrate, by sitting with them, that you are not embarrassed or disapproving (even if you feel a little of both these things), as this will encourage them to gain a healthy understanding, appropriate to their age. Learning to discriminate between accurate information and sensationalist information is an important skill for all children to develop, and they need to learn it by experiencing searching with an adult who can help them identify key elements of a trustworthy site.

Ensure that they can access the level of information they need to support their home education environment, but that they are not able to access social networking or entertainment sites during the learning day. You may need help in establishing these controls; most parents are naive about what their kids get up to online. Schools have good controls on their computers and networks; you need the same thing, at least on the computer you are using for their working day. If there is only one computer in the house, you might need to be able to disable access and then re-enable it at the end of the learning day. Some parents consider social networking while they are working as a useful learning tool, particularly if they are chatting with other children from their learning network (other home-educated children with whom they keep in contact and sometimes complete tasks or share their work with).

Thinking more widely about gadgets, we would recommend that there are no computers or phones/tablets in their bedrooms, and that you develop and agree with them restrictions on where and when they are used at home, bearing in mind that most inappropriate use happens when you are not there to see it. If you leave a child alone during the day with a computer, check the browsing history on your return – and do this with them. Don't read any emails they have sent, unless you have concerns. Do the same with their phones; check on activity during the day as a matter of course. You are doing what any school or sensible adult would do. Of course, age comes into it and, like other elements of privacy, greater trust is given with the passing of time and as they prove themselves to be responsible.

If you don't have a computer, or you feel you would rather not use one, the local public library can be used to gain computer access, and you could build this in as a standard activity within your week, going on supported visits when the your child(ren) are little but then on their own when they are older. You will need to build in good habits before you offer unsupervised visits, to ensure that they are there when they say they will be – and have not headed off for a trip to the shops – so keep checking that they have used the allotted time for the task or purposes decided upon beforehand.

If you feel they are not doing as much as they should be, bear in mind that sometimes looking things up does not produce much on paper – and they should not be encouraged to print things out before working out whether or not they are useful to their general topic under exploration. Lots of sheets of printed paper do not necessarily equal effective understanding. Learning to format a question that will yield the right kind of information takes practice, so work with them on this, as part of their learning experience. All the while ask questions, ask what stands out, or what – looking back – it would have been helpful to do first, and so what use they are making of their time. Some children need particular help in relating from one area of learning to another; for example, how a maths recording process could be useful for making sense of a survey on traffic. Encouraging them to reflect on their progress in broad terms might enable this, so instead of asking 'What did you learn?' you could ask 'How could you use what you learnt in a real-world situation?' (see the note on using Bloom's Taxonomy in Chapter 7).

At all times, encourage them to keep their notes, sketches and workings out as part of the learning journey. What they produce does not have to be finally finished to be useful.

On the theme of creating something worthwhile, think about how you are going to store what they produce. It's a good idea to keep all related notes and scribbles, printouts and lists of books consulted, and combine them in a box file.

Then, when the project is over, they can get it all out again and think about which bits to keep and how to now turn it into something useful. You could compile a scrapbook, or an online resource book, or covert it into an (access-limited) website for sharing – it's easier to do this than you might think, and managing the website could become part of your child's education. You might want to make it available within your home–school network, and so hopefully get responses from other families or home-educated children. You might also think about making it available within your family – showing it to Granny so that she knows what your child has been up to and can come back with a comment. It's important to think about who comments and what kind of comments you are seeking – negative comments can be destructive and may be difficult for the child to handle.

### FIVE ASPECTS TO PLANNING

When planning an effective environment for home education, think about the following:

1. Even though in a home environment, where communication might be assumed to be informal and therefore easy, every home educated child needs a 'planner'. This probably works best if it is a physical document showing what you have agreed, the progress made and what is going to be done next. Filling it in makes a really good end of the learning-day routine and it can be the starting point for deciding what to concentrate on the following morning.

2.  If you are at home all day, the heating arrangements might need to be reconsidered. This can make a significant difference to the family budget. If this is a big consideration, think about where else you could go and study during the day: local libraries, education centres, and so on.

3.  If you have one computer, that is shared across the family (perhaps positioned on a trolley), who will have priority of access during the time when the home educated child still wants access but it is not necessarily part of the agreed learning day? Will you open up your own computer/laptop/tablet for use by others to make up the gaps?

4.  How will you accommodate the relaxation needs of other members of the family that fall within the home educated child's day? Does everyone need to rethink their coming-home processes, such as not making lots of noise on arrival? At what time does the television go on?

5.  Children do not necessarily have the same needs as adults. Some like a noisy creative environment, others prefer quiet and calm surroundings. Interestingly, many young adults study better when music is playing than in silence, as it keeps one part of the brain busy and stops it interrupting the other part of the brain. Explore with your home educated child(ren) what works best for them in which situations, and find ways to help them make it the way they like.

## Questions and answers

**Q:** *War has broken out. My 14-year-old daughter attends the local secondary school but, regrettably, her 11-year-old sister did not get into the same school and was offered a place a long way away. As we live in a rural environment, and transportation is difficult, we decided that it was not feasible to take up the place offered at a school so far away, and to home educate her until she can have a place at the same school. She's taken it on board and is enjoying the experience; she is working hard and we are proud of what she is producing. But she is now saying that as she is working at all hours of the day, with no time off, she feels she needs a lot more space. Our house is small, and she has the smallest bedroom over the front door – which does not permit her to have a desk in there too. She has been suggesting that she should swap rooms with her sister, so that she can have a desk in her room, and this is – quite understandably – meeting considerable resistance. What do you suggest?*

**A:** We would begin by asking her sister what she thinks. It could be an opportunity for her to redecorate and have a new location, but a move will work best if the swap is made voluntarily rather than through confrontation. Another solution might be to get one of the cupboard desks that are available, with doors that enable the working space to be hidden – and for this to be placed in a space downstairs, or perhaps in your bedroom (if you are the last to go to bed and the first to get up). Trolley desks are a good idea too, as they offer a flexible solution to the need for a temporary desk – and can be wheeled out of the way when no longer needed. You can also buy a desk bed where the bed is raised and accessed by a ladder with the underneath kitted out as a desk and shelves. In our experience these are often available second-hand.

Garden sheds are another possible alternative, and can provide a good working space – as can putting up a stud-wall to partition part of the garage (if you have one). But you did mention that you see home educating as a short-term solution, so it might not be worth moving everyone around if the situation is not going to last long. Resentment at being forced to move out of her bedroom from a teenager who sees her space as sacrosanct could last much longer.

**Q:** *I work part-time and my partner works evenings, so we managed to make sure there is someone at home at all times for our two home-educated children (10 and 12), but now my hours have changed slightly and I have to leave them alone for two hours on one afternoon a week I have noticed that there is much less indication of work being done on that one afternoon than I would normally expect. We have talked to the children, who are full of excuses, and they tell me that they are working just as hard as ever and that I am being over-sensitive. I want to be able to trust them and I can't afford to pay someone to look after them.*

**A:** While the law does not currently specify the age at which a child should be left alone, it is important to be safe. Get on to your home network and find out if someone in your network is happy to have your children sit with theirs one afternoon a week, with a reciprocal agreement that you will watch their children at a suitable time when you or your partner is available. Alternatively, perhaps a family member might be willing to supervise, to be at your home and happy to take an interest in their work. If children say you do not trust them, they are partly right, but it's about safety and security, without an adult present for that amount of time. Another alternative is to make that one afternoon 'own time' for both the children on the understanding that they make up the two hours by slightly longer working sessions throughout the week. Of course a lot of time is wasted in the school day, so a home-educated child really doesn't have to complete anything like the same hours of study to complete an equivalent amount of work – they could have this time as a craft afternoon or even as video-watching time. Choose your videos in advance to fit in with the themes that they are working on.

**Q:** *I am home educating my five-year-old for the next couple of years at least, as I feel she is far too young to be away from her parents all day long. In order to provide the most stimulating and fun environment I could I bought sand trays and water trays, and other people have donated to us all kinds of lovely things, such as an easel, a trike and a sit-and-ride bulldozer. But it feels a bit like we are now living in a nursery school. My husband and I love our daughter dearly, and are totally committed to this plan, but I can see the look on his face when he comes home and I have to admit that there is very little space left for us.*

**A:** Do you have a garden or outside space at all? If you do, simply moving the larger equipment outside at the end of the learning day (say tea time) and covering it all over with a waterproof cloth held down by a couple of handy bricks will work perfectly well. Your daughter should help – certainly the trike and bulldozer are light enough for her to move and 'We have to tidy up before we can have tea' is a good motivation. If you don't have any outside space, get a couple of sheets of MDF or similar to cover the sand and water trays, push them together in one corner and pile everything else underneath or in boxes on top with a throw over the lot. It might be a bit unsightly, but it could provide more room with a less 'play-centre' vibe. Of course, if you have an outside space and can spare a little money, a shed could solve a lot of problems.

Invest in some large plastic boxes with covers and wheels. Your local hardware store will have plenty at low prices – don't bother with the expensive 'toy box' versions. If you can't afford them, get on to your local Freeshare network via the Trash Nothing app. Someone, somewhere will have what you need for free, if you can wait a while.

See the Appendix for some tips from a former reception teacher on creating a stimulating home-learning environment for a primary- or nursery-age child.

# 6

# Developing a Curriculum

One of the many challenging things for any home-educating parent is deciding on the curriculum for their child to follow: what they are hoping to achieve in the longer term and, hence, what they are going to do on a day-to-day basis. These decisions will, of course, depend on the child's age, needs, abilities and interests, and on whether or not you plan to reintroduce them to school at a later date.

## Priorities for four- to seven-year-olds

For younger children, the priorities will usually be about instilling a love of learning as well as developing certain skills, abilities and interests, such as:

**Everything starts with fingers.** Young children need to touch, feel and explore with their fingers. Use different textures and materials to expand their understanding of the physical world. Sort things by rough and smooth, hard and soft. Let them invent their own descriptive words – wiggly or swishy, flat or humpty. Try wet/dry sand, shaving foam, cornflour and water and finger paints.

**Dexterity.** Model with Plasticine or playdough, either bought or home-made (or even pastry!) and practise kneading, stretching, rolling twisting and pinching.

**Hand-eye coordination.** Start with chunky mark-making materials, such as thick crayons, chalk and giant marker pens. The friction against the surface of the paper or chalkboard helps children feel the movement of the implement and associate it with their body movements. Try stringing beads of different sizes or following a pattern of colours as they string (red, yellow, blue, red and so on). Picking up objects with tweezers or tongs, using scissors, measuring spoonfuls into a bowl or weighing vegetables in a supermarket all offer practice in hand-eye coordination.

**Writing.** Start with tracing shapes or big letters/numbers with a finger, tracing patterns on a rug or lines of print in a book. Move on to tracing over shapes and letters with a pencil or crayon, colouring in and, from there, move on to copying letters and numbers underneath. Don't rush them – let them develop their skill over time, and give lots of activities to practise. Be creative: draw a road on paper and let them run a car along it; make it twisty, and so on. Play mats, alphabet and number posters and cards are all good for this. Don't push them to write until they want to try.

**Social skills.** Sharing, cooperating, empathy, turn-taking, and so on, can only really be learnt by interacting with others, so play, play, play is the answer, and preferably in groups of children of different ages and with minimal supervision. Let them learn by sometimes doing the wrong thing! Read more about social skills in Chapters 9 and 11.

**Sequencing, sorting and creating sets.** This can be done by working with objects by size or colour, actions in stories, numbers, biscuits on a plate, types of leaf, getting dressed, a trip to the shop – and in many other ways. Get them to retell a simple story with everything in the right order (this is harder than you might think for a five- to six-year-old). Draw some simple pictures from a well-known story and mix them up for them to sequence and colour. Collect pebbles on a beach and, when home, sort them by size, then again by colour, then again by patterns (striped, plain or mottled). Draw circles on paper to put the sets in. Count how many there are in the set and put the number in too.

**Stories and books.** You cannot tell a young child too many stories or read them too many books. When reading, sit next to them or have them in your lap – this means they have to engage with the words you are using and not just lip-read or watch your expression to understand the words being used. As you move along the line, underline the words with your finger. Look at the pictures together and talk about them. Ask them to describe things. Ask, 'What do you think happens next?' (even when it is a story that they know well). Get them to tell you the story and turn the pages as they go. You can buy commercially made games with character, setting and event cards to make up your/their own stories. Use a clothes line and pegs to sequence events. Libraries often have story-telling sessions, which make a great outing and a chance to choose new books, too. Loving stories is the first step to loving books and, even in our digital age, a love of books is the first step to loving to read and to learn. In the long run, those who read for pleasure have consistently better outcomes in life (for example, they are healthier, safer, more empathetic, articulate and so on).[11]

**The natural world.** You can grow plants from seed, watch birds and small animals in the park, and develop an understanding of the growth of fruits, vegetables and grass. You can discuss animals and how we rely on them for food – from the bees that ultimately contribute to all life on Earth. Grow something and then cook and eat it together – there is lots of scope for gathering, comparing and measuring along the way. Modern children are often unaware of the natural world, but understanding its role in life as we know it has never been more important. Photos, scrapbooks, leaf-prints, pressed flowers and leaves, bark rubbings and observing mini-beasts (or bugs) are wonderful activities to do with young children.

**Science.** You could try making and observing ice cubes and how they behave in different bowls, liquids, and so on. You could design and/or make 3D objects – a bridge that the billy goats can cross, a shelter for a giraffe. You could make a simple electric circuit (using batteries) to make a light come on or a wheel to turn.

**Learning numbers.** Begin with counting to five, guessing, teaching number bonds (plus and minus) to five and then the same to ten. Ask them to find seven yellow things and bring them to you, or to count the ducks on the pond or the books on the table.

**Awe and wonder.** Teach them to look at rainbows, flying birds and planes, a sunset, blossom-covered trees, baby fruit growing on a tree, a bumble bee with pollen bags on her legs, baby animals too small to walk. All offer considerable scope for conversation.

Young children should be encouraged to have some 'sitting down and doing' time every day – particularly if they are to attend school in the future. Three or four 10–15-minute activities a day sitting at a table doing anything from colouring to mixing cakes is probably enough for a four- to five-year-old, increasing to four or five 15–30 minute sessions for six- to seven-year-olds. In between, offer lots of play, building, drawing, kicking and throwing balls, skipping, hopping, climbing, visiting people and places, shopping, taking photos to look at later – all these make a full and developmental programme.

## Priorities for seven- to 11-year-olds

If children have had lots of practice with sequencing, following text from left to right with their eyes and tracing and drawing/copying, they should be starting to write for themselves by the age of seven. Some children, however, may need a bit more of a push. By seven to nine years they should know their letters, the names and the sounds of them, the common pairings and syllables 'ing', 'ang', 'th', ' ch' and so on. And by the same age they should be able to read and write at least simple sentences. Every child is different, and while many children in schools are writing long and interesting stories unaided at seven, others by this age can barely write their own names. Good groundwork and a love of learning are, however, far better indicators of eventual educational success than how many lines they can read and write. In some countries children don't start formal education until seven and yet, by the age of 11, they have similar and sometimes higher attainment levels to those who started at four. A slow start full of fun and exciting things is a great way to begin.

Some activities that you might provide include:

**Handwriting practice.** There are lots of books available in high-street bookshops or online for children to trace over or copy beneath letter forms and writing patterns. Many children enjoy this, especially if they are allowed to use colour pens. The idea is to build an automatic 'muscle memory' of writing so that it becomes easy. I know they all want to use keyboards, but writing by hand matters too.

**Spelling.** Often considered old-fashioned, spelling, like handwriting, needs to become almost automatic. Practise spelling everything from the words on packets and tins in the supermarket to the names of the streets as you pass. Get them to try to read words all around themselves wherever they go. If there are words they frequently misspell, give them a spelling book to write them in so that they can look it up in there. If they like tests and getting marks out of ten for things (and many children do), a weekly spelling test – or even a daily one for the very motivated – may help them learn words really well.

**Writing for purpose.** Get them to complete a learning journal about their day, every day. This can link in with target setting and self-assessment, too, once the habit is established (see pages 152–155). If they struggle, divide the page into sections such as, 'What I did', 'What I liked', 'What I could do tomorrow to follow on'. This helps to guide their thoughts. In time, they should be able to use this template without having it written down. If they are part of a home school network, sharing with their work group via social media or a website created for the group gives them more reason to share and present.

**Creative writing/storytelling.** Some children's brains work so fast that it is hard to write things down before they forget them. Writing is important, as currently almost all exams require written work, and writing in a sequence so that the reader can understand is also important; however, great thinking and creativity matter, too, and should be encouraged. Let your child record their thoughts for scribing later, let them tell stories out loud that they can later illustrate, ask them to add another chapter to that story they liked and so on. If they cannot write alone yet, get them to tell you while you write. They can copy the writing in their own way if appropriate.

**Numbers and maths.** Counting, money, telling the time, basic functions such as addition, subtraction, etc., fractions, shapes and angles, measuring accurately and mental maths are all key themes. Most children can count, add and subtract pretty well by seven using blocks or counters, and some can do amazing things in their heads. Having lots of fun with numbers, and lots of real-world application (adding up the supermarket shopping in the basket to see if they can get it right when it goes to the checkout, for example) can make maths fun and meaningful. Steer clear of too many maths books unless you need them – they can be very dull. Cooking is a great applied-maths activity, particularly baking, where measurements need to be so precise. If a recipe is for one cake, how can we bake three? Other activities include building things (a bird table, a bookshelf), model-making to scale (Globe Theatre, my room, a zoo) involving a lot of calculations, 'guesstimating' how many 5-litre buckets will fill the paddling pool and then checking it out. If you are not mathematically minded, you might need to train yourself to spot the opportunities to use maths, but there are lots around. (Let's each guess how many leaves are on the branch, then count to see who was the closest.)

**Topics.** These can follow and reflect the child's own interests. All children are interested in something, and the trick is to make that the starting point of a journey that includes science, maths, language and literacy, creative thought, design and technology, history, art, geography and some appreciation of the way the modern world works, too. You won't always get everything to fit easily, but by mind mapping with your child and revisiting and adding to the map regularly you might be surprised at how many of these subjects can be covered through topics as diverse as otters, football or mythical beasts. An example of a topic-planning mind map is given on page 149. Topic work can be shared with your wider home-school network, which may add some interesting ideas to what could be included, and so inspire others. Sharing their work at the end of the project can also encourage care in presentation and recording.

**The world around them.** Understanding the seasons, including the weather, climate change and its implications globally. This offers lots of possibilities for creative development (perhaps they could even have their own weather-monitoring station) the world of people and the effects of culture on thought and behaviour. They can explore why people behave as they do, and the importance of personal freedom and rights balanced with responsibilities. Other themes include: citizenship and being part of a society; inequalities and 'causes'; law, justice and human rights; the exploration of space and our understanding of the universe; the leap forward in technology in the last 150 years and its wider implications.

**Understanding the human body.** As appropriate, including: the bones, organs and their functions; the immune system; the oxygen/blood systems; the digestive system; growth and maturation (puberty); reproduction; the brain and its functions, processes and changes (such as the pruning down of existing neurons and the laying down of myelin sheaths connecting the remaining linked neurons that continues from adolescence onwards, perhaps making it harder to learn new things as we get older); how we learn; the causes of illness; genes and DNA.

## Priorities for 11–14-year-olds

This is the period of development when it is vital that children are exposed to as many ideas and experiences as possible. After adolescence, many of the character traits and interests of a person become quite 'set', so making sure they aren't already fixated on one thing, by providing a wealth of stimuli, will help them to become adults with a range of skills, interests and abilities – for life.

It is also the period in their educational development where they should be further developing their independent study skills, developing questioning and reasoning in their studies, and learning good research practices.

They should be able to work unsupervised for 30 minutes at a time (at 10–11 years) to an hour or more (at 14), and should be able to spend four to six sessions of 30 minutes to one hour working at their table, other workspace, such as a music stand or art space, and computer, with some physical activity in between.

From 2017 the GCSE subject list has changed a great deal, so if you and your child are looking at taking GCSEs, make sure that you know what the available subjects are, and design some exciting taster lessons or day trips around these. New subjects such as astronomy or film studies may well fire up the imagination of a young person, and the 11–14 stage is all about considering pathways and options.

This is a good time to start to learn a musical instrument if your child hasn't already done so. Like much of education, starting too early and being pushed too hard has put many people off many things. Adolescence is a great time to begin something new, as it can often become a lifelong pastime or passion. It is also a good time to enrol them in outside classes or groups for things such as creative writing, drama, dance, sound work, animation or graphic art – anything that allows for creative personal expression, as this is the age where the need to be seen as an individual begins to assert itself strongly and needs creative and expressive outlets.

It is also the age where a child's relationships with parents become conflicted, as they need and want the love and protection of their parents while rejecting any sense of obligation or ownership by them. This, therefore, makes an excellent time to engage a tutor for some of their work, if you haven't already done so. Individual tutoring can be expensive, but in many areas small-group tutoring is available, which is cheaper and allows for a degree of social interaction with others they may not know. Creating themed or managed groups within your local home-educating network is also an option, with parents volunteering to manage a particular theme or topic at their home on a rota basis.

## Priorities for 14-plus years

This is the age at which young people should be taking responsibility for their own learning and progress. It is also the age at which social relationships begin to become more important to many than family (at least while all is well).

They should continue learning literacy skills and maths, as these are extremely important core skills, but they may decide what other options and directions to follow. This will depend on the individual and their thoughts (if any) for their future, if they intend to sit GCSE or equivalent exams in the coming years, their talents and passions and their willingness to participate in learning.

For some young people at this age, learning to manage, maintain and understand social relationships is an almost full-time occupation, and that is understandable. This is the best age for exploring such issues before adulthood makes meeting new people and interacting with them more difficult.

For most, the desire to explore relationships and the wider world without supervision can easily be balanced with study and developing skills and interests related to their future plans. It is usual to expect young people to perform well in both areas and to respect priorities and boundaries so that study comes first.

At this age young people should be designing and managing their own programme within boundaries set by parents and/or tutors. These may be time boundaries or related to accomplishments, so a plan for the week with clearly defined expectations and outcomes will help both student and parent manage the process. At this age the young person should be able to keep a learning journal in which they reflect honestly on their progress as well as identifying areas of weakness or the need for further support or practice.

## CASE STUDY: PRISCILLA

We introduced Priscilla and her husband on page 29. Their eldest daughter went to a Montessori school at the age of three and stayed there until she was almost six. At that point, she was home educated until the age of 16. Each of their other girls followed a similar pattern, going to the Montessori school for a while (until it closed), but then returning for their full-time education at home. This was not something that had been planned ahead – Priscilla had loved school, been happy at the boarding school she attended from the age of 11 onwards and enjoyed her teaching career – but educating their family at home was rather shaped by the parents' chance meetings and Priscilla's growing interest in home education.

When her first child was about four, Priscilla met a mother at a party who was home educating and had a really interesting conversation with her about the benefits. As a family, they routinely had other families to stay, and a little while later she was struck by the children of one family, only finding out at the end of the weekend that they were home-educated. Visiting children could at times be fractious and demanding. These children rather struck her as calm and serene, assured of their place in the family without needing to demand attention, and confident enough to integrate with others, both adults and children. They had an innate self-confidence and clearly knew where they belonged.

Priscilla was also perturbed by hearing parents talk about how eager they were for their children to start school, or go away to boarding school – with the benefit being to the parents rather than the children. It seemed such parents were not really engaging with their children, and she felt that this was an abdication of parental responsibility. Her thinking was also influenced by the introduction of the National Curriculum in the UK (in 1988), which she thought implied that all schools had to be teaching the same things at the same time. As an independent spirit, she resisted this, thinking that learning should be adapted to the individual's interests and talents rather than centrally prescribed.

While they were still making up their minds about whether or not to home educate, Priscilla visited a number of potential schools and used the opportunity to find out more about what head teachers thought. In general, they were willing to talk about it and were positive. She read as much as possible about the subject, and was particularly influenced by a book called *I Saw the Angel in the Marble*,[12] which proposes that each child is special, and suggests that as you work with them you recognise both who they are and see their capabilities and interests.

Priscilla established a schoolroom at home where the children worked together, but on age-appropriate activities related to wider topics. To start with, she led it all herself, but as the girls got older they brought in specialists to support them. They regarded English, maths and French as the core subjects, and recruited specialists to teach music, art, French and maths, and later some science. They tried to be in the schoolroom by 9am – preferably having had some fresh air first – and to cover the 'high-energy' subjects by lunchtime. The wider curriculum – history, geography, art and so on – was fitted in around the core subjects.

Priscilla would often read aloud to them all, and discussions of what they had been covering would continue over mealtimes – always with a dictionary on the table so that they could look up things they did not know. Their strong belief was that education involves life-long learning and everything became relevant and an extension of what they were covering in the classroom.

When they had been going for about six years, they formed a group for those home educating in the area, gathering every Friday to work on a project together or specific areas of the curriculum where they all needed support (often in science). They took it in turns to organise this and found the sharing a fascinating experience, as it drew out hidden talents.

## Needs

There are certain things that need to be part of the child's programme, whatever their age. These not only fulfil physical needs but also offer opportunities to mix and meet with other people, of all ages, but particularly of roughly the same age as themselves.

### Physical activity

Home-educated children need some physical activity built into their programme. For younger children this should be on a daily basis, and could include running around the garden, a trip to the park or walking a dog (see www.borrowmydoggie. com, if you don't have your own). Older children will need longer sessions, perhaps a couple of times a week. This could be swimming, a trip to a gym or sports club or trampolining at a local sports centre. Not everyone likes physical activity, and a decision to home educate might have in part been fuelled by a desire to avoid such shared physical effort, but it's important to continue physical involvement of some kind, in order to provide a balance in their day and keep up their energy levels, and we know that physical exercise can also influence mood. There's usually some kind of exercise that everyone will enjoy, even those who are not sportive in any way. Bear in mind too that this can be varied with an appreciation of the value of mindfulness, being still and truly in the moment, which has been shown to impact positively on both mood and learning.

## Social skills

Learning social skills is important (see Chapters 9 and 11), but so is using them in real-world situations. Make sure that your children's week includes several opportunities to mix with others of roughly the same age. Clubs are good, but they don't always provide much chatting time. Research on emotional resilience suggests that too many clubs are as bad as none – children need unstructured time together with their peers. The less they can manage it, the more time they need. Shared projects that they can take part in with others, trips and visits with a group of others, weekends camping with others or joining an action group or a charitable group to work alongside others for a common cause are all good.

## Talking about real-world issues

Opportunities to discuss, reflect and experience the wider world first-hand in an appropriate and age-appropriate way are helpful ways of encouraging a child to consider issues and develop their values. Sitting around the meal table or during a car journey are good times for this. Encouraging young people to discuss, debate and even argue can help them develop their sense of identity. Drama groups, discussion forums (real world or online), attending public meetings and belonging to a junior or teen book club or film group are all helpful. If you don't have any near you, consider starting one.

## Abilities

It is important to think about not just your child abilities now but also what you want them to develop in future. And their ability level does not have to be, or potentially be, of an international standard – just things that you would like them to try or experiment with. For example, learning a musical instrument develops the brain and is therefore something you might want to include, without expecting them to be performance standard afterwards – but it will also require an honest assessment of your support skills, and perhaps additional expense if you have to provide lessons with a specialist teacher.

Other areas of the curriculum that might need specialist support are art and design, writing and maths, and if your child has a particularly obvious interest in one area, it might be worth providing a tutor who can develop that area. Having full-time tutoring for a child can be an expensive option, so for most home-educating parents deciding where you do need specialist help and where you or part of your network can supply what is missing will need to be discussed. You can make arrangements to swap time and skills with other local parents from your network.

Finding specialist support is getting easier all the time, and with the rising numbers of children being home educated there are networks of (often former classroom) teachers who are available. How you schedule their involvement will, of course, depend on what involvement you want from them, when they are available and how much time they can offer.

With children between the ages of eight and 13 the best way to approach the curriculum is through broad and wide-ranging topics, not a lesson on each subject. You might establish a series of stimulating and interesting topics together with your child, which overlap without going over too much common ground, but which ensure you are covering all the elements of a balanced curriculum over a period of time. Each subject does not have to be done every week, and you might want to do core subjects (maths and English) more often, but overall you should be looking to create a balanced, stimulating and personalised educational experience for your child.

## Locating resources

There are a great many resources available from high-street shops or specialist services online. Some of these are useful, others are not, as you might expect. Exercises that encourage a child to think are better than those that don't, and workbooks that provide real-world examples for concepts or explorations (for example in science or maths) will be better received by most children than those that simply explain a process and provide endless practice.

If you want your child to be following the UK's National Curriculum (and there is no need for them to do this unless you choose to), you can download copies of the national curriculum documents for stages and ages from www.Gov.uk along with resources and materials commercially available. Online, there are places where you can get lesson plans and worksheets for the National Curriculum quite cheaply, or for free, but do bear in mind that these are probably not enough on their own. Children don't learn through worksheets, so use these as a back-up to more creative and hands-on experiential learning rather than on their own. They can be a useful tool in assessing how much a child has learnt, rather than being used to provide the teaching.

## How to find a tutor for your home-educated child

Agencies are a starting point for finding a tutor, and you will then ensure that the tutors you employ are qualified to teach the subject in which they offer tuition (depending on the level being sought – you would not necessarily expect subject specialism for children of primary or early secondary age) and to be DBS checked.

You will also find that the tutoring available, and the associated costs, vary according to parental objectives. For example, for those who are using home educating as a means to prepare their children for a specific and very selective school to which they want to ensure their child has access, tutors offering preparation for a particular exam may find themselves highly desirable in a very competitive market, with fees for their services in the £80–90 per hour bracket. There may be lower rates for group teaching. A regular commitment to teach a home-educated child over a longer term period might cost much less.

You should also be aware that those opting to be tutors to home-educated children might find the situation overly pressurised, due to either parental expectations of what can be achieved or previous experience of difficulties in establishing a relationship with a home-educated child. One tutor reported arriving at the house of the child he was going to tutor each week and the child refusing to leave their bedroom – the mother was emotional and the tutor felt pressurised and embarrassed. He was always paid for his time (which had been pre-booked and allocated to the child) but it felt an awkward situation, and he has since reverted just to teaching children who are in full-time schooling but are preparing for a specific examination stage (school entrance at 11, GCSE or A level).

All the tutors we spoke to did, however, talk of a real boom in demand for their services, from children who are already high achievers where parents are seeking tutoring to supplement their children's formal education, to home educating parents who want to employ a tutor, all are competing for the services of a group that are increasingly in demand.

## Interests

A child's interests can be of primary importance in encouraging their development. A common reason for embarking on home educating is a child's feeling of alienation within the classroom. Building not only their self-confidence but also their intellectual development through encouraging their interests can be a very positive thing to do.

---

### CASE STUDY: LEO

Leo did not get on well at school. He learnt early on that he 'could not read' and would tell people so. Many people at school and at home had tried different methods to get him to read, but he would become agitated and panic at the very mention of words or letters. What finally enabled a breakthrough was his grandfather taking him to an otter sanctuary and him falling in love with the creatures. His parents built on his passion for otters by getting books from the library, looking for otter clips online, and helping him to make otter models and pictures. Within a few days he could recognise the word 'otter' among the most crowded of texts and he began to compile all he was

---

learning into a book. His parents and other family members secured him a range of different materials on otters, including a junior supporter pack for the sanctuary he had visited. It was a desire to learn everything he could, and not miss out on information available to him, that provided the starting point for him learning to read. Although he would still balk at a pile of flashcards, presented with a new article about otters he would sit for a long time working out the text using his own carefully crafted system until he had read most of it. Within a very short space of time he was reading well and able to read the kind of material most of his peers could not. He had also completed writing some 50 pages of an encyclopaedia on otters he was making for his grandfather.

If your child has something they are passionate about, build on this. That's their window into the world, so it's a good idea to find ways of using that passion to encourage them to learn. Your local library could be a starting point, but also getting them to write their own books, printing out and stapling them together to offer a permanent record of their interests.

Along similar lines, for a child interested in trains, time-tables can offer a great way to develop their maths skills, or you could investigate the different engine specifications for railways around the world and where they go; these have been covered in documentaries and offer information on which you could build, thereby bringing geography, history and science into their explorations. You could add to this with visits to some of the sites of early development, or mapping out the first transport links, or working out how to get around the Monopoly board in the minimum time possible. The process of learning can involve a variety of general and specific knowledge – it's amazing how much can be shoehorned in – and may be one involving the whole family.

## Reintegration into conventional schooling

If your longer-term plan is for them to reintegrate into conventional schooling, you will need to think about the stages and ages of the National Curriculum and when would make the best point at which to do this. Ideal times are when there is more general change within the educational system, and other children may be coming and going, so the end of junior schooling, the start of year 10 (as the GCSE curriculum starts) or for the start of the first-year sixth form/at sixth-form college, whether for A levels, a course leading to the International Baccalaureate or for NVQs. Moving them in and out of primary school is not such a big deal and providing their standards of reading, writing and number work are up to scratch, it's not such a barrier to entry, and given that the children share a common teacher for most of the day, their accommodation to a new environment can arguably be more quickly achieved.

**A MOTHER COMMENTS**

Due to my husband's very peripatetic job, our children moved primary schools continually, usually at one- or two-year intervals. What they learnt was that not every school works in the same way, but primary school teachers who have a new child in their class usually ask for a volunteer to look after a new arrival, and this was always helpful in enabling them to feel established. What we learnt as a family was that fitting in can generally be helped by involving yourself in after-school activities.

Some schools are particularly flexible, and it might be possible for a child to partially reintegrate, for example, by going to a school to study sciences, which are harder to do at home. This creates an issue of whether the child is 'on the roll' of the school or not. Your ability to have a partially enrolled child will depend on the head teacher's attitude to inclusion but also it will probably relate closely to how much demand for places there is in the local area. To find out attitudes towards partially enrolled children, talk to your local school. Once they are in the sixth form, more flexibility will almost certainly be possible. See advice on flexi-schooling in Chapter 3.

## Preparation for reintegration

If you are planning for your child to re-enter school or college for the sixth form, you might need to find out if there are any additional classes that need to be taken before doing so, and which are a requirement before further study (for example GCSE English, if they are going to enrol for the A level). But bear in mind that there are many subjects that are completely new at A level (for example psychology, philosophy and art history) and so may be entered on the same basis as the rest of the school. The range of subjects offered by sixth-form colleges may be particularly broad.

If there are stages that have been missed out, you could look into access courses, which are not time-limited, and are tailored to diverse needs. You could talk to your local school about taking the odd course before your child(ren) rejoin to find out the options (and any potential costs) first.

Often joining the school first and then looking at any catch-up needs might be the best way forward. Attending school will provide a suitable motivation for the child to work at the additional learning in most cases.

## A MOTHER COMMENTS

My 11 children mostly transferred to secondary schools when we moved to South Africa, largely because by then they needed more maths and science content than I could either offer or realistically support – and there were no tutors available at a price we could afford. But once the children transferred, the schoolteachers were always really surprised at how well they fitted in. I think that having lived in lots of places, our children were broadminded and flexible, and where we had lived they had often got involved (where appropriate) with the community project we were working on; for example playing with the local children, delivering meals and putting on little shows for the hospital residents.

I like to think that these attitudes rubbed off on the younger ones. Certainly, by the time they transferred to school they were all well ahead of where they were meant to be by that age, and after initial tests several of them went into classes above their calendar age. This was not because we had been pushing them, but because home education means you can progress much more quickly – you don't have to wait for everyone in the class to be heard, and there is much less administration. We also went out a lot – on expeditions and visits, wherever we were living – and this too enlarged their understanding and practical skills.

## How to design a curriculum

It's a good idea to start with timing: how and when you want your school day to run. There is no need to stick to the 9.00/9.30am to 3.00/3.30pm structure. You can design a programme to fit your child's energy levels and peak learning times – as well as your availability. Some people learn better later in the morning, some are buzzing first thing. Teenagers often don't wake up fully until mid-morning, and some of us are more active in the evening. Design their day around their peak learning activity times. The school day for a home educated child also does not have to be as long as that within conventional schooling, as the administration, travel time and group activities (such as assembly and form time) do not need to be scheduled.

Draw up a list of all the essentials first, and include exercise sessions, relaxation, socialisation and outings such as library visits. If you have any tutorial or network group times, add those to the plan. The rest of the time can be divided into suitable chunks to fit your aims and objectives – but for many it would simply become 'topic' time.

### Step 1: the time plan

This plan is for a 12-year-old boy named Matthew. The timings have been decided by trial and error. Matthew prefers to start later and finish later. The long break at lunchtime allows for additional time to extend 'out and about' time.

Figure 1: Sample timetable

| | 10.00–10.20am | 10.20am–12.00 midday | 1.30–2.30pm | 2.30–3.00pm | 3.30–4.30pm | Additional |
|---|---|---|---|---|---|---|
| Monday | Review of Friday and setting targets and outcomes for the day | Out-and-about activity: • Cycling • Swimming • Gym • Walking | Topic 1 | Piano lesson | Topic 2 (with small group from network) | None |
| Tuesday | Review of previous day | Topic 1 | Library | Piano practice | Maths tutor | 6.00–7.00pm Football |
| Wednesday | As Tuesday | Topic 1 | Out-and-about activity, visit a: • Museum • Gallery • Cafe • Topic-related activity | Maths – work set by tutor | Free | 6.00–7.00pm Topic 2 with small group |
| Thursday | As Tuesday | Weekly blog Reading | Out-and-about activity | Maths – work set by tutor | Topic 1 | 6.00–7.00pm cooking dinner |
| Friday | As Tuesday | Art group: painting, sculpture, clay work, drawing, drama and puppets, etc. | Art group | Topic 1 – no break, finish at 3.30pm | Free | Board games – friends and family |

## Step 2: the topic plan

The topic plan is not a rigid or set plan, rather a way of joining up ideas and experiences through a common theme. It can take some practice if you have never used such free-flow forms before. It is the absolute opposite of the 'list' approach as it has many branches that frequently join up with each other or branch off into new areas altogether. Children frequently find this way of mapping ideas easy as it echoes the way a neuro-typical child's mind works – leapfrogging from idea to idea.

You might find it helpful to create a checklist, real or in your head, of the 'subject' headings you want any and all topics to cover. A list might include:

- History – what went before
- Geography – the natural environment and links to the wider world and people around the world
- Social studies – people and their interactions and life choices,
- Maths – how many? How much? How big/small? Movement, time, size, weight
- Language – description, terminology specific to the topic, recording discoveries, experiments, trips, observations, etc.
- Science – how things work, asking questions 'What would happen if . . .' 'How does it work?'
- Drama
- Literature and reading
- Biology – the living world of plants and animals, how they live, grow, reproduce and die
- Diversity – how different people do things, feel things, behave and believe

A good topic plan is not set in stone; it is something that can be added to and may even evolve into something entirely different. For example, after a visit to the Albert Docks in Liverpool one 12-year-old was inspired by the International Slavery Museum, which charts the history of slavery and its relationship to the growth of the city of Liverpool, to write a book looking at slavery (historical and modern day) in the UK. Copies of his book were given to local primary schools where he also gave talks to pupils about his findings.

Once a basic topic plan has been produced (Gill draws them freehand on large sheets of paper with thick pens of different colours) it can be added too and filled in with adult and child additions.

A topic like 'Water' could occupy a family for a full year as it might cover all kinds of creatures, plants, history of human settlements, great rivers of the world, climate change, needs of plants and animals, cooking and all manner of other things. It might also make an excellent topic for a networking group to work on as each parent/child can have part of the plan to explore and can feed back their work to the others, as well as providing opportunities for trips and visits together to anything from a pond to look for mini-beasts to Roman Baths.

Smaller topics such as 'Food' or 'the Vikings' may be more limited and take a shorter time. One of the advantages of home education over any other types of education is that it can be tailored around the interests and curiosities of both parent and child so that some of the learning can take place together, with the adults taking a facilitator role rather than the role of 'expert'.

Figure 2: Topic plan (mind map) for topic 1 in timetable above.

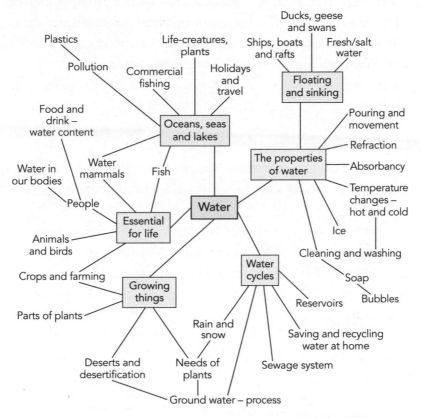

## Step 3: planning activities

Once the topic plan (mind map) has been drawn, it can be used to form the basis for planning some specific activities. Here is a sample of some activities designed from the above mind map for water, in rough planning form.

Figure 3: Activity planning based on topic plan (figure 2)

| Focus | Activity | Recording | Resources | Visits, etc. |
|---|---|---|---|---|
| Floating and sinking | Design and make a raft capable of keeping a 5kg weight floating in a paddling pool of water for 1 hour using only items found in your room. | Photographs of materials found and attempts to complete task. Create document on computer with photos in sequence explaining process. | As given. Paddling pool filled with water in garden. | Science museum or historic dockyard, port, docks, river or canal trip? |
| Floating and sinking | Using materials provided, can you: (a) Decide which items will float and which will sink. Sort accordingly and test them. Were you right? What about turning things the other way up, such as bottle tops – do they still float or sink? (b) Using one of the corks, can you devise a way to make it float halfway down a bowl of water so that it is not touching the bottom in any way or breaking the surface in any way? | Draw and label items that float, and items that sink; and indicate any that tricked you. Draw your attempts before testing. Photograph the cork floating in the middle of the bowl if you succeed. | Box of small items of different materials: corks, metal bottle tops, small plastic toys, Kinder egg middle, coins, paper clips, foil container, cardboard box, etc. Clear glass or plastic bowl of water with plastic sheeting underneath. | Science museum or historic dockyard, port, docks, river or canal trip? |

| Focus | Activity | Recording | Resources | Visits, etc. |
|---|---|---|---|---|
| The properties of water – ice | Freezing times. Fill an empty ice-cream container/small plastic box with 250ml water. Place in the freezer and estimate how long it will take to freeze. How long did it actually take? Add different substances to the water, such as salt, baking powder, food colouring, fruit juice, cleaning fluid, washing up liquid and so on. If you have room, put all in same-size containers with 250ml water and estimate if any will take longer or shorter than plain water to freeze. Were you right? Once you know how long 250ml takes, estimate how long 500ml in the same container will take. Check it to see if you are right. Now try 1 litre in the same container. Estimate and check your guess. | Photograph each stage for creating a detailed record later. Once you have all your results, create a chart to show your results. How you do this is up to you. | 6–10 empty ice-cream or takeaway containers. Ask friends for some. Range of kitchen and household products to be chosen by the child. | Ice skating or a trip to an indoor ski slope, or a visit to an ice-cream shop with a look at how it is made? |
| Floating and sinking – ducks, geese and swans | Once a week, visit the pond in the park and make a note of the number of birds on the water, and the number around the pond. Identify the types of bird using an online reference or a bird book from a library. Keep a regular log of the birds seen, the date, the types of bird, etc. in order to map their habits, such as nest building and egg sitting. Emergence of young? Families and survival? Independence of young – no longer with parent birds? Migration? Return? | Create and maintain a detailed log that gives information by date of bird behaviour on the pond. Log can be on the computer, on paper, a wall chart, etc. | Binoculars? Notebook and pencil? | RSPB wildfowl centre or a pond or lake known for its wildlife, or a natural history museum? |

## Step 3: topic 2

This is a shared topic devised with parents and children from the home education network. There are currently seven children in this network ranging from five to 13 years, so the topic has less structure than topic 1, as the group itself devises the work and who will be responsible for what, with supervision from two adults. The adults rotate on a monthly basis. The group has a network WhatsApp group to share thoughts and ideas, as well as its own website where members post their work together and weekly personal blogs. The website is shared with several other network groups that occasionally meet up to share thoughts and ideas for a day event or weekend camp.

At the moment the group is working on the topic 'The impact of human beings on planet Earth'.


## Child-centred target and goal setting

This includes personal reviewing and evaluating performance – and all can be done in the nicest and most fun ways. For the home-educating parent the challenge is to get the child to see 'work' or learning tasks as something they want to do rather than something they have to do. The very fact that it is at home means freedom to many children, especially those who are left to their own devices much of the time. The home-educating parent probably does not want to lean over their child and point out their mistakes, or become a firm disciplinarian who polices the time spent concentrating. Rather, they aim to encourage their child to monitor their own progress, to review what they have done with their day, to set targets for the next day and further ahead, and to think about what they have not done for a while or avoided, in order to ensure coverage of all the subjects they want to progress in.

Depending on the age of the child, the home educated young person can then get on with much of their learning on their own. The parent can assist through:

- Discussing settling down routines – or procrastination habits.
- Helping them decide what they will do first – and the basis on which this decision is made (do they like to do the thing they enjoy most first, or leave it until last?).
- Helping them plan their day: some simple guidance on mixing tasks and topics to make sure every session has some fun elements might be helpful at the planning stage.
- Helping them get started: an established 'first-task' routine every day can help them transition into learning more easily, perhaps by completing a simple time or task planner.

With a younger child, going through a planning process with them for 10 minutes or so at the start of each day is helpful so that they understand the stages of creating a plan. It also involves them in saying yes or no to some things, gets them excited and interested in others. Children should probably be told clearly that some things must be done whereas others are optional, although what the 'musts' are is up to you and your curriculum and aims. But even 'musts' can be exciting and fun learning events with the right planning, resourcing and activities.

Crucial for your planning or supervision is some kind of evaluation to enable you to give more experience or clarity in some areas or to provide more instruction and advice in others. To do this we need to have some kind of evaluation system – a way of knowing what was hard or easy, interesting or dull, what made the time fly by or drag, as well as knowing which areas of a subject or topic were being explored and how effective the learning was.

The only simple way of doing this is by having clear learning intentions or aims for each activity or time slot. For parents pursuing the 'life as education' model, this might simply be creating shared intention for a whole week or month such as 'helping others' or 'being kind to others' or something more personal, such as 'thinking before doing'. In such instances, every family member simply shares what they have done or noticed or felt in relation to their intention at a family get-together at the end of the day, perhaps over their evening meal.

For parents pursuing a more home-based learning experience, similar intentions can be identified as personal-growth targets, but some more academic learning intentions can be created in relation to the curriculum they follow. For example, 'knowing and recognising the numbers 1 to 10' is a straightforward learning intention for a young child, whereas 'understanding the role of sugars' is a far more open-ended learning intention for a young person requiring research and organisational skills in order to define what needs to be covered to fulfil the brief.

Once we have a learning intention, it is possible to decide when something has been learnt. For example, if our learning intention is for the child to learn the numbers 1 to 10, we can provide lots of activities to help them learn and then observe if the child knows the numbers 1 to 10 by presenting them with a range of counting and recognition tasks and seeing that they can do them without too much difficulty. Likewise, for the young person who has been given the task of finding out about the 'role of sugars' we can demonstrate that the intention has been met by first outlining what is to be covered in the work the young person is to undertake and checking that this has indeed been completed. They might keep a reading log for this so you can see which books and websites they have used to get the information they require. Also, by expecting them to demonstrate using words, pictures, diagrams, downloads or any other method that they choose so they have indeed got a clear understanding. You can always round up such a piece of work (which might represent many hours of study) with a quick verbal or written test based on their own work, just to make sure that they have understood, and not just copied things down. Sometimes young people love a test – usually when they feel they know the answers.

When you are satisfied that your child has learnt something from your curriculum list, cross it off and choose a new outcome for them or encourage them to think about what else they need to learn to complete their knowledge and understanding; for example, the history of sugar is a very human story that embraces most of the world. You might extend this by looking at the geography of sugar (where it grows and where it is mostly eaten), the sugar industry, the current trend for substituting sugar with other substances and its effect on diet, and you could develop some related cooking and eating activities (can you make bread without sugar? What does it taste like?).

## Questions and answers

**Q:** *I am home educating my nine-year-old son. It's going really well but he doesn't like writing. Whenever I give him a task that involves writing he tends to disengage completely – and usually walks away in a strop. It got so difficult that I started employing a tutor who does writing with him once a week. But this is an expensive solution and I also feel that he should be doing writing more than just once a week. What should I do?*
**A:** It is good to hear it is going really well. Getting a tutor was

a good way around the issue of how to get your child to do some writing, but obviously it would be better if he would do more. Writing is a skill that everybody who can needs to learn.

It's important to think about what's going on. Writing is a multi-faceted skill that requires several things to be done at the same time. Given his age you probably won't get much out of him about why he doesn't like writing, but in order to think about how best to support him, it's important to try to unpick what's going on.

Is it the physical activity he doesn't like – in trying to control the pencil? Or is it the requirement to be creative? Or is he not confident about what he has to say, and therefore what he should write about? Does he find it boring and slow? Is it that his hand can't keep up with his brain, and he needs to think more slowly? You need to play detective, so perhaps chat to the tutor about where he or she feels the difficulty lies.

In the meantime, although being able to write is a very important skill, there are temporary solutions. You could help your child record his stories on a voice recorder or computer. You could then go through what he has captured with him and decide which bits of the recording he wants to use. It's important for him to learn how progression works in a narrative – the sequencing of what happens and in what order, and what the most important parts of the story are. But progression is a skill that younger children find difficult, and it needs to be practised in order to be developed. You can help him with exercises, which are available commercially if you don't want to make your own. Many of these feature pictures (some with accompanying words, depending on the age of the child) that tell a story and which have to be put in an appropriate order.

If the issue is a physical difficulty, you could try handwriting practice. This has to be learnt as a drill, but practice will help him develop the fine motor control that is a key skill for writing. Handwriting practice books are easily available, and as letter formation is taught in a particular way, you will probably have to unlearn some of your own writing practices as you work with him.

If he has problems with spelling and can't remember or sequence words, he may have a form of dyslexia, in which case using a computer that will spell for him will build his confidence – and in the long run there are spell-checking programs that he can use. But it's important that using a computer does not enable him to avoid handwriting completely. He can write out sentences on the computer, print them out and then copy them himself in his own writing.

Perhaps he sees writing as boring, in which case you need to help him see how useful it can be in a daily context. Suggest activities out of the home education situation where writing is needed – perhaps with you looking in cupboards to find out what is needed for the shopping list and asking him to write it down, or helping him to write birthday and Christmas cards on behalf of the family.

You will also need to inspire him so that he wants to write more, perhaps through enabling him to take part in a joint project with other home educated children so that he can both contribute and see his efforts included within a bigger whole. Reading aloud from books he likes will also help his writing, and listening to audio books can play a very effective role in this. Is it possible for him to go to listen to a writer talking about how they came to write stories he enjoys? Many writers did not find writing easy to start with, and this might help him to see that he is not alone. The writer might also have a website talking about this, which you could explore together. Share with him the joy that comes from reading, and he may be keener to participate himself.

Above all, don't give up. Whatever his reason for not liking writing, and there may be several, he does need to learn how to do this, not only as a key communication skill but also for the effective development of his brain.

**Q:** *I have been home educating my 12-year-old daughter for a couple of years now with the intention that she will go back into mainstream school in time to study for her GCSEs. I've been using the National Curriculum and downloading worksheets and lesson plans, confident that there was enough material to keep her going and to save me having to do it, because I work part-time.*

*Recently, however, through my daughter's regular swimming class, I met a mother with a child of almost the same age, who resources her daughter's entire learning plan herself, putting together a programme of work but alternating this with day trips and projects that they do together. I felt it sounded so much more exciting than what I was offering our child. What should I do?*

**A:** Some children like worksheets. They work their way through a prescribed and achievable piece of work, and receive a response at the end of it; it's what school work means to them. Many home-school packs include a self-completion certificate at the end of the book, and parents often under-estimate how much pleasure these can give.

But the beauty of home educating is that you have much more freedom and can use the time how you want, so it's not a bad idea to think about the learning preferences of your child, and how you can best work with her through home educating.

You need to both observe and ask your daughter whether

she is finding her learning stimulating. Is she being stretched by her experience or is she finding it a chore?

An intermediary solution might be to team up with your friend and see if you could collaborate for one project, and see how the girls work together – perhaps in return for you offering some sedentary work that you could coordinate and supervise. You could then talk to your daughter about what learning style she prefers. If she finds a more experiential style of learning more engaging remember, however, that she will still need to record and annotate her experiences and learning. When she is preparing for GCESs or other formal examinations, she will need to consider the examiners' requirements. But whatever her route, all pathways are best supported by encouraging her to develop a love of learning.

---

**A MOTHER COMMENTS:**

My five-year-old son had a teacher who would write comments on every piece of work he handed in, and he really appreciated this. Looking through the portfolio of work he arrived home with at the end of one term I spotted a piece where 'good Ben' had been written on it in rather a shaky hand. He had added the comment himself in order to make the teacher's response to his work complete. It was clearly a part of the learning process he really valued.

---

**Q:** *I am German, living in the UK, and used to children starting school when they are seven. My six-year-old son has always been home educated, because I felt he was not mature enough to start mainstream school, and I did not want him to be pressured into having to sit down and conform when* *he was still so little. For now, I want him to play as much as possible, and my intention is to integrate him into school for Key Stage 2 when he's seven.*

*I have tried to find educational toys and games, but as at yet he's not shown any interest in this, and has no interest in formalised learning. He doesn't like drawing, and is still at the scribbling stage. Although he is a happy, outward-looking child, and very friendly, it does worry me that perhaps I should be doing more formalised things, getting him used to sitting down and doing what he's asked to do, particularly as the long-term aim is to integrate him within a mainstream school.*

**A:** In the long run, children who don't start school until they are seven (which is what happens in much of continental Europe) are indistinguishable from their earlier schooled peers by the age of 11.

You might introduce some fun activities – perhaps just once a day to start with – where your son is expected to sit at a table with you for about 15 minutes just to get him used to a little structure. Introduce cutting and sticking, planting things in pots, sorting and counting. If you are worried about the educational content of what he is doing at home, you could increase the amount of reading you do with him: getting him to act out stories and look at their sequencing – what happens and in what order. You could work with him on some of the exercises that are available, cutting up pictures in a cartoon-type exercise (thereby working on his manual dexterity) and then getting him to put them in order. These exercises can be bought in shops and online.

From there you could try sequencing with texts as well. Depending on his familiarity with reading you could get him to look for words he can recognise, or names that begin with capital letters. If he is already reading, you could get him to draw characters from a story and write their names, cut them out and make a frieze – lining paper used for decorating can make a very good basis for this. Stories that have a range of characters work well, such as the Gingerbread Man in which he meets a series of people and animals, or the wonderful *Very Hungry Caterpillar* by Eric Carle. If writing is still emerging, you write the captions first and get him to trace over them (bearing in mind that you will need to write characters the way he is learning to do so, not in your usual handwriting).

Above all, don't worry too much if he is not yet at the same level as his peers. Being back in the school system will enable him to catch up quickly. But just as important is not to forget that an early part of schooling is socialisation, so provide him with plenty of opportunities to play with lots of other children. You playing a game with him is not the same as him playing a game with other children.

# 7

# What Constitutes 'Quality Learning'?

Schools consistently debate the issue of 'quality learning' and whether some learning is superior to other types. There are those that maintain that all learning is equally valid, whereas others place greater value on some areas and types of learning than others. Partly, this is driven by what comes next – with testing and exams being the means by which learning is measured and directions for the future decided upon; however, this is by no means the only way of deciding what is and isn't important. Education only for exams and tests leaves out a lot of what makes life exciting and surprising. Recent evidence clearly shows that teaching social competencies and promoting well-being effectively can boost academic achievement by up to 11 per cent[13] although we also now know that the level of social competencies of a child at seven years old is as reliable an indicator of academic success as IQ – or even more so.

Educating children is as much about teaching them to be learners as it is about the knowledge or skills acquired, so in this chapter we provide some pointers on maximising your child's learning by building their sense of self-worth as a learner. We also explore learning processes and skills, as well as how to make a simple activity a deeper learning experience all round.

## Teacher or educator?

Dictionary definitions offer little difference in meaning between the words 'teacher' and 'educator', and you will find that a thesaurus offers the words as alternatives to each other. In general understanding, however, the term 'educator' has a more formal association than 'teacher'.

When we think of teachers we tend to think of schools, although, of course, the number of those involved in teaching is much wider: parents are teachers, as are grandparents, friends and neighbours. The television and the Internet teach us things, and the concrete step that gets slippery may similarly teach us something if we are not careful. But that does not make the concrete step an educator, as it does not have intention, skill or application to our learning process. If we slip and twist our ankle, we become our own educator, because we learn to recognise cause and effect: the experience of slippery pavements or very high-heeled shoes may lead us to change our behaviour in the future. But our involvement in our own learning depends on our readiness to absorb it. Whereas for some it might take many experiences over a lifetime to create learning, for others just one experience might be enough. An educator seeks to open the mind and develop a whole range of thinking processes to enable learning to happen within an individual or group. A teacher provides a lesson, which may or may not create learning. The best educators are also teachers, and the best teachers are also educators, because the two processes work best in harmony.

## What makes a great educator?

Most of us carry answers to this question in our own life experience. Take a moment to think about some of the people in your life who have inspired you.

- Was there someone who 'opened you up' to music, art, history or perhaps just being kinder to yourself?
- Was there someone who inspired you to love reading or writing?
- Was there someone who showed you something familiar in a whole new way? Perhaps it was the growing cycle of plants, the stars in the sky, the food on your plate or the relationship between numbers.
- Was there a coach or instructor who helped you believe in and master your own physical abilities?
- Was there someone you've never met whose life story or creative influence inspired the choices you made?

Now ask yourself what these different individuals had in common. What was it about these people and these life events that had such a powerful impact? Jot down on a piece of paper the first three thoughts that come to mind.

The answers for each of us will vary, but when using this exercise Gill has found that common threads frequently occur, such as:

- They believed in me.
- They taught to me to believe in myself.
- Their passion for their subject/abilities was catching.
- They spent time with me/they helped me learn.
- They never gave up on me.

- They always gave constructive and helpful criticism – never negative.
- I thought: *If they can do it, so can I.*

A great educator opens doors and inspires others to step through them; they hold your hand until you are ready to run by yourself; they never give up on you and never let you give up on yourself; they help you to be the best learner you can be; they also provide a wonderful role model.

## The role of the educator

**To provide safety.** In order to learn, a child needs to feel safe: safe from harm, of course, but also safe to make mistakes without shame or criticism; safe to express their own thoughts and opinions, knowing that they will be valued. It is the educator's role to create and maintain a relationship and environment that allows learners to safely and effectively pursue their own personal interests and ideas.

**To guide the learning experience.** It is the educator's role to guide the learning experience; to ensure a suitable context and environment that fosters the creation of a knowledgeable, independent, resourceful and socially adept individual as is possible.

**To support the individual's understanding of their learning process.** Each learner needs to understand their own learning process and learning styles while developing good learning habits. The educator assists them with this.

## An effective learning environment

As we have seen, it is the educator's role to provide a suitable and effective learning environment, and this will vary from family to family, and from educator to educator. This may be a physical space or a virtual one in which agreed behaviours and processes take place regardless of where and when learning is facilitated. Regardless of the limitations or extended facilities offered by the environment, learning will follow certain routes, whether it is a walk in the town centre looking at advertising in everyday situations or watching a television documentary on foxes. The planned learning needs to be organised for times of the day and locations when it can be both available and best absorbed; thus spreading out trips during the week and watching the documentary at a time when the learning environment is quiet.

Terry Heick, founder of the professional development agency for teachers, TeachThought.com, provides an excellent list of the ten key characteristics of a highly effective learning environment, which, although geared towards schools and teachers, holds equally true for all learning environments. They are reproduced here with permission:

**1. The student(s) ask the questions – good questions**
Questions should be recorded and valued. Good questions should direct the learning, not just get an answer from the educator.

**2. Questions are valued over answers**

**3. Ideas come from divergent sources**
Sources might include community members, professional and cultural mentors, academics, bloggers and personal recollections.

## 4. A variety of learning models is used

## 5. Classroom learning 'empties' into a connected community
What has been explored is shared and reshaped by working with, to and for others.

## 6. Learning is personalized by a variety of criteria
I think ..., my view/opinion ..., how I see/hear/imagine this to look like ...

## 7. Assessment is persistent, authentic, transparent – and never punitive

## 8. Criteria for success are balanced and transparent
How will I know I am doing well at this?

## 9. Learning habits are constantly modelled
Cognitive, meta-cognitive, and behavioural positives are constantly modelled. Curiosity, persistence, flexibility, priority, creativity, collaboration and revision are good places to start. So often what students learn from those around them is less directly didactic, and more indirect and observational.

## 10. There are constant opportunities for practice
Old thinking can be revisited; old errors reflected upon. Complex ideas are reapproached from new angles. Divergent concepts are contrasted. Bloom's Taxonomy (see page 172) is constantly travelled up and down, from the simple to the complex in an effort to maximize a student's opportunities to learn – and demonstrate understanding – of content.

For advice on the physical aspects of creating an effective learning space, see Chapter 5.

## Setting learning goals and measuring success

Not everyone likes the idea of setting goals or measuring success, but whether they are using a trampoline or learning to measure the angles in a triangle, goals and targets used well create a clearer focus, and this generally results in better learning.

If your child is completing a daily journal of their activities and learning experiences (or if they are young, you are doing it for/with them) it is relatively straightforward to adapt this process to provide simple methods of measuring success. This process helps the child see themselves as someone who is growing and developing, and it provides a record for you, clarifying their strengths and areas for development. As they get older, records can help the young person begin to recognise for themselves what they need to master or practise further.

The simplest method of measuring success is to make sure that there are some clear learning objectives for each lesson/activity/visit/work period in a way that fits with your overall vision and methods. These may be decided by you, they may be decided by the group, if that is the context, or they may be decided by your child themselves.

Some examples of learning objectives might look like this:

- I can find five things that sink and five things that float in the activity box (age five).
- I can list some of the reasons why the suffragettes were not popular and some of the ways in which they changed public opinion (teen).
- I can spot 5–20 (specify as appropriate) things that begin with the letter R in the park (all ages and

incidentally the basis of the popular word game *Scattegories* from Hasbro).

- I can work as part of the team to devise a documentary on the moon based on the work we have been producing in our project (all ages).
- I can come up with smart questions about cakes and choose four to explore next week (age seven).

There might also be some process objectives, such as:

- I will look up all the words I don't know in the story (age nine).
- I will draw a copy of my favourite picture in the gallery (all ages).
- I will double-check my spelling and grammar to ensure both are correct (teen).
- I will write on the lines (age 6).
- I will make sure everyone has a turn to speak (all ages).

How many objectives you establish will depend on the age of the learner and the activity taking place.

A really good start to this as a learning process is asking the child to come up with some objectives. Older students will find this quite easy on the whole, although they may be inclined to 'under-stretch' themselves on occasion. If a piece of work is based on a dynamic and growing mind map or project diagram, objectives may be the answers to questions already identified within it or arising from it, for example:

**How do plants grow?**
Identify the factors affecting growth in plants by:

(a) Guessing what they might be (hypothesising), then
(b) Devising an experiment to test this out (such as
    sequentially removing water, light and warmth).

Recording success can be by cross-referencing the objectives with work completed, such as 'fully completed – see notes on suffragettes in project folder', writing the questions devised or items spotted and so on, in the learning journal, or pasting work into the journal if it is an electronic document or scrapbook-style document.

After objectives and what they have or have not yet met, you might like to have an 'effort and enjoyment' reflection. This can be as simple as them giving themselves a mark out of ten for their effort and another for enjoyment (an interesting reflection is to notice if there is a correlation between these marks over time), ticking or ringing a supplied emoticon from a range of five, from sad to neutral to very happy.

Finally, you could add a section for questions/ideas/thoughts to explore next time; in other words, how to continue this stream of learning or to move it into another related area.

## Developing 'habits of mind'

The reasons most often given for home educating children include feeling that the current education system does not encourage individuality, creative thought or problem solving within a real-life context; however, just educating a child independently will not necessarily provide the stimulus for these. Children need to be taught to be learners and thinkers.

Plenty of structured play and managed experiences that promote questioning should be provided for very young children – no matter what their age. In an ideal situation, this natural curiosity is developed and honed as the child grows, and the role of adults working with children should be to provide tools, resources and learning frameworks to help the child develop their abilities. One such tool is known as the 'habits of mind'.

'Habits of mind' is a set of 16 qualities or behaviours that intelligent people bring to a challenge or problem. There are many useful online free resources and books devoted to using the habits of mind with children, so you might want to explore what's available. It is notable that quite a lot of schools have begun to use these with pupils in countries all over the world, with some surprising and positive results.

The most common way in which they are used is by educators taking time to explore different 'habits' from the list with children so that each child is fully aware of what is involved for each habit, what works for them and what they find most challenging. The structure offers an excellent framework for helping children think things through for themselves or plan a piece of work for themselves. Gill has found it particularly useful when a child is stuck and doesn't know what to do next with a piece of work, or for encouraging precision, care and diversity of thought. You might choose to focus on only one or two of the habits to start with and increase the child's repertoire over time. The 'habits' also offer an excellent framework for reflection: asking the child which habits they used to complete a task carried out during the day might form a part of their daily self-assessment.

## THE 16 HABITS OF MIND[14]

1. Persisting – stick to it.
2. Communicating with clarity and precision – be clear.

3. Managing impulsivity – take your time.
4. Gathering data through all senses – use your natural pathways.
5. Listening with understanding and empathy – understand others.
6. Creating, imagining, innovating – try a different way.
7. Thinking flexibly – look at it another way.
8. Responding with wonderment and awe – have fun figuring it out.
9. Thinking about your thinking (metacognition) – know your knowing.
10. Taking responsible risks – venture out.
11. Striving for accuracy and precision – find the best possible solution.
12. Finding humour – laugh a little.
13. Questioning and problem posing – how do you know?
14. Thinking interdependently – learning with others.
15. Applying past knowledge to new situations – use what you learn.
16. Remaining open to continuous learning – learning from experiences.

## Bloom's Taxonomy

Another widely used tool for encouraging children to develop critical thinking skills is Bloom's Taxonomy. In its simplest form it provides six levels of learning and thought. These are:

1. Know (for example, remembering facts, such as grass grows).
2. Understand (for example, grass needs water and light to create roots to grow).

3. Apply (for example, let's grow some grass and look after it).
4. Analyse (for example, what is happening with the grass we are growing?).
5. Evaluate (for example, is our grass as good as it could be? How do we know? How does it compare with other people's grass? What would improve it?).
6. Create (for example, let's grow a perfect patch of grass on an everyday object).

Bloom's Taxonomy provides an excellent framework for educators for planning and extending activities to maximise learning at all ages. Stacia Garland, a US teacher specialising in gifted pupils, says:

When children are moved beyond Bloom's lowest level, **Remembering** to the next level of **Understanding,** they are answering questions which ask them to organize previous information, such as: comparing, interpreting the meaning, or organising the information. Therefore, children are basically just retelling information in their own words, which is not helping develop critical thinking skills.

As parents, we want to encourage our children to think for themselves and to avoid peer pressure and fad thinking. We want them to have the skills necessary to listen, analyse and interpret the information that will be a constant part of their lives. Memory and understanding are part of this process, but to succeed in further processing this flow of knowledge requires higher level techniques.

**Here are some examples of how to use Bloom's Taxonomy with your child:**

Most questions asked of children fall in either the Remembering or Understanding level. I encourage parents to move to a higher order in the taxonomy when questioning their child, which are Bloom's next four levels. These include:

**Applying.** Ask your child how they would solve a given real-life problem. Ask why they think something is significant. Ask your child to continue a story or predict what would happen in a given situation. Encourage your child to make a diorama or model of what they learnt on a given topic.

**Analysing.** Ask your child to identify motives or causes from real-life stories. Encourage them to conduct an interview or survey. Have your child make a flow chart, family tree, or role play a real-life situation.

**Evaluating.** Ask your child to form and defend an opinion on a subject. Kids, especially teens, are pretty good at this one. Example: encourage your child to write a letter to an editor or evaluate a character's actions in a story.

**Creating.** Ask your child to put together several bits of old information to form a new idea. For example, ask them to create, design or invent a new item, proposal or plan. This requires a bit of creativity and the ability to think in the abstract.[15]

You can find many excellent representations of Bloom's Taxonomy online, with most recent versions including lists of words associated with each stage. You can also find versions of the taxonomy that include questions and examples of use. One version designed for very young children uses 'I can' statements in the petals of brightly coloured flowers. Most are free to download.

In conclusion, educating your child or children at home is a learning process for you, the parent, as well as for them. Doing it well takes time and a willingness to self-review against your original aims and intentions. If what you want is to produce a confident, happy child with a curiosity and interest in everything, you will need to ask yourself if this is truly happening and if there is more you need to do, or to learn yourself, in order for your answer to be a resounding yes. If what you want is a young person able to study alone and to design and manage his own learning schedule and curriculum, likewise you need to think about how this can best be achieved. Education is about opening up a person's thinking, not facts and figures – so to be a great educator takes time to open up yourself to the new possibilities and to be honest about the results.

## Questions and answers

**Q:** *My eight-year-old son gets very upset when I critique or mark his work in any way. I feel it's really important that he knows what is going well and the areas he needs to work harder at. How do I get him to accept that criticism is part of learning?*
**A:** Up until about the age of nine most children feel hurt by criticism and don't like getting things wrong. They generally learn best when we highlight their achievements and what they do well rather than concentrate on where they need to improve. It would seem that at the moment he's too young to understand the principles you are trying to get across to him.

You might try to notice what he needs to learn and think of enjoyable and creative ways in which to practise those skills with him in a way that allows him to succeed. When he gets a bit older, research shows that from the age of nine or ten children do find some constructive criticism helpful; what makes it constructive is not dwelling on mistakes but offering pointers for how to get things right in future.

**Q:** *My 14-year-old is dyslexic and has problems with reading and writing. We took her out of school and now have a fun and practical life together. Although she learns all the time, writing things down and formalising information remains very hard for her – she's inclined to have a panic attack at the very thought of writing. I worry that if our local council decides that it wants to see evidence of her learning, short of hearing her talking about it, there will be very little to look at.*
**A:** Learning occurs when experience is shaped by reflection – so it is important that she does reflect, as she is clearing doing verbally with you. Some formalisation is, however, needed so that she, and others, can see how she is reflecting on her learning processes, but it's possible to do this in a creative way that both encourages her particular learning style and reflects her educational experience.

It's important to note that there are other ways of record- ing words than writing or typing. Gill writes using dictation software because she has arthritic hands. Although it's not perfect, it's not bad – and you could try to use that with your daughter. As you speak, it can be empowering to see what you say appearing as fully formed text on the screen in front of you, and if you ask her to consider how the spacing and presentation might be improved (for example, should you offer justified text or leave the right-hand edge ragged; what typeface would she like to use and how big should it be?) this will really make it feel like her own work. You could also use photographs of learning materials or experiences, encouraging her to make her own picture books and support these with captions and dates. Blogging her daily learning journal (to a chosen audience, of course) using pictures and captions might encourage her to want to add more text for others to read. Overall, we tend to embrace skills either because we enjoy or value them, or because we enjoy or value the outcomes we get from them. Changing who gets to share her experiences might stimulate her desire to communicate them more fully.

Taking the pressure away from her to produce everything in a written format, while enabling her to maintain her joy in learning, will be a consistently tricky balancing act. You need to develop her ability to record her achievements, however difficult this is, and to do so in a way that avoids pain and pressure. In the long run, enabling her to see the value of reflecting and learning from what she has done will be an immense support to her future development, in every sense – not just educational.

**Q:** *I didn't do too well in school myself and have no formal qualifications of any sort. Therefore my family are very negative about me home educating my own children. They question whether someone who did so badly at school can teach anyone else. This really upsets me. Meanwhile, my children and I have a really good time at home and they really seem to be learning. What can I say to convince them?*
**A:** Well done you for not letting your own lack of educational attainment lead you to believe you are any less able to educate than anyone else – and have the self-belief to keep going.

There is a world of difference between teaching and learning. Learning happens because the learner engages both with the topic being presented and with the world around them.

Teaching in a school is actually a difficult location in that the teacher consistently has to make links to the wider world. Were they on a school trip, they would be able to point to what they are talking about; in the classroom the link consistently has to be made. The skill of the educator is in providing opportunities for learners to engage in the real world – and anyone who provides learners with opportunities to learn can do that. Good luck as you continue with your role, in providing access and open-mindedness, and allowing lots of experiences and associated reflection. One of the benefits frequently quoted by parents involved in home education is the opportunities it offers for the personal development and growth of all involved, adults included.

# 8

# Discipline

We are used to the concept of discipline in schools – and in general it means sticking to a set of rules based on clear principles that ensure the effective operation of the organisation for everyone, with various sanctions to ensure everyone remains on track. Discipline within school takes up a lot of time: creating and writing rules; ensuring they are understood; implementing them; responding to those who don't stick to them; and managing frequent low-level disruptions that if left unchecked would impede the learning or participation of others.

Discipline in schools is necessary to allow the main purpose of school – learning – to take place. It is therefore the responsibility of school staff to ensure adequate discipline to enable the maximum learning to take place. In the home education environment the learner needs to take far more responsibility for their own learning, which requires the development of self-discipline. In school a bell sounds for the end of the day but at home it is frequently the completion of the set task or tasks rather than the clock that determines an end to schooling.

**A 14-YEAR-OLD GIRL, WHO IS NOT ENJOYING
HER SECONDARY SCHOOL, COMMENTS**

Home education sounds great, but I think if I was here by
myself all day there would be too many distractions.

## Creating agreed boundaries for
## the learning environment

Depending on the age of the home educated child, the param-
eters of the learning day need to be established; for example,
how much of the day will be taken up with learning and what
are the best times to start and finish? Given that learning can
be flexible, and considerable time can be saved by not having
to travel to school, attend registration or assembly, or have
implemented breaks, it's possible to start and finish according
to the biological clocks of those involved: late starts and early
finishes, if that suits the child's metabolism, or timings to fit in
with a flexible work schedule of the parent who is organising
the home education environment.

There is considerable evidence showing that many children
are not getting sufficient sleep, which, while detrimental to
their health, also affects their learning and behaviour. This
is particularly noted in adolescents, for whom a minimum of
nine hours sleep a night is recommended. The early school
day, combined with both the sleep biology of adolescence and
the desire of many young people to be up and about as long
as possible, results in the majority performing at considerably
lower levels than their capability. But while the flexibility of
the school day and the ability to adapt and respond to the

weather or provide a new environment or enrichment activity are among the advantages of home education, it's a good idea to establish a base schedule and location for the learning: a set space, and a length of lesson that suits the child.

Young children frequently get tired in the afternoon at school, so for the home educated child making mornings the time for the bulk of their structured learning would seem to be sensible, with afternoons left for play and outdoor activities. With older students, a start time of 10.30 or 11.00am with a break for food at around 1.00pm and an end of structured learning around 2.30pm, followed by physical activity, clubs or groups, hobby time or continuing an ongoing interest-based project until 5.00 or 6.00pm would seem a stimulating and rigorous timetable.

Because every child is different, the duration and timing of your child's schedule will be entirely individual to them. If they consistently have problems starting at a certain time, staying motivated and on task during sessions, or if they frequently express tiredness or boredom, there are some things that might be worth considering.

- Are they getting enough sleep?
- Are they getting enough of the right food and plenty of water?
- Are you providing enough variety of subjects and topics?
- Are you creating a sufficiently engaging curriculum?
- Are you providing enough opportunity for your child to self-direct their learning?
- Are the individual learning times too long?
- Are they frequently distracted by toys/TV/phone or gadget?
- Are they getting enough exercise and time outdoors?

- Are they getting enough time with peers/friends to socialise freely?
- Are they being presented with enough new subject matter to keep them interested?
- Are they being sufficiently stretched and challenged?

The answers to some of these questions can easily be found online, where guidance on sleep and diet are readily available, but others only your child and you can answer. If you are new to home educating, don't worry if you don't have it all worked out from the beginning. Try things out, be honest about how well they worked, and ask for your child's view, and keep adjusting until you are satisfied. As an example of how this can work in practice, the following text comes from an interview in the *Financial Times* with the music prodigy Alma Deutcher, by Laura Battle.*

Both Deutscher and her younger sister Helen (who is herself an accomplished musician) are homeschooled. 'I think that I learn at home in one hour what it would take at school five hours to learn' she says. Private music lessons are taken with teachers from the nearby Yehudi Menuhin School (an academy for musically gifted children) and most other subjects are taught by their parents: she is currently reading *The Odyssey* with her mother, and working to improve her German.

She enjoys wholesome pastimes – playing with her sister in their tree-house, where they have a 'dryad school', and meeting up with friends from a local home education network for swimming and ballet – and she is proudly out of step with the iGeneration. 'Lots of children spend all the

---

* 16–17 December 2017

time on video games, I don't like that at all. I don't have a phone or computer or anything, I just read a lot,' she says, listing Philippa Pearce, Joan Aitken and Shannon Hale as some of her favourite authors. 'I don't really know what they do – *Minecraft* or whatever – some of my friends do that but I think it's a complete waste of time and it ruins your brain as well because you can't imagine anything for yourself.'

## Creating a home education contract

Once you have found a suitable daily structure, it is time to create your home education contract with your child. Like any contract, it should contain guidance on what will be provided by everyone involved, and what the expectations of both parties are.

This is a contract between a mother and her six-year-old high-functioning autistic son, Jack, who sometimes has very angry and sometimes aggressive outbursts, particularly if he doesn't get his own way.

Figure 4: Sample contract for a young child

**MUM AND JACK AGREE THAT:**

- We will only use kind words and touches with each other.
- We will have four lessons every day.
- We will set the timer for each lesson and we will work until the timer 'pings'.

- We will play a game for 15 minutes every time we finish a lesson.
- If we get upset or angry, we will have some time out alone until we are ready to continue.
- We will have a reflection session for 10 minutes every day after tea.

The contract is simple; it is about both Mum and Jack (and therefore 'fair' to a child) and spells out the structure of the day, the expectations on behaviour, the built-in rewards (in terms of 'play') and the all-important reflection time. Like all good contracts, it is positive and helpful, providing a good basis for reflecting on the day after tea time.

A contract for Poppy Aldis (13) and brother Zac (15), below, looks very different, as they are alone together for most of their 'school day' twice a week and spend one learning day supervised by their father and two by their mother. They also have a two-hour individual tutor time once a week to look at their work and set some targets for the coming week.

Figure 5: Sample contract for an older child

### HOME EDUCATION CONTRACT

**We, the Aldis family, agree that:**
- Our school day starts at 10am every day and finishes at 2.30pm on Mondays and Thursdays, and at any time between 2.30pm and 5pm on Tuesdays, Wednesdays

and Fridays. The end time on those days will be decided when everyone participating agrees to stop for the day.

## Mondays and Thursdays

- Zak will see Gitika (tutor) alone from 10am to 12 midday every Monday in the dining room.
- Poppy will see Gitika alone from 10am to 12 midday every Thursday in the dining room.
- The dining-room can be used for quiet study by both Poppy and Zac except during tutor times. If both are working there, each can use half the table space only. They must show consideration and kindness to each other when using other spaces in the room.
- The dining room is to be left tidy and clear by 5.00pm – any books or equipment left there will incur a fine of 10p per item to be put in the charity box.

## Working agreement

- The kitchen is a social space for chat, preparing food and drink, or eating and drinking. It is not to be used as a workspace for anything else without adult supervision.
- Each child will be expected to spend a minimum of 3½ hours a day working on tasks set by Gitika, Mum or Dad. They will keep a diary of start times, break times, work times and topics, which will be looked over every day after supper.
- Each child will pick a subject for 'own study' that they will work at on Wednesdays. They will discuss with Mum at the start of the day what they will be doing

and how they will be working. This may change as the day progresses, but all changes are to be discussed with Mum, who will be available all day for support and inspiration.

- Tuesdays are for trips and extension activities. Family members together will create a list of 'things we want to do on Tuesdays', which will then be worked through until complete. No activity should cost more than £15 to complete and all outings will be recorded by a post on the family blog from each child.

- Fridays are for home-based skills learning such as cooking, painting, drawing or other creative pursuit, music practice, carpentry, electronics and design. Both children will participate in each activity unless agreed in advance by an adult.

- Poppy and Zac may work in their own rooms when they wish but may not engage in personal calls, emails or other communication. An occasional 'phone and email' check will take place without warning.

- Music or multimedia devices may only be played if wearing headphones.

- Sunday evenings is family time, and all family members are expected to sit down together to eat at 6.00pm. This will be followed by a general family meeting to discuss how the past week has been, any problems arising and any challenges in the week to come. We shall also choose our Tuesday activity from the list.

The Aldis family has spent a lot of time over the couple of years that their children have been home educated refining the programme and the working agreement. Disputes and areas of conflict have been discussed through regular family meetings, and the contract has been reworked, adapted and added to many times. It is clear to see that they have tackled issues, such as who gets to use the dining-room table, and books and papers being left all over the house, in positive and transparent ways. As each child receives a small allowance every week, it was agreed at a family meeting that any item left in the dining room after five would incur a 10p fine, with the money being put in the family charity collection box. Since agreeing this, only a couple of 10p fines have been made and the dining room is generally clear.

What is important about these examples is that they both provide a clear contract that is regularly reviewed by all involved and updated or altered accordingly, and that it is a helpful document for everyone as it clarifies boundaries and expectations. It is important to build in expectations time and to review how things are going in relation to what is trying to be achieved. How this is done will again depend on the child's age and the family structure. For Jack, a thumbs up, down or in the middle might be enough feedback for the day; for the Aldis children, a learning log completed daily provides monitoring information for their parents and tutor, as well as an insight into their engagement, enthusiasm and effort.

## How to create the rules and expectations

Most of us have a sense of what we would like the rules to be, and children are no different. Any that have attended school will be well aware of the lists of rules that appear in classrooms and in school diaries, so simply asking your child 'What should our rules be?' will probably result in a very long list of don'ts: 'don't swear', 'don't kick anybody', 'don't scribble on the table', and so on. These are not only negative instructions (to be avoided) but unhelpful for the home educating environment.

One way to create rules is simply to work out your timetable and then begin. At the end of each day review what went wrong and what went right, what each person found difficult and what each person would like to change. Talking things through and then writing down solutions to the problems in the form of rules creates a working set of boundaries rooted in shared experience.

Good 'rules' should be:

- Inclusive – and that means the adults too.
- Offering guidance not criticism – what to do, not what not to do.
- Written in language that helps everyone understand.
- Concise but clear. Overly general rules, such as 'work hard' or 'be nice' might be a little vague and unhelpful.
- Relevant to the situation, and regularly adapted to avoid or minimise difficulties.
- Easy to reflect on. Did I keep the rule or didn't I?

## What to do if they break the 'rules'

The whole process of rules or expectations should be a shared one. Likewise, we should be sharing thoughts and decisions about what to do if the rules are broken. In both the sample contracts above there is some indication that these families have considered how to manage certain behaviours. For Jack and his mum, when either is unable to manage his or her emotions, it has been decided that a period of time out alone is the best course of action. Eventually it might also be decided that once that period of time out is over, the person whose emotions got the better of them might apologise. Or some reflection process might take place about what happened during the emotional overload, and how in future it could be avoided, perhaps by changing the stimulus or reaction, or letting the other person know when things were getting to boiling point before they actually did.

For the Aldis family, procedures have been put in place to reduce the amount of arguing that might ensue when trying to decide where to go on a Tuesday outing (and how much money Mum or Dad will have to provide), as well as who gets to use the dining room table.

Sanctions designed to punish are not considered effective, particularly with children under the age of nine or so, where rewarding good behaviour is proven to result in improvement as is providing opportunities to 'do over again' with a different outcome. With children over the age of nine, a degree of constructive criticism can be helpful, as it involves letting them know how to do better next time rather than telling them what they have done wrong in the past. Simple, straightforward sanctions are also helpful in weighting one choice against another, and as we see for the Aldis family, a monetary fine has been decided upon as a simple sanction for leaving the dining room table untidied at the end of the day. Money as a reward is probably not ideal, but it might work well as a sanction for young people who have an allowance or pocket money of their own.

## Sharing lessons with other families

We suggest in various parts of this book that it is a good idea to build a home educators' network and consider sharing lessons with other families. If this is done, you will have to tackle issues that might impact on the experience, and this is best done upfront, before problems arise. What is your attitude to timing (how strict are you going to be about the agreed timetable, what constitutes punctual, how late is late?) and to rescheduling commitments (how often, how tolerated?). It's a good idea to have a back-up plan in existence (in case of long-term unavailability or illness). Networks can start to break down if resentments form ('he is always late', or 'she always asks her own child the easiest questions', and so on).

Discipline styles will depend on what type of home education you provide, from the very informal to the very formal, and what role you are playing at any given time. Below is a chart listing the ways in which head teachers, teachers and parents react and support children. For the home educating parent (swap 'home' or 'family' for the word 'school') there may be times when you are in any one of these three roles.

## Figure 6: Discipline styles

|  | Head teacher | Teacher | Parent |
|---|---|---|---|
| Discipline style | Universal: uses a reflection of the child within the peer group to get appropriate behaviour, 'This is the second time you have been sent to me by your teacher. What have you done to result in being removed from class this time?' | Pragmatic: uses the relationship with the child to get appropriate behaviour, 'I'm disappointed in your choice of behaviour, I expected more from you.' | Emotional: uses the relationship with the child to get appropriate behaviour, 'I'm so angry you didn't do what I said.' |
| Demeanour | Kind, stern, precise and detached | Kindly (but not friendly) and precise | Friendly, exasperated or angry |

|  | Head teacher | Teacher | Parent |
|---|---|---|---|
| Responsibility to the child | Maximising performance of each child by ensuring staff are following policies and practices laid down by government (national and local), helping teachers manage discipline where appropriate in order for children to learn, and achieve as close to their learning potential as possible. | Education as defined by government, time management, personal development as defined by school policy, keeping and maintaining clear boundaries so that the child will achieve as close to their learning potential as possible. | Love, safety, cleanliness, health, time management, personal development, keeping and maintaining clear boundaries, forgiveness in order for the child to grow into a self-regulating and empathetic adult. |
| Key roles | To manage the day-to-day running of the institution. Overseeing staff needs and development, ensuring that the school has sufficient expertise and resources to provide the best education and welfare to pupils or students. Liaising between a range of agencies providing care for individuals or groups. Collecting and sharing data, and developing and maintaining policy. | Creates an accessible learning programme and environment. Inspires children to learn. Secondary role model for some. Uses discipline, differentiation and encouragement to ensure fair access to learning and freedom from harm for all. Helps pupils and students become more independent in both learning and relationships with others. | Provider of physical needs: food, shelter, clothing and so on. Principle role model for child. Protector of child from external harm or poor choices. Nurturer and guide. |

|  | Head teacher | Teacher | Parent |
|---|---|---|---|
| Key skills for their roles | Managing a large institution of many staff and many children. Patience, listening, clarifying and explaining, organising events time and people, able to keep an eye on the whole school at once – scanning, discipline – able to command respect, creative thinking, record keeping, reading body language, empathising, making tough decisions that may affect others. | Managing a class of up to 30. Patience, listening, clarifying and explaining, asking inspiring questions, organising time and people, able to keep an eye on the whole room at once – scanning, discipline – able to command respect, creative thinking, record keeping, reading body language, making connections between ideas, objects and people. | Managing a family. Patience, multi-tasking, organisation – everything! Food prep, first aid, able to manage stress and pressure well, planning for the day/week ahead, keeping track of individuals' needs, wants, likes and dislikes. Soothing, challenging and supporting. |

## Questions and answers

**Q:** *I have been home educating my 13-year-old daughter for three months, having had trouble getting her to school every day for months, and with her being very unhappy about attending when she did get there. I took her out of school on the understanding that she would still have to do work at home. But since being officially home educated she has refused to do any maths work at all. We had agreed that she would have a tutor, and I managed to find one, but when he came this week she refused to meet with him, ending up with me having to pay him even though he had not done any work. What do I do now? I think it's very important to keep maths going but feel resentful about paying for her not to be taught.*
**A:** It must be frustrating to pay the tutor when nothing has happened, but of course it is not the tutor's fault and they need

to be paid for their official delivery time (which will include prior preparation), even if they have not taught anything. (Naturally, you don't have to pay if they don't attend for any reason.) You are in a difficult situation, because home education relies on getting your child to participate. Ideally, you will have made a verbal or written 'contract' or agreement with her when you began. Bringing this to her attention now is the starting point for discussing how to proceed.

If you haven't got a written or verbal agreement, it's never too late, and now is the time to create one. Sit down with her in a cafe or somewhere else casual – so that she is less likely to walk away – and talk about what she needs to accomplish educationally over the next few years in order to meet her desired outcomes. Start the conversation by asking where she sees herself in five years' time: what does she want to be doing? How does she want to be living? Does she want to be at home, in her own rented accommodation, or in a shared flat with others? Does she want to go to college or university? Depending on her answers, work backwards – if she sees herself at college doing a course in beauty therapy or media studies, for example, there will be entry requirements or expectations, without which she will not get in – as will be the case for any course she wants to do. Work backwards to the present time. How can we make sure that she gets what she needs in order to achieve her desired outcome?

It is important that you ask her questions to think through and respond to in small steps at a time rather than telling her – the brain operates in completely different ways when answering a question than it does when listening to something being said (particularly in a teenager and when the person asking the question is a parent).

It may be that she does not want to go on to higher education and would rather get a job with training as soon as she can (16 for an apprenticeship in England). There are lots of useful websites designed for young people showing what you need in order to be a hit in the job market these days: skills, aptitudes, standards (resilience) quality traits – but also a certain level of academic achievement, numerate, language skills, reading and writing, and person skills. When you have drawn up with her where she needs to be, redesign your curriculum and home education programme to meet her direct needs, and think about how over time you will provide opportunities for her to learn what she needs to do. Write the contract together, and tell her what you will provide (such as tutors, computer access, visits and trips, and so on) and decide what she will do in return, such as meeting with tutors, trying her best, reflecting on her own learning and performance, and so on. Add a clause on what you will do if either you or she breaks the agreement. Differentiate outcomes so that a small non-compliance, such as refusal to come on a visit that is planned because she is feeling tired that day, has a relatively small sanction like restriction on her phone for a day/week. If a larger non-compliance occurs that has cost you money (such as refusing to meet with the tutor), reducing her allowance until the money, or at least part of it, is made up is appropriate, or restricting the amount of spending she can do. Otherwise, agree with her a penalty that reflects the seriousness of what happened, such as doing additional chores for a week. The sanctions need to be negotiated and agreed between you, or the contract will not work.

If, when you employ a tutor, you involve your daughter in the selection process, she may be more likely to cooperate in future (see page 139.) If she has input, she may be more willing to take part. It may also take away some of the apprehension when meeting this person for the first time if she has had the opportunity to ask questions about their approach in advance.

**Q:** *I am home educating my twin eight-year-old sons after years of problems at school because the boys have always been highly active and tended to cause some disruption in the class and at playtime. To be honest, I always felt the school wasn't doing enough to help them. We made the decision to home educate until they are due to start secondary school, and I gave up my job so that I could be here with them all the time, but I'm not sure it was a sensible decision. I find myself getting so angry with them that there are times when I feel like I hate them! The bad times are usually whenever I try to do anything with them that might be termed educational, or even getting them to sit down together to talk is a nightmare. They constantly bicker and play-fight with each other – they don't hurt each other, it's how they've always been, but they wind each other up until a fight starts, then I'm called on to break it up and they begin all over again.*

*Left to their own devices, they spend a lot of time playing video games together or kicking a football around in the garden together and, although they bicker and tease as usual, they still seem to prefer playing with each other than with anyone else.*

*Right now I feel they are running wild, and although I start every day with a new resolve to stay calm and deal with things sensibly, by about ten o'clock I just leave them to get on with it.*

**A:** It sounds as if your sons have no idea that they are being home educated. They just think they don't have to go to school anymore and can stay at home – yippee! It also appears that being at home equates to doing what they like most of the time and that discipline at home was, as now, merely about sorting out their fights and arguments.

You used the word 'we', and I'm assuming there is at least one more adult in their day-to-day life, so it is time to call the family together to talk things through. Firstly, there needs to be an agreed structure to your days. Not every home-educated child needs clear and consistent structures, but it seems that here it is essential. Be sure to include start times, number of lessons, and so on. The boys do not get the final say in these because they are eight and because, given the choice, they will only play games; however, building in plenty of active time so that they can use up some of that energy is very important, with extra physical activities thrown in as rewards for doing their school work. Perhaps three 30-minute 'lessons' or work times a day is enough to start with, and see if you can try to timetable these during the morning session.

Secondly, don't try teaching the boys together, because, at the moment, they are unable to be together and do anything but what they are currently doing. It does make your job harder in one respect, but hopefully in time you will be able to bring the boys together more. You'll need two learning areas, and I know that can be a strain for some families, but perhaps the kitchen table for one and a desk in the bedroom for the other? If this causes problems or arguments, change who works where on a weekly basis (or similar). Provide each workplace with a timer – preferably one that cannot easily be tampered with – and divide your time between the two boys in small chunks. Whenever possible, design tasks that are physical rather than just pencil and paper, such as building a simple model to exact proportions as a way of practising measurement rather than just drawing lines on a piece of paper. You'll find that the more you get into your role the more creative your thinking will become, but do talk it through with that other adult in your life, who may be able to come up with some different ideas.

Be clear about the learning intentions for each task you give them and ask them to assess their own performance at the end of each task, then record it in a notebook or on a chart. Gill usually asks children she works with to give themselves a mark out of ten for how well they did what they were supposed to do, but if this is too difficult, they can use colours such as red, amber or green, or pick from a predetermined choice of emoticons, and so on. The reflection is not about how well they achieved the end result but in how well they worked towards the end result.

At the end of each 'lesson' bring the boys together for a 10-minute kick around in the garden, a local park or free choice of play, if they have completed the tasks they were set. If they haven't completed them, they will need to continue work on them during their play break. This might mean that one child has finished while the other has not, but do your best to keep them apart during the break. It is the desire to be together as often as possible that will eventually get them to work better. Use it as a reward for doing what is asked of them.

Make afternoons a time for physical play, and include trips to the park, the swimming pool, the adventure playground or whatever else is available as part of your programme, but make these trips conditional on the behaviour and work completed during the morning. By all means let them play in the garden in the afternoon rather than trying to keep them working, but the next day make sure that they are clear that if they want to go out – to the park or for a swim – they will need to complete all the work set.

Consider the afternoon part of their school day, and don't on any account allow them to use gadgets or play video games. When you make your contract or set of rules, make clear that playing with video games, gadgets of any kind or toys during their 'school day' is not permitted just as it was not at school. There will be times, of course, when they will be using computers or tablets under your supervision but not free playing with them.

You can download the National Curriculum programme of study from the Gov.com website, which is probably a good idea if you are intending to reintegrate them into mainstream school later. You don't have to do all of it, of course, but it will help with the important things such as maths. Lots of reading with, to and by the boys will do a lot to improve their literacy skills and, again, the programmes for study will outline what they should be learning if you want to use it as a guideline.

# Section 3

# Social Skills

# 9

# Developing Your Child's Social Skills

Developing social skills is one of the most important aspects of child development for any age, but it's also one of the most difficult to quantify or monitor. Whereas it's possible to assess a child's ability at maths, according to the extent of their understanding and their ability to recall and apply specific techniques to problems, with social skills you might not grasp the level of their understanding – or lack of understanding – until they are older and problems arise.

Social skills also need a level of constant revisiting as the child ages and the complexities of situations they have to deal with change; what works for a young child will need new levels of understanding and skill as they get older; for example, it may be appropriate to teach a five-year-old to tell an adult when they have a problem with the behaviour of another child, which the adult can then sort out, but continuing to direct them to inform adults of their issues when they are nine or ten might be pointless, as no adult is likely to intervene for minor disagreements or problems such as turn-taking for children of that age. It is often at the point where the old strategy becomes ineffectual, that it becomes apparent to a parent or parents that their child might have limited skills in working on conflict or disagreement themselves, because they have become so used to relying on adults.

---

## CASE STUDY: RACHEL

Rachel is the eldest of three children and was home educated for the last two years of primary school, missing years 5 and 6. Year 4 is frequently the year when relationship problems and social bullying tend to become problematic in schools, particularly among girls.

'My family made the decision to home educate me because there were friendship problems at school, and the school wasn't helping me, and the teachers didn't understand or help me enough. At one time a teacher ridiculed me in front of the whole class for giving a wrong answer to a question.

'Being educated at home didn't make any difference to my educational standards. I was in the top set in primary school and went into the top set when I went back to secondary school. I kept in contact with many of my friends from primary school who were also at my secondary school, but I felt somewhat out of touch. There were ways of doing things or saying things that my school friends all shared, but I just didn't always know what these were or understand the "rules". I think this was because I was home educated for those last two years.'

---

A child's ability to manage social skills progresses as they get older. We wouldn't expect a six-year-old child to be able to manage skills such as taking turns as easily as a 12-year-old. A six-year-old might want their own way a lot of the time, and sometimes being given an extra turn enables the game to continue and may make them happy. A typical 12-year-old, on the other hand, is capable of understanding how it feels to be treated unfairly, what will seem unfair to others and the need to comply in order to be part of a group. It follows that although we can't look at social skills as simply a list, because they need to be tied into development, there are certain abilities and understandings that we need to keep an eye on, whatever their age.

One of the big issues for home-educated children is where they are to develop their social skills. Children learn the majority of their social skills through interaction with those of the same age or slightly older. They learn through interaction with other children (either as a participant or observer), from their immediate friendship and sibling groups, and their wider peer group and family – not through being taught in lessons or having things explained to them by adults. Many children who are used to adults explaining the ways of the world to them from an early age may in fact become quite anxious as they get older, as they are unable to perform in the logic-based complex world being presented to them by the parent. Of course, some well-meaning advice, or even some clear instruction, such as 'Perhaps you could ask her what the problem is?' or 'Try not to dwell on it right now. Put it out of your mind until tomorrow' will not pressurise a child. But as they get older, such advice might make them feel unheard or patronised – and the extent to which they are willing to listen to or accept advice or instruction will, in any case, probably depend on their age.

Well thought-through advice (although not instruction) can, however, be valuable with older children, as long as it is tied in with listening at length to the young person's viewpoints and wishes; as the child moves into young adulthood, it should be possible to talk together through the best way to handle a friend, for example, and to offer advice. The advice may not be taken, but your child may be interested to hear your viewpoint. Adult advice for a younger child, on the other hand, often feels like 'being told what to do' by an adult and may disempower them. Being offered a solution that they can't implement themselves (because they are only seven) can make them feel that relationships are overly complex and hence they feel unable to act. Such children often feel that the fault lies with them, that they are not 'smart' enough to manage the world around them or lack some magical quality that allows others to make and keep friendships. This can be devastating to the self-regard and self-esteem of a child. They may also start to notice the social competencies of those around them, and feel that they are much less skilled, and hence further disempowered.

This means that some of the most important aspects of home educating are the times when the child is mixing with others, and how this is structured or facilitated to maximise their opportunity for developing their inter-personal and social skills and social awareness.

Sometimes children are home educated because they lack social skills and confidence around others. They might find school overwhelming or social relationships too complex and difficult to manage. At other times it is the cruelty of their peer group, or individuals within it, that has prompted a parent to find another way to educate their child. For many parents who see their child struggling with relationships, and responding negatively to the behaviour of others at school, it is probably instinctive to support them by taking them away from what is causing pain. But for children who struggle with social skills this can be counter-productive, especially if you want your child to reintegrate at a later date. They may not get better at social skills just because they get older, although it is probably true that children who cannot relate well to other children, but have no problem relating to adults, will probably find things easier as they get older – because eventually their peers will be adults.

## How are social skills learnt?

Ideally, social skills are learnt by social immersion. In other words, we learn how to behave around other people by being with them and experiencing their reactions to our actions; for example:

- If I am grumpy, perhaps others will not want to spend time with me.
- If I am rude, others will not like listening to me.
- If I always have to be in charge, others will not want to be in my game or group.

We learn by both making mistakes and having successes, by observing others both making mistakes and managing things well, and by balancing our own personal wants and needs with those of a group – or other individuals.

For today's highly supervised children, very little social immersion takes place without adults setting the boundaries or managing outcomes. Children who behave in an unacceptable way are chastised by an adult and then encouraged to carry on playing with the group. In a more natural setting the group itself would let the individual behaving unacceptably know the boundaries by punishing them, admonishing them or excluding them. Children learn quickly how to keep in with the group by following group mores and developing their skills as they grow older, in line with the complexity of the group or groups they belong to.

The notable exception for constant supervision lies in the online world, where many children interact freely, and frequently anonymously, with individuals and groups that may be unknown to them in the real world – while following rules or procedures that may be predatory or cruel. This may change the way a child understands social conduct in the real world – or perhaps make interacting in the virtual world feel more exciting and affirming.

Ideally, children should have more unsupervised time to interact in the real world, and considerably less time unsupervised online – or even none! Parents often feel reassured that a child 'playing' a game online is at least playing. But while computer games may have some coordination or strategic-thinking elements, which are overall helpful developmentally, they are the absolute opposite of social. Even playing with a friend (if not present) does not count, as individuals don't interact in the virtual world the way they do in real life. Social skills tend to have optimum learning periods – a time when the brain is developmentally geared to learn certain things – and not learning key skills at certain times might hinder later learning and behaviour. Many children who do not have adequate socialisation before the age of five will struggle when they get to eight or nine with friendship and group dynamics. Others may be unable to manage social politics and values in early adolescence (at about the age of 12 to 13).

As a society, we are seeing big changes in the resilience of young people, which research suggests is due to less free socialising, more adult intervention and close supervision, and greater social isolation supported by gadgets and TV.

Social media sites offer young people instant approval in the form of 'likes', or similar pocket-sized feedback, but they may also offer powerful disapproval by giving negative feedback or comments (or persistent negative feedback through 'trolling') or blocking an individual from communicating again. Many believe that there has been a notable change in the way young people interact with each other since the advent of social media, with face-to-face interaction becoming seemingly more supportive and kind than perhaps in other generations, while online bullying, trolling and shaming are widespread and increasing at an alarming rate year by year.

For children being educated at home it is imperative that they spend time interacting with other children of different ages in environments that are conducive to free-play and conversation with limited adult intervention. Classes provide excellent opportunities for home-educated students to mix with others, but they might not provide enough social opportunities for learning complex social skills and group behaviour.

Providing some age-appropriate 'lessons' around social skills helps children to reflect on their experiences and observations, and it is this reflection that helps them develop their competences.

## What is age appropriate?

All children develop at different rates in terms of their skills and abilities. Life experiences, friendships and position in the family are just a few things that can make a difference to how a child acts and learns. For example, many eldest and only children have behaviour that seems more 'adult' than children of the same age with older siblings, so it can seem that the child is therefore more advanced for their years. Other children can be more easily upset than others and so might be referred to as 'highly sensitive' or immature. Whilst it is true that all children develop at different rates there are some things that are fairly standard in the development of a child. The immature 'sensitive' child and the older than their years 'adult-like' child are not as different on the inside as they might seem, but have just had very different influences and stimuli which have led to different behaviour. They will often be treated very differently, too, with the more adult-seeming child having higher standards of behaviour and responsibility expected of them whilst the sensitive child is treated with extra cossetting and gentleness, but as far as their development goes they are in fact at the same level.

It is not behaviour alone that determines maturity; it is determined very much by brain development and this can be charted and has some key milestones along the way. We can see the outward development of a child but the brain development and therefore the real capabilities of a child are hidden and may be masked by learnt behaviours. It is important to remember that the brain is not fully developed until the early 20s.

Here are some of the known milestones that affect a child's learning.

## Children under five

The concept 'theory of mind' says that very young children don't understand that others have their own thoughts and feelings, and that these are different from their own.

By the age of four to five, a neuro-typical child will begin to understand that their thoughts and yours are separate and different, but this might still be somewhat limited. Trying to talk to a child about empathy or fairness when they don't have a theory of mind is like talking in a different language. When trying to explain what they should do and how to do it we therefore talk about 'kind' and 'caring' behaviour. We can show them how to stroke the cat, ask someone to do something, or talk to someone else – all in a 'kind' way. If we disagree with someone, it can similarly be done in a 'kind' way, without going into too much detail about how they are feeling – which a child of that age will not understand. Talking things through, using logic or concepts that they don't have, might enrage a child, confuse them or even make them anxious.

A child's inability to appreciate or care that we don't all think and feel the same thing, might indicate a delay in the development of theory of mind, which might be an indicator of issues to be explored.

### Children of around seven and eight

Children of this age generally understand that individuals think and feel differently, but what they might find difficult to do is recognise whose wants and needs should be at the top of the list. Their desires tend to remain the most important to them. For children of this age it's important to help them recognise the truth or what is going on in a situation, to work on listening to each other's points of view and to find fair solutions. They may be able to recognise an essential truth or appreciate how a situation is working but find it hard to suggest a solution or see a way out of a difficult situation – so they might need to be helped in order to make further progress.

As always when helping children at this age to learn social awareness and social skills, it's important to ask rather than tell. Ask them to notice the behaviour of others on TV, in stories, in the playground, and to reflect on the motivations and feelings of others.

## Children of around nine to 12

From about the age of nine or ten, children start looking for their new 'tribe': a group to belong to that gives them a sense of belonging. This increases throughout the pre-adolescent and adolescent stages, and includes wondering where and how they fit, where they belong and the process of moving away from the familial tribe in search of their own. At this point the family is no longer the child's only marker, and it will be important to look at the game play that goes on in groups; how to manage conflict, rivalry and power play, and the important role of informal conversation and gossip.

## Children of 13 and 14

By now, the young person's tribe is becoming everything. Spending time with family members decreases and they may find their parents and siblings extremely challenging. Trying to 'teach' them about social skills might become increasingly pointless, as they operate in a different world from their parents. Relationships are new and often complex with strong behavioural rules, and will be influenced by the morals, habits and behaviour codes of the different generations and the particular tribe to which the young person belongs. Parents may not necessarily understand or appreciate the mores of the social group their child is in, so the role of the parent may be to provide opportunities for general discussion, reflection and emotional support.

## General guidelines

Teaching social skills is an ongoing process, not something that can be taught once and left, because the child's under-standing will develop with age and experience. As a rule of thumb, 'Ask, don't tell' should be the motto of every home or school educator. When we tell someone how to act or how to operate in their life, very little brain activity – and therefore learning – takes place. But when we ask them their opinions, coping strategies or suggestions for change, much more neural activity is evident.

Asking hypothetical or 'what if?' questions might be a helpful strategy: 'What if he was not there when you arrived?', 'What if someone is talking behind your back?', 'What if some-one borrows something and does not give it back?' Asking hypothetical questions, for them to think through, might also be a good way forward, as it enables them to think objectively rather than concentrating on social skills face to face.

'Change' questions offer another great way of opening up thinking in different situations; for example, 'How would your life be different if Charlotte stopped being your friend?' Questions like this might provide a good way to encourage a child to take responsibility for their part in a relationship upset. 'What would happen if the Internet stopped working for 24 hours?' could be a powerful question to ask to start a conversation about Internet security, global interconnected-ness or just how the world works today.

Occasional 'magic wand' questions can help a child clarify outcomes or paths that they find confusing, and these come in particularly useful when a child is weighing up the difference between what they want and what seems right. When children get stuck for solutions to their relationship and friendship problems, asking them what kind of outcome they would like (before asking what they can do to achieve it) helps them gain perspective; for example, with younger children asking them 'If you had a magic wand, what would you like to change between you and Charlie right now?' while with teens 'If you had a magic wand so that you could jump forward six months, how would you like your friendship with Evie to look?' might help them to project forwards.

Once the child has identified the outcome, understanding the choices they might make to help achieve this, or what they could do to make it happen, can become clearer. Asking them what they will do to achieve this outcome, or inviting them to create a choice chart with you (see the Chapter 11), will help them to feel able to take things forward for themselves.

It might also be helpful to allow others to influence them; to absorb other points of view – perhaps from other friends and family or even strangers by allowing them to participate in question-and-answer online forums. For example, you can spot appropriate questions on Yahoo Answers and you might read through responses together, while talking about how the person asking for advice might manage the situation. You might decide to introduce into your home educating regular access to an online agony aunt, to help them understand the world they are part of and also to think through what appropriate behaviour might look like and offer care and support to people they don't know. In the process, depersonalising the social interaction can help them develop their own thinking.

On the other hand, a regular music or discussion session with a trusted individual from outside the immediate family can offer an outlet for a young person to develop their thinking; and this opportunity can grow without the basic need for any associated skills to be developing at the same rate. For example, Alison found that the jobbing musician she employed as a drum teacher for one of her children offered a very valuable take on the world during adolescence – although the amount of drum instruction got less and less.

Our general conclusion is that it's appropriate to teach social skills on an ongoing basis, as the child develops, and to keep checking on their levels of understanding as they grow older. This enables them to function effectively within the wider society, of which they are part, even if they do not attend one of its major and most unifying social constructs – school – on a regular basis.

## Skills for children with particular social needs

The following advice for teaching social skills to a child with a limited understanding of others – and those identified as having an autistic-spectrum disorder – has been adapted with kind permission from the work of Carrie Clark of Speech and Language Kids.[16]

Techniques for teaching social skills that were helpful:

(a) Teaching social scripts
  - Learning the specific rules that govern these activities.
  - How to make introductions.
  - How to enter a conversation.
  - Sitting with others.
  - Phone conversations.

(b) Modelling and role play
  - Watch someone else do it first.
  - Practise the skill on their own.

(c) Differential reinforcement
- Give reinforcement based on their behaviour. This could be verbal praise or corrective feedback, or the reaction of the listener.

(d) Peer involvement
- Use other children with different social needs.
- Use 'typical' peers.
- Use siblings.

(e) Multiple 'trainers'
- Try to use other adults or children so that they don't get too used to the same communication partners.

(f) Practice in natural environments
- Use peers to help with introducing the skill into a 'natural' setting.
- Talk through the skill before the child enters the situation.
- Review how it went afterwards.

(g) Foster self-awareness
- Watch videos together of the child using a particular skill.
- Talk about how it went.
- Encourage discussion of how it went.
- Encourage the child to notice the other person/ other people's reactions.
- Encourage the child to judge if it went well.

How this might look in practice:

1.  When working with the child on social skills, tell them that this is what you will be doing, and invite peers, friends, other children with autism, siblings (if possible).

2.  Observe natural social interactions within the group, or use the child's own experiences to choose one target, such as entering a group conversation.

3.  Observe the children with typical age-appropriate social skills in a typical situation that allows for the specific action being worked on – this can be filmed for group discussion. Learning points to observe in this instance include:
    *   If body language of group individuals is closed off, don't enter,
    *   Stand quietly by the group to see if they are willing to let you in,
    *   Watch body language to see if they're OK with you being there,
    *   Listen for the current topic,
    *   Make a comment that is relevant and on topic,
    *   Keep to the topic – don't change the topic straight-away
    *   Ask others questions and let others take turns – don't hog the spotlight.

4.  Write a social script/social story to show the stages of the interaction.

5.  Read the story with the group and discuss.

6. Act out the story with different people being the person approaching.

7. Provide reinforcement and positive feedback about how each child performed.

8. Ask other group members to rate how the other child performed in relation to the written script.

9. Send home information to parents of other group members, if appropriate, so that they can practice/talk about it at home.

10. Take that skill to a real-life setting with the same children or young people.

11. Have your child rate their own performance.

12. Take your child to a natural setting without the group to interact with whoever is there.

13. Talk about the skill being practised before they go in.

14. Have them rate their performance after they have finished, and give feedback.

15. Maintenance:

   • Discuss periodically to keep fresh.
   • Keep copies of social scripts to refer to.
   • Provide feedback on what you observe.

## Questions and answers

**Q:** *My nine-year-old son won't talk to people he does not know. Sometimes it's so bad that he just won't come down from his bedroom. He's fine with people he is used to, but I worry that as he gets older he is going to get isolated if he does not start meeting new people.*

**A:** You have not mentioned whether or not he has special learning needs. You might find the advice in the past few pages useful, as it lays out steps and procedures in a very precise way. He has clearly missed some of the development phases for learning social skills by trial and error – and if he is not prepared to trial, he is not going to make errors, so we would recommend that you teach him some simple strategies for greeting people; for example, you could cover:

- What to do when you meet an adult you don't know.
- What to do when you meet a professional adult you don't know (such as a doctor, dentist or tutor).
- What to do when you meet someone new of your own age.

It's a good idea to teach this in steps, a little at a time, encouraging him to watch how other people interact – in soap operas, in books, on public transport or in the street. You might also find some of the commercially produced material for ASD (autistic spectrum disorder) children useful (see the Learning Resources section at the end of this book).

**Q:** *Whenever she has any free time, my 13-year-old daughter is on social network sites. I can't get her to go out of the house to clubs or activities either – apart from the occasional*

*meeting with one or two old friends. She has been home edu-
cated for two years, but we are part of a collective. There are
12 children involved, so we team up and teach them together.
Although she chooses to see some of these children during the
school week, she never chooses to talk to them during down
time, although she may sometimes be in social media contact
with them over the weekend.*

**A:** If she is spending her time during the week with lots of
others, the fact that she is socially networking for the rest of
her time is fairly normal for a 13-year-old. Make sure you
have built into your home school agreement at least one or
two clubs a week, so that at least she is meeting in person
some other people of her own age. Offer her some options like
pizza and movie nights, or sleepovers, to encourage her to feel
better about being at home. She might also enjoy it more if
you are not there (or in another room). Give her some space,
but make it her home space.

**Q:** *My four-year-old son is a nightmare. I took him out of
school because he did not settle well, and my intention was
that I would integrate him back again when he got a bit
older. But he is very aggressive with other children, and if he
does not get his own way he will hit, bite or kick. He tries
to do the same to me, but I have learnt how to manage his
behaviour. As a consequence he doesn't get asked to parties,
no one wants to come to play dates, and if I try to arrange
outings, no one wants to come with me. I am worried about
how he will reintegrate and him getting further isolated as
he gets older.*

**A:** It's very hard to say what is going on for your son just from
this slim information, but it might be that the boundaries you
provided in his very early years have not been clear enough to
him. Now you need to reward his correct behaviour and steer

his poor reactions: reward him when he gets it right, show clear disapproval when he gets it wrong and show pleasure in improvement. As a response to his behaviour, physical aggression and anger won't work.

Keep an eye on it, bearing in mind that you might need professional help, either now or when he gets a bit older, if things don't improve – particularly when you want him to reintegrate into school. It is possible that there is something in the way his brain works that is producing his behaviour. Sometimes the clues to this might be found in the family histories of you or his other parent – has there been anyone else in the families with similar behaviour?

For now, he's only four. And whereas 'theory of mind' is generally in place by now, it's not always fully developed. Until a child has theory of mind in place, they don't really get that hitting and hurting is not OK; rather they are abstaining in order to please you. You need to provide a safe growing-up space, but it's important not to over-explain things to him, 'In this family, we don't hit, it's not kind' is sufficient. Make a big fuss when he gets things right.

# 10

# 20 Key Social Skills and Some Tips on Developing Them at Home

We have compiled a list of the social skills that we feel are important. Our list is not exhaustive; we have simply chosen 20 of the most frequently used skills with some ideas for ways to practise or reinforce them in a home environment.

## Embedding the development of social skills

Ideally, learning about social skills and exploring them should form part of a thematic piece of work or project so that the areas being discussed form a natural part of ongoing learning. This is probably most easily done through books. Discussing why particular characters in a book behave the way they do, and how a different choice of behaviour might have led to a different outcome, can lead to really helpful conversations about how your child or young person does – or does not – relate to the issues being raised. Books and stories are great doorways into discussion, observation and reflection on the way we interact with each other and the world around us. No matter whether it is the *Hungry Caterpillar* or *Othello*, Lyra or Gandalf, when characters make choices or speak to others, we can learn from them.

One of the easiest and most enjoyable ways to ask a child to reflect on a book or story is to get them to draw, from a single picture to a whole comic book, with speech and thought bubbles, as well as notes. The way in which they do this, however, will depend on their age and their facility with drawing.

Any topic or theme that includes human beings interacting with others, or the world at large, can offer opportunities for social learning. Figure 7 shows the very first planning stage for a project on communication

Figure 7: Theme plan for communication

What are the key social skills to be learnt?

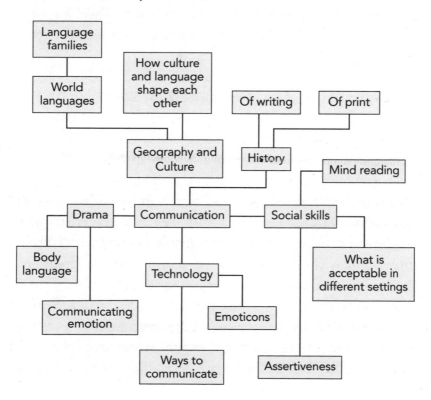

that provides a wonderful opportunity to look at everything from secret codes to satellites, pictograms and cuneiform,[18] to Caxton and Cawdrey.[19] A simple spider diagram can make an excellent starting point to look at any topic – with the inclusion of a category marked 'social skills' appearing as a matter of course.

## 1. Sharing and turn-taking

The best and simplest ways to encourage children to share and to take turns are by playing old-fashioned board games (which were designed for exactly that purpose in many cases) and by cooking and eating together. It may take time, but family cooking is a great 'easy-chat' situation where cooperation and sharing are required for a good result. Regular group cooking strengthens family bonds and reduces competition too.

How about a regular evening where the family cooks together and then plays board games?

## 2. Communication skills

The term 'communication skills' covers a wide range of skills that children might lack if they are growing up in time-poor households where more time is spent watching or interacting with screens rather than interacting with others. Effective communication skills might include:

- Talking to people in a way that is engaging.
- Showing interest in the other person as well as speaking oneself.

- Taking turns in conversation.
- Demonstrating that you are listening.
- Understanding the nature of the audience and that, depending on whom you are talking to, the method of optimum communication will change.

Opportunities to use words in as many ways as possible will be helpful, particularly for describing:

- Their own emotions and feelings.
- The behaviour and emotions they have observed in others.
- The world around them.
- A sequence of real events.
- Imagined outcomes or consequences to real events.

Simple ways to practise these might include:

- Retelling a story that they have been told, or outlining the plot of a book they have read.
- Trying to relate an event or incident from their life in sequenced detail – perhaps a visit to a friend or a trip to the park.
- Playing a game where one person closes their eyes and the other gives a detailed description of something they can see, so that it can be clearly identified by the non-speaker when they open their eyes. Trying to describe one tree among many, one market stall or shop in a busy high street or one flower in a flower bed can be very challenging.

- Asking the child to guess what happens next in a story at a crucial point or how they think a television plotline might end – and to outline this in detail.

Figure 8: Communication activity

**Intention** To help your child or young person identify how they listen, what affects their listening and recall, and the possible impact this might have on others.

**Preparation** A set of slips of paper or small cards, each with a question on one side only. Questions are personal – about likes, dislikes, experiences and viewpoints. Here are some possible questions:

- If you had to have another first name, what would you choose?
- What is your favourite and least favourite subject?
- What is your favourite television programme?
- What is your favourite meal?
- What is one thing that you have done that you are proud of?
- If you could spend an hour talking to a famous person, who would you choose?
- If you had to live somewhere else for a year, where would you live?
- What do people most like about you?
- What is one thing that you'd change about yourself if you could?
- If you won a million pounds, what would you do with it?
- What is one way in which you would like to change the world?

- If you could be famous for something, what would
  it be for?
- What is one thing about you that annoys people?

Don't show the slips to the other person/people, but shuffle
them and place them face down on the table. Take turns to
pick up the top slip, read the question aloud and answer it.

(If they are not able to read the questions, pick them up
one by one and read them aloud. Let your child answer first,
then answer the same question yourself.)

When all the questions have been answered, ask further
questions to prompt reflection:

- What were the easiest questions?
- What were the hardest questions?
- What makes these hard or easy (generally likes and
  dislikes are easy, self-regard questions are harder)

Finally, ask them to recall as much as possible of each
other's answers in turn. If there are only two of you, ask
them which of your answers they recall – and don't help.
Ask them to reflect on why they remembered some answers
better than others and why they can't recall all the answers
(almost nobody does).

If appropriate, reflect on why we listen better to some
people than others and how it feels when you are not listened to equally.

Ask them how what they have just been talking about
could help them when they are engaging other people in
conversation, or trying to.

This might lead to discussions.

## 3. Showing care and concern

With younger children, we tend to use the word 'kind' as a general 'care and concern' word. Whenever an opportunity arises, invite your child to be kind; for example, when a sibling is crying (and the other child is not the reason!) ask them what they can do for their sibling that would be kind and would comfort them. When it is Dad's birthday, ask them what the family could do to show Dad how much he is loved.

When reading together, ask the child how one character can show kindness to another. Encourage them to mind-read; for example, by asking them to notice how others might be feeling when out and about. This is a great activity for all ages, and with older children it can be expanded into a game where the participant makes up a back-story to explain the current mood of a stranger they have observed through the 'people-watching' game.

Teens and very young children can sometimes be oblivious to the feelings of others because they do not yet pick up on facial and body-language cues. If talking to them about your feelings, or the feelings of anyone else, be sure to be clear; for example, 'I'm puzzled by your answer, I don't understand why you are saying that?' or 'I'm sad that you didn't think to ask me too.'

As children grow, it is important that they learn to show care and concern, not only for those in their immediate circle, but also for those they have never met. Looking at an age-appropriate news programme or news website regularly together is an excellent way of helping a home educated child stay in contact with the world around them. When terrible things happen, such as hurricanes or floods, ask the child how they think it would feel to be in such a situation and how they would manage if it were them. Move on to ask them to think of ways in which they, and perhaps your whole family, could help. Perhaps they could organise a fundraising event? Perhaps they could sell some toys on eBay and send the money to a charity helping victims? Perhaps they could write a poem or story for you to post on social media to encourage everyone to help?

## 4. Managing conflict

Conflict is a side effect of living, working or playing in groups, and it exists to a greater or smaller degree whenever people get together. But it does also provide an opportunity for greater understanding between group members if handled well. Good conflict management leaves everybody feeling OK at the end. This is an important principle to consider when managing conflict with or between children: they don't have to feel good but they shouldn't feel bad.

We live in an age of revenge and retribution; somebody is made to be responsible for anything that happens that we don't like – and punished accordingly. Most conflict arises through disagreement or conflicting wants; the desire to be in charge for younger children or to be seen as the group 'alpha' with older young people (and adults). Revenge and retribution tend to lead to more revenge and retribution, and so enemies are formed and lines drawn in the sand.

The first principle of behaviour management for all of us is that we always have a choice about our own behaviour, but we don't get to choose anybody else's. It is important when working with children around conflict that we make clear to them that there is no one right answer in any situation, but the best solution is the one that leaves everybody feeling OK at

## Figure 9: Choice chart

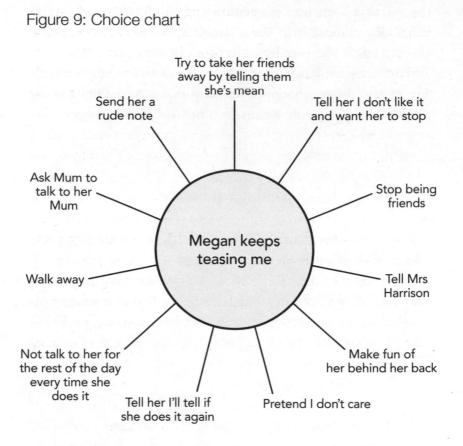

## A simple choice chart

1. The child is encouraged to think of as many options as possible and no censorship or disapproval is shown – in fact we encourage all the possible answers, its fine to imagine being mean.

2. Then we ask the child if there are any solutions listed that would never be a 'good solution' – these we cross out.

3. Then we ask the child which one they might want to try first.

With older children (10 or older) we might look at what the consequence of each of these choices might be and grade the choices accordingly out of 10. The choice with the highest score is the one to try first.

the end of it. One way of encouraging children to understand behaviour choices is to use a simple spider diagram called a choice chart. The problem is written in the centre of a circle and as many choices as possible are listed around the outside. These can be anything the child chooses and they can be described by the child themselves or by an adult helper. The point is to keep encouraging them to think of other choices without too much comment or judgement. Therefore, we would not say 'that's a silly choice' or 'that's a sensible choice', otherwise they will simply put down the answers they think we want to hear. Rather, the activity is about acknowledging the enormous range of options open to them – including some that they definitely would never use.

Then we consider all the choices that have been suggested and ask if there are any on this diagram that can never possibly leave everybody feeling OK. If there are, we simply put a line through them to acknowledge that they exist but that they are not suitable choices to be made.

## 5. Negotiation and fair solutions

A fair solution is any solution that leaves everybody feeling OK at the end of it. They don't have to be pretty and they don't have to be achieved the way adults do them. Whenever the opportunity arises to make a decision where there is more than one viewpoint, it's a good idea to find a way to make a fair choice and recall the method used on a list headed 'fair solutions'. Whenever a situation arises where there is a conflict of interests – perhaps in a story or book, perhaps in real life or on television or in a film – ask the child to consult the 'fair solutions' list and see if they can find a way of resolving the conflict. Below is an example of a fair solutions list created by a group of children to give an idea of what it might look like. Please don't be tempted to use this list yourself – the process of thinking through potential options is far more important than the list.

Figure 10: Sample fair solutions chart

**WORKING OR PLAYING WITH
OTHERS – FAIR SOLUTIONS**

Fair solutions include:

- Volunteer
- Test for the best person for the job
- Identify three or four options, and choose between them
- Agree on what each person says
- Agree by discussion – keep putting forward your points of view
- Work together as a team
- Vote
- Adapt what is happening to include everyone
- Take turns
- Share
- Tell the truth
- Be supportive
- Leave it to luck – rock, paper, scissors, dice, flip a coin, and so on
- Share the responsibility/blame
- Own up to something and apologise – appreciate the honesty and forgive
- Apologise
- Share

## 6. Being assertive

Children who are assertive (that is, not aggressive or passive) are less likely to be bullied or picked on by others and are generally considered by their peers to make excellent friends, as they can be relied upon to be honest and to stand up for what is right, even when things get difficult.

When working on assertiveness, whatever their age Gill uses a simple computer drawing of three faces, which represent different kinds of behaviour. We find children have very little problem with looking at the faces and responding to the question, 'What kind of behaviour might this person do?' (for younger children). For older young people, you could ask them to suggest what kind of behaviour might fall into specific categories.

With pre-teens and teens Gill sometimes use a fourth face to represent passive-aggressive behaviour, which is massively on the increase among young people these days and which includes many online behaviours: revenge, spreading rumours, lying, and generally being underhand and deceitful in a hidden way.

The faces chart can be kept and added to whenever a new behaviour occurs in a story, in real life or just in the imagination of the child. Eventually it becomes a comprehensive list of all the different kinds of behaviour choices a child might make – but the only behaviours on the chart that leave everyone involved feeling OK are the ones in the assertive category.

If a child displays this behaviour, we might ask them which category they are operating in or which style of behaviour they are showing right now. If they correctly name the category, we praise them but ask them to rephrase or amend their behaviour in order to leave everyone feeling OK.

# Figure 11: Assertiveness

**Passive**

- Shy
- Says "I don't know"
- Quiet
- Gives in
- Blames themself
- Says "If you like"
- Follows others
- Copies others
- Gives up quickly
- Lets others have things their way
- Gets left out
- Cries
- Says "Whatever you want"
- Waits to be asked
- Lets others boss them about – might have bossy friends
- Clingy

**Aggressive**

- Boses people around
- Mean/rude
- Demands
- Threatens
- Has to win
- Organises everything
- Shouts
- Does as they please
- Takes what they want
- Pushes in/pushes to the front
- Has 'cronies' rather than friends
- Upsets others on purpose
- Blames everything on others
- Physically hurts others
- Doesn't care about the feelings of others

**Passive-aggressive**

- Vengeful
- Tells tales – doesn't keep confidences
- Feels hard done by
- Insincere
- Changes friends and allegiances
- Passes blame to others
- Lies
- Manipulates people and situations
- Spreads rumours
- Presents as a victim "poor me!"
- Gossips
- Enjoys drama (and may engineer it)

**Assertive**

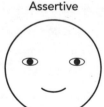

- Kind
- Friendly
- Reliable
- Negotiates
- Listens to others
- Comforts others
- Forgives easily
- Has good manners
- Honest but kind
- Admits mistakes
- Loyal
- Shares
- Collaborates
- Takes turns
- Sticks up for themselves
- Non blaming
- Polite
- Shows and feels empathy

The simple explanation of assertive behaviour is that it is any behaviour that leaves everyone feeling OK. In the everyday world, the term 'assertive' is often used as a kind of code word for aggressive, a more polite way of saying someone who always gets their own way. In its truest form assertive means being able to stick up for oneself without overpowering anyone else. The simple explanation of speaking assertively is that it is honest but kind. There are lots of games that can be played to practise these traits. Our favourite is the 'What would you say if ...?' game. Each person takes it in turns to give a really hard situation to the other, who must try to give an honest but kind answer. Such situations could include:

- Somebody cooks you their favourite meal. You take one mouthful and it makes you feel sick, it is so horrible. What would you say?
- Somebody invites you to their house to watch television with them for an evening, but last time you went round it was really boring and you don't want to go.
- Someone invites you to their party, but you have already told a friend you will see them on the same day. You would rather see your friend.

## 7. Integrity

Integrity is a rather old-fashioned value that is important for children to understand in the modern world. Essentially, it means being true to your belief system and applying it to your own behaviour choices – even when the going gets tough. Having integrity means that if you believe lying is wrong or bad, you don't lie even when others do; it means that if you believe stealing is wrong, you don't take something that isn't yours even when others do; it means that if you believe bullying is wrong, you don't bully others – or ignore it when you see it.

Of course, the world of children today is seldom so clear cut, and most people have times when they have done something against their own code of conduct, perhaps because the pressure to do so was so great or the impact of the right action was so much more complicated than the wrong action. Essentially, integrity has two parts: recognising our belief system and how we want the world to be, and living up to those same ideals ourselves, even when circumstances are difficult; however, all of us know that there are times when we break our own rules of behaviour.

---

### CHANGING YOUR BEHAVIOUR AS A PARENT

One mother wrote about how she recognised the need to change her own behaviour in relation to her son if she wanted him to react honestly:

'The other day I was having a bit of a rant at my nine-year-old son for putting the empty milk container back in the fridge after he'd used it all up. He swore that it wasn't him, although I knew it had to be, because he and I were the only people at home, and it certainly wasn't me. While I was giving him a talking to, I found myself telling him that lying was never the right thing to do and that he really shouldn't lie to me because as a parent there are times when it matters to know the truth. I was suddenly struck by a memory of my parents saying exactly the same to me in very similar circumstances and at a very similar stage in my childhood.

I consider myself an honest person and a person who values honesty in others, but I had a sudden flashback to a lie I told at work a few years ago of the, "Yes, I finished it and mailed it to you yesterday" variety, when in fact I hadn't even begun the work. I realised that lying, even when you believe in the truth, happens almost instantaneously when faced with the fear of criticism, disappointing others, or getting punished or disapproved of in some way. I realised that if I wanted my son to be honest to me I needed to change the way I questioned him and the way I responded to his answers. I knew he had finished the milk and yet I still asked him if he had finished it, which was unnecessary and pushed him into a corner where the lie response kicked in. I vowed from then on that when I knew the answer I would simply state my request for his future behaviour, "Can you rinse the empty milk container and put it in the recycling when you finish the milk rather than back in the fridge please?" I want my kids to tell the truth to me, and I recognise that if I pressurise them, sometimes the age-old human survival instinct immediately kicks in with whatever will get someone out of trouble!'

Teaching children about integrity has two parts, the first is simply thinking about how we want others to behave. Regardless of whether your child is three or 16, there will be many times when other people display actions they find distressing or annoying. Whenever this happens, simply ask them what is the behaviour they would have liked from this person and jot it down on a list in their social skills folder, under a heading of 'How people should behave' or 'Desirable behaviour'.

Whenever your child is faced with a dilemma or whenever they have behaved in a way that goes against the criteria they have previously identified in the behaviour of others, get out the list and have a discussion on the relevant point, without criticism or anger. Ask them to remember when other people have behaved that way towards them, how it felt, and ask them to guess or identify how you might be feeling right now. Point out to them that it is unrealistic to expect others to behave in ways that we don't ourselves and that the only behaviour we have any control over is our own. If we want the world to be an honest place, a fair place, a kind place, and so on, the way to make that happen is by each person taking responsibility for their own part of the world. I'm a great believer in Gandhi's maxim of 'Be the change you want to see in the world.'

Sometimes children take the view that if other people are going to lie, why shouldn't they? If other people are going to steal, why shouldn't they? If other people are going to be mean, why shouldn't they? As to how to respond, listening without anger and acknowledging that we all feel that way sometimes is a good starting place, but then ask them to con-sider how they feel about people who lie, steal or are mean to others? Do they really want to feel the same way about themselves? Do they really want other people – including their family – to feel that way about them?

Having family discussions about morals or values you hold dear can be effective around the dinner table or when driving in the car. Some tricky questions thrown in will help them know and understand the importance of values and of living by them.

## 8. Keeping secrets – and how
## to gossip successfully

Gossip often gets a bad press, and most people would probably say they think it's not a good thing. Certainly, young
people frequently complain that others 'talk behind their
back' while younger children between seven and 10 years old
are incensed about the things people have said about them to
each other and the 'secrets' they have shared.

Gossip is actually a really important part of social groupings and is often the way in which group members reaffirm
their shared values – as well as providing opportunities to
chat. Of course, there is always television, the news or the
weather to talk about, but being good at gossip, having things
to gossip about and knowing more than anyone else rank very
highly in terms of social currency.

The art of gossip when young is to do it within a framework of values. If we talk about someone's eating behaviour
in order to gain cachet with friends or to sensationalise and
judge the behaviour, it is wrong. If we talk about someone's
eating behaviour because we are showing genuine concern
for them and want to create a climate of care among the peer
group, then it is probably acceptable. Of course, there is a
difference between genuine concern and feigned concern.
One seeks to understand and support, while the other seeks
to make the speaker the centre of attention for a while. The
problem with gossiping in order to be the centre of attention
is that in order to maintain that attention, the speaker frequently has to embellish their story and add new particulars
as it goes along.

Helping children understand the difference between good
and bad gossip is probably best done without reference to their

own personal behaviour. We talk about gossip in an abstract way. 'When is it good to gossip?' or 'Is gossip ever right?' are excellent questions to consider as a starting point. Asking your child to write/dictate/draw a cartoon strip of a situation in which gossip is helpful and another illustrating when gossip is harmful can help them reflect on what they already know about the effects and power of gossip.

Gossiping about oneself – what we did, what we thought, where we went, who we interacted with and how – is always acceptable. We have the verbal rights over our own lives even where they criss-cross with the lives of others. We also have the verbal rights over things we have read or seen in the public domain. We don't have the verbal rights over everything we are told by others, including things on social media that involve people within our social systems. It may be OK to share a scandalous story about a celebrity (if you really want to) but it is not OK to share a scandalous story about someone from your football team or music class, even though you have read both stories on Facebook.

Asking your child to create a set of rules or guidelines for gossip would be an excellent social skills task, starting with a brief discussion and perhaps some 'what if?' scenarios.

Keeping secrets comes with one rule: all secrets should be kept at all times, except those which are about harm or could lead to harm for the person who has the secret.

Such secrets should always be shared with someone trust-worthy, usually an adult, because adults have the capability of resolving a damaging situation, whereas other children don't. There are many excellent books written about secrets for all ages, which can be given as a reading book or a starting point to social-skills work about secrets. To find a good book, simply enter 'books about secrets for kids' or 'books about secrets for young people' into your search engine and read the synopsis and reviews for those that look promising.

## 9. Collaboration and cooperation

It is almost impossible to teach a child about collaboration and cooperation if they are working alone. If your child is isolated from others for a lot of the time, wait until they do meet up with peers before exploring these issues.

The easiest way to get children to recognise and value collaboration and cooperation is by giving a task to a group of children to complete individually and to record in some way how effective they have been. This may be by timing them or by measuring the amount of output. Suitable tasks depend on age, but it can be anything from stacking bricks on top of each other to create a metre-high tower to making an outfit out of toilet paper! It can be a fun task, such as gathering as many leaves as possible in one minute, a creative task, such as making a mural or collage, a piece of writing or a science experiment. The important point is that first they do it alone, then they do it as a group, then you compare the outcomes. Ideally, with older children from seven or eight to teens, the task should involve a range of different skills or activities so that the participants begin to recognise how individuals can bring their talents, skills and interests to the group to enhance the outcome.

Of course, there are many examples in history where collaboration and cooperation have contributed to world change in positive, and occasionally negative, ways such as during Second World War allies, the suffragist movement and the operation of parliaments around the world. In sport, we can see that teams where members don't cooperate with each other don't do very well; for example, in rowing, working together is essential, and being able to read your teammates' intentions has huge advantages in doubles tennis and bowls. There are many opportunities to consider the advantages and challenges of working with others as well as many opportunities for helping young people to explore collaboration.

## 10. Working in groups, and managing relationships in groups

Some home educated children have a history of finding it difficult to work within groups or managing relationships within groups. There are many styles of home educating, but whatever you choose, it is essential that your child spends some time working with others. It is not enough for them just to meet up with friends and family for play or socialising sessions. Learning to work with others takes time and a set of skills and understandings specific to completing tasks with others. When children play or socialise together, they can keep changing what they do in order to suit everyone or split into smaller groupings of like-minded individuals. But when working together in a group, differences have to be resolved in such a way that everybody stays engaged.

Where many schools go wrong with group work is in assuming that simply working in groups is enough to teach children the core skills required. Many children never learn to work well in groups because they have never been asked to think through what is required or how to manage when challenges occur. Not everyone finds working in groups easy, and children with specific learning or behaviour needs, such as those with ASD or ADD, might regularly find themselves being left out when others form groups either from the outset or as the group evolves. It is important for children with a negative history of working in groups to understand that they can work with others as long as everyone sticks to some principles to ease things along.

When working with groups, Gill always discusses some form of guidelines for their behaviour. These may be referred to as 'rules' – but they don't have to be. She usually begins by getting children to identify the behaviour of others that they find most difficult in a group setting and they list these. Once they have a list to work with Gill asks the group to think of guidelines or rules to make sure that things on the list cannot happen. She usually acts as the scribe for this to enable everybody to share equally. Here is an example of some guidelines created by a group of young people and scribed by Gill.

Figure 12: Group rules

**RULES OF THE GROUP**

- Make sure everyone is included
- Work together
- Let everyone talk
- Respect others
- Always be honest and kind
- Listen to each other
- Agreements must be fair to all
- Use only constructive criticism with everyone
- Take part
- Treat others the way you would want to be treated
- Move up in the big circle to let others in
- Keep trying
- Be cooperative

Initially, when working with a group, Gill keeps tasks small and very clear, with a firm agreed (and activated) time boundary. The idea is to allow the group to succeed in working together and to build on that success with more challenging tasks or longer time periods. Expecting very young children to work together in a group for more than about 10–15 minutes is unrealistic at any time, so tasks need to change, adapt or develop in clearly marked chunks of time.

With children from seven up, Gill asks them to reflect at the end of each task using the rules or guidelines they came up with. She then asks them as a group to give themselves a mark out of ten for their performance. This may take into account the end product of the activity, but it is essentially about how well they worked together. If there is a variety of views within the group on performance, groups might need help in deciding how to score themselves, but using the previously devised list of 'fair solutions' might help them choose an appropriate strategy. Alternatively, they might decide that when choosing for a group, what constitutes fair looks quite different, in which case they might add new things to their fair solutions list.

Keeping a record of the group's scores can help those involved see what is working and what isn't. Any discussion on how a group works should be carried out without blame: every member in the group is responsible for the group's performance.

Sometimes groups need a little extra help in understanding which behaviours are helpful and which aren't, in which case Gill uses a little card game where the object of the activity is to sort the cards into helpful or unhelpful behaviours. With groups where assertive behaviour has been discussed (see above), she asked the group to sort the cards using the 'faces' for assertive, aggressive and passive behaviours. They then discuss which of these categories provides the most helpful behaviour.

The sorting cards contain the following behaviours:

## Figure 13: Sample sorting cards

Note these have been mixed up and are not in any particular order.

| | |
|---|---|
| Complain to others about someone else while being silly themselves | Make fair decisions |
| Sulk | Complain about everything everybody else says or does |
| Make an effort to help someone who isn't joining in to feel part of the group | Laugh at some ideas |
| Blame other people for what is wrong in a group | Make fun of people or their contributions |
| Take time to include everyone | Refuse to join in |
| Talk only to one or two particular friends | Mess about |
| Leave people out then say it was their fault when they get upset | Take control |
| Make silly suggestions | Leave all the decisions to everybody else |
| Say 'good idea' or 'I like that idea' | Only listen to some people |
| Chat about other things | Keep on doing something even if someone has told you it is annoying them |
| Complain about a member of the group to another group member | Help everyone to share ideas |
| Tell someone what to do | Call someone names |

To encourage good working in groups also requires the adult(s) supervising any activity to leave the group to operate in its own way – but then to manage reflection sessions in which group participants can be honest, but kind, to one another about what works and what doesn't, as well as reflecting on what they contributed that was helpful or unhelpful themselves. Although this can be frustrating with younger children, or with individuals who find group work particularly difficult, perseverance will help them to learn and develop their skills.

## 11. Coping with teasing and being laughed at/with

Most of us are sensitive to being laughed at unless we have tried to elicit laughter intentionally or have related a funny story about ourselves in which we highlight an amusing flaw. We often refer to this as the difference between being laughed 'at' and being laughed 'with'. Some young people understand the difference, but many do not.

Encourage your child to tell funny stories from their day by sharing some of your amusing moments and mistakes – and encouraging them to laugh with you. Sometimes, having a question that each member of the family has to answer, such as 'One thing I did well today was ...' or 'One thing I'm proud of today is ...', can provide a useful way of encouraging shared laughter by occasionally asking 'One silly thing I did today was ...' or 'One funny thing I did today was ...'.

Although this can help children grow up with a sense of perspective about everybody's mistakes and silly moments, it's fair to say that most adolescents find being laughed at (when they haven't chosen to be) very difficult. Creating a choice chart (see page 230) using examples either from their real experience, or made-up ones to cover aspects of embar-rassment, can provide a good way of discussing options and possible outcomes. Once they have listed all the choices of behaviour they can think to suggest, go through each choice and ask what the best outcome of that choice would be and what would be the worst. These can be added to the chart. It may be that they can think of only one outcome for some of the choices, which is enough. No decision needs to be made unless they want to formulate a perfect answer. Simply exploring the options by asking them to think through pos-sible behaviour routes is enough to help them have some choices, should they find themselves in a similar situation in future.

Remember that, unlike adults, children do not necessarily see similar situations as having the same options. We can see that being laughed at and teased for spilling your pencil case all over the floor might have similar choices to being laughed at or teased for having your cardigan buttoned up incorrectly, but for the person on the receiving end of the teasing it might feel quite different. Therefore, we don't just work through one or two social-embarrassment options, we ask them to think them through frequently during social skills discussions throughout the period of their schooling.

## 12. Maintaining friendships

For some children friendships are mysterious, and making friends in the first place can be really problematic. For such children, it can be really helpful to be taught how to look for behaviour and body language that signals a willingness to engage with someone new.

Most children at some time have problems with maintaining

friendships. Children who have been taken out of school might find maintaining friendships more difficult than most because they are not with their friends all day in the same way as they were, but the friends are still seeing each other. Friendship groups often have a strong dynamic that can leave people behind if they are not regularly part of the group.

As with all social skills, helping children to maintain their friendships and to understand how friendships are maintained involves a lot of questions being asked, rather than explanations or descriptions being given. If a child has established friendships, asking them to consider ways in which they can keep their relationships current will be helpful.

Problems often occur when children are around year 4 to 5 (about 8–10 years old) when friendships begin to take on a whole new meaning. Up until that age they are simply playmates who enjoy each other's company, but once they get a little older, friends become desirable 'properties', and how many friends you have or who your friends are can change the way others see you. This continues into adolescence for many young people whose friendships in the teen years have been shown to be highly influential on behaviour. Young people tend to make friends with others with whom they have a common ethos – those who see the world the same way as they do. And once friendships are formed they can exercise a powerful influence. When things go wrong during the teen years, many parents blame their child's friends – he or she got in with a bad lot – but often the truth is that he or she chose those people because at some level they represented and supported an aspect of the young person themselves. Because of this, we want to work with children on maintaining friendships with those who bring out the best in them rather than excuse the worst.

If a child is having problems with a friendship, listen, ask and listen some more would be the most helpful approach. When they have explored the issue from as many angles as they can, which can take a while, ask them to think of the options and choices they can make and the potential positive and negative consequences of each choice – time for yet another choice chart. Using examples of friendship issues that arise in your life and other family members' lives, books and literature, television, film and social media can provide an endless source of examples of friendship issues to discuss and dissect.

Occasionally, encouraging your young person to read and respond to questions on online forums such as Yahoo Answers can give them an opportunity to think through options and be helpful and thoughtful to others.

## 13. Taking responsibility for their own behaviour choices

Home educating at its best encourages children to take far more responsibility with their learning and time than their peers in mainstream schools. The home-educated child should be working within clear guidelines and to an agreement with everyone concerned with their well-being and education. It is therefore much more difficult for such a child to deny culpability when it comes to their learning or output.

Encouraging them to take responsibility for their other behaviour choices comes down to having clear expectations and a 'no blame or shame' approach to poor behaviour choices where reflection is based on asking what happened and not on why it happened followed by an expectation that the child will rectify the situation themselves. This, of course, depends on what has happened and what the poor behaviour choice was, but it might include playing with a sibling until they cheer up, apologising sincerely, writing a letter of apology, doing chores or kind acts for someone – the list of possibilities is endless.

Practising this approach, by looking at scenarios where individuals behave in unacceptable ways and having to put things right again, will make doing it for real much easier. For younger children, the use of puppets allows even a single child to role play. Characters or figures that can be moved around, or made-up plays, provide great opportunities for exploring extremes of behaviour as well as restorative techniques. Once children reach the age of nine or so, having clear sanctions for certain actions might be helpful, and these can be continued and expanded upon as they grow older. Working out with the child themself what the boundary should be, and how it should be maintained, is similarly helpful.

## 14. Adaptability

Like most social skills, adaptability – managing your place and your relationships within different situations – is really only learnt by being in relationships. Those who struggle with understanding differences and prefer to learn by using lists, such as ASD children, can be taught by rote. They might find it very helpful to be told that when you visit a friend's house you do XYZ; when you visit a relative's house you do ABC, and so on. Some excellent resources are available online for teaching social skills to ASD children – see Resources at the end of this book.

Helping a young person to be more adaptable in relationships is best done by frequent exposure to different people in different places. Therefore, it's important to build into a weekly plan plenty of opportunities for visiting libraries, coffee shops, parks and outdoor spaces, exhibitions, galleries, sporting venues, the cinema and theatre, dance classes, book clubs and any number of other events where people gather together for some shared purpose. Lead by example and use every opportunity to chat and involve your child in taking an interest in the people they meet. When home again, ask them about the conversations they had, what they enjoyed about them or learnt from them, and what worked or didn't work in terms of getting others engaged in conversation. Of course, they will go out and about without you during their non-learning times too, so asking some friendly and open-ended questions when they come home again can help increase their understanding of relationships in all their variety. If, however, it feels like an interrogation, they will be wary of telling you.

## 15. Managing attraction-based relationships

Home education is a choice some parents make because they want more control over what their child is learning. One thing they would be learning in school is Relationships and Sex Education (RSE). During these lessons, of course issues of biology are dealt with, but the best RSE schemes spend lots of time talking as children grow older about the changing nature of relationships. They will also be exploring aspects of attraction-based relationships from a surprisingly young age, including aspects of sexuality and sexual behaviour, from flirting to what you can and can't do with your friend's boyfriend – and this largely by talking with, and going out and about with, their friends.

Most young people say they get most of their information about sex and sexual behaviour from friends and other young people – and very little from parents or school. This isn't because schools and parents don't give them information, it is more that they get the information they want from friends as they want it in small, easy-to-understand packages – whereas adults tend to give too much information or too much of their own opinions. It is important, then, that you provide appropriate support to this side of your child's development, in line with your belief system, of course, by finding a good website designed for young people where they can access information and chat or ask questions in a safe and closely monitored online environment. This is really important for all young people, as asking friends alone might result in some very unhelpful or even risky answers. Having a website they can access freely without any restrictions will support their development when they need it.

## 16. Relating appropriately to different relationships with adults

Many international languages use different forms for addressing elders or those in positions of high respect within the community (e.g. in French the formal: informal *'vous'* and *'tu'* and in German *'sie'* and *'du'*). Modern English does not – or at least not formally; however, there are ways of addressing individuals that are more respectful and polite than others, and although it is increasingly acceptable to use more informal language, children need to learn what is and what isn't appropriate in different settings. This can be particularly difficult for some children who find it challenging or impossible to pick up cues from those around them.

With younger children, a simple sorting activity using small cards with actions or phrases on them and a diagram of overlapping circles representing key people in their lives, will open up the discussion for what is and isn't to be talked about and how we speak to different people. For children who find differentiation difficult, creating a simple list for each of the key people who they interact with, which tells them what is and what isn't appropriate, will be extremely helpful. In fact, for any child who really loves lists, compiling one can be a great learning opportunity.

Figure 14: Things it's OK to talk about – sample

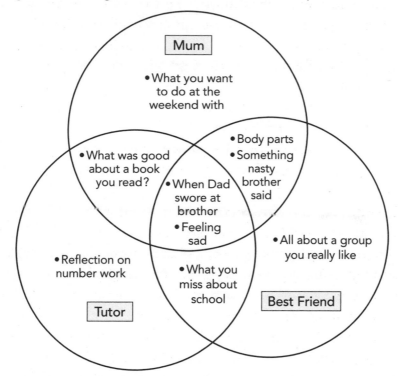

Ideally, the activity above would have 20–30 cards with different conversational topics on each for the child to sort. For this example Gill overlapped the three key people being discussed: mother, tutor and best friend. This allows for some items to be placed where best friend and tutor overlap, where best friend and Mum overlap, where Mum and tutor overlap and where all three overlap. With children under six or seven, overlapping circles would not be appropriate. Keep the circles separate, but duplicate cards where necessary to show that some things are appropriate to more than one person. It is probably extremely complicated to have more than three overlapping circles at a time, but you could always ask the child to devise a method illustrating areas of commonality.

## 17. Personal space and boundaries

We all have different feelings of personal space, which change according to who we are with, how comfortable we feel generally wherever we are and how those around us are behaving. Young children have little understanding of personal space – at least for that of other people, and they will cheerfully climb all over people or barge others out of the way. By the time a child is six (although possibly considerably sooner), they have some understanding of appropriate behaviour towards others that includes respecting their bodies, and some may be beginning to understand that we are affected by things close to us – not just by what is happening directly to our skin.

For older children, boundaries become extremely important when thinking about:

- Attraction-based relationships and appropriate/ consensual touch.

- Showing affection appropriately to peers and adults.
- Intimidation or threat.

One of the simplest ways of describing how feelings change according to circumstances is by using a simple comfort-zone diagram.

Figure 15: Comfort-zone diagram

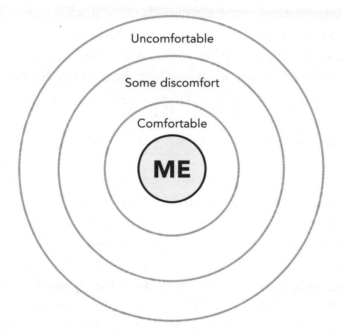

Simply drawn as a series of circles around a central 'Me' or name, the comfort-zone diagram can be used for discussing types of language and how comfortable or uncomfortable the individual is with them. It can also be used for different people, different types of approach or touch, or different subjects from the curriculum. It can be used by the child by simply placing their finger in the circle ring that represents how they feel, so if discussing language, for example, we might ask them to indicate how they feel when somebody laughs at them. Or you could use small cards with statements or names on them for the child to sort into the appropriate place. If using flipchart paper, large sheets enable people to write directly onto the circle and thus keep a lasting record.

Another interesting discussion point using the comfort-zone diagram is how big the respective areas are at different times; for example, there may be times when the child feels they have a very tiny 'comfortable' area and a very large 'some discomfort' area. If this is a particular issue for an individual, before any formal work takes place, asking how their comfort zone is looking today might be a good way of avoiding meltdowns or upsets. If need be, create a new chart.

## 18. Being supportive to others

As anyone who has read one of our books before will know, we are great fans of family meetings – regardless of how large or small the family is. One of the ways that children learn to take the feelings of others into account is by understanding what they can do that will upset or please another person that they care about. In a good school there is a great deal of discussion about how to help each other, particularly in schools that use Circle Time or well-organised PSHE[20] sessions. For the home-educated child, regular family meetings are extremely important, even if it is only a family of two. A good family meeting allows everyone to express how they feel about issues within the family without blaming anyone else or complaining about anyone else's behaviour. It then offers an opportunity for everyone to come up with possible solutions that are then carried out over the following week. It is a place where dissatisfactions can be aired as well as good things planned and organised. By sitting down together, and listening to each other respectfully, family members learn about each other's feelings and how they can help to support each other.

A family meeting should be formalised and should happen ideally at the same time on a regular basis, perhaps after dinner on Sunday afternoon or just before that cooking and board game evening mentioned earlier.

## 19. Managing anger in oneself and others

Most adults learn to manage anger well enough in their everyday lives, but even the calmest of adults has moments when they flare up. If an adult struggles to maintain a calm demeanour at all times, it stands to reason that children find it extremely difficult. Just as with adults, tiredness, stress, emotional upheaval and being told what to do when you don't want to do it, are all common triggers of anger.

Managing anger is not straightforward – there is no one solution or recommendation that works for everybody, but below are some tips on managing anger that might prove helpful.

**Children often get angry because** they can't adequately say what they are feeling, so asking them why they are angry might just make things worse. In which case, try verbalising for them such as, 'I can see that you are feeling really annoyed with your sister for knocking down your bridge because it took you so long to build and you did it so carefully. It was a really unkind and unfair thing for her to do.'

**Help your child develop 'emotional literacy'** by encouraging them to identify, name and express their feelings. You can help by naming your own, by questioning the feelings of characters in books or on television, or by talking about the feelings and behaviours of friends.

**If your child gets angry,** stay calm yourself: model the behaviour you want. You'll almost always have some physical reaction to their expression, perhaps a feeling of tension or faster heartbeat. Be aware of why this is happening, but stay calm and reasonable.

**Don't use platitudes** like 'Come on now, calm down. You're getting yourself in a state.' Such phrases can often make the child feel worse, not better. Instead, try to show acceptance and understanding of their feelings; for example, 'I can see that you think I am being unfair and I can see this is making you feel very angry.' The time to discuss the issue is when they are completely calm again. They cannot hear you when they are angry, and they will not listen to you either.

**Be firm and consistent** about aggressive behaviour. We are not responsible for our feelings, but we are responsible for our actions. Place restrictions within a family context such as 'In this family we don't think it's OK to hit each other – even when we're angry.'

**Work with your child** to recognise the triggers for their anger. What is it that sets it off? Once you can both recognise some of the causes, it might be possible to limit or divert an outbreak of uncontrollable anger before it starts, using another activity such as a punchbag, kicking a ball in the garden or blowing a balloon. Physical activities may work best, but some children may respond to drawing a picture of what annoys them and then scribbling all over it or tearing it into little pieces, or writing slogans or comments on paper to destroy or discard later. What you *never* do is give in to them to avoid a scene.

**Older children or adolescents** might prefer to do their anger alone. If they storm off, let them go, but always check on them after a short period to see if they are ready to talk. You could just sit with them to let them know you care, even if the anger they are expressing is towards you. Any rudeness should be dealt with after the anger has dissipated – never during.

**If your child storms off** in a huff at any slight criticism, or shouts at you when they mess something up ('stupid bike'), then try to show love and kindness to them – a big hug if possible. Sometimes young people get angry when they feel shame or when they feel helpless. At these times they need reassurance and affection.

**Sometimes what triggers a person's anger** is actually anxiety; for example, if you are going out somewhere, or visiting a new place, and they throw a hissy fit, they may need to understand and feel safe in the new experience. What might help is lots of reassurance, lots of talking about how you are both going to manage things in advance – and most of all how you are going to be there for them throughout.

**Teach children how to 'use their words'** to express how they feel – and teach doesn't mean tell. Read stories where characters get angry, tell them about times when you got angry and how you managed it.

**When they get it right** make sure you let them know that you've noticed.

## 20. The line between pride and boasting

There is a simple rule of thumb that everyone should learn in order to differentiate between pride in one's own accomplishments and achievements, and boasting.

Pride that comes from something we have done is a good thing; it is an essential component of self-esteem. Being able to recognise ourselves as the source of all our accomplishments really matters, and we should all encourage children to recognise the feelings that come with it.

Boasting, however, is mean behaviour. Boasting is using one's own achievements to belittle or put down the achievements of others and as such is a form of bullying. Often the only difference between celebrating an achievement and putting someone down with achievement is the way in which it is said, so use role play with your child to practise some simple phrases said in different ways to imply pride in oneself or a put down to someone else.

You can find plenty of phrases in everyday life, but here are a few to start the thinking process with:

- I got ten out of ten
- I've got some really excellent new trainers
- I scored two of the goals
- My mum's got a new car
- I'm getting a new phone for Christmas

Once you have practised the different inflections used to share good news or to boast, try softening these statements so that they cannot be misinterpreted, such as 'I'm so relieved I got ten out of ten this time. I worked so hard to try to remember everything because I'm really not very good at spelling.'

Practise sharing achievements with each other on a regular basis, perhaps at bedtime, when you might ask every family member to say two things they've done well today or one thing they are proud of about themselves.

## Questions and answers

**Q:** *I recently married and inherited part-care of my partner's ten-year-old daughter. We get on well and are shortly taking her travelling with us on a world trip for a year, and the plan is that I will be responsible for her schooling and education while she is away. The only bit that really worries me is how I will manage her social skills, as I don't know her very well. What on earth will I do with her?*
**A:** How exciting, and what a wonderful mother to trust you with her daughter for a year. This is likely to be a very bonding shared experience. On your travels, you will all be meeting lots of different people, and watching how you do it will be excellent modelling for her. You can give her little observational tasks to do around culture and behaviour – an excellent opportunity for her to learn how things are done differently around the world; for example, how people say hello and greet one another. Don't worry about her social skills, she will learn a great deal from creating a friendship bond with you. Although it's up to you all to set the boundaries and help her stick to them, your role is to help her blossom and be who she can be.

**Q:** *We took my eight-year-old daughter out of school earlier*

*this year because she was having great problems with bully-*
*ing, and the school was not taking it seriously. Which are the*
*most important social skills to work with her on?*
**A:** For a child being bullied, do lots of work around self-esteem,
because that's usually a problem. Self-esteem influences how
she will view the world, so you need to spend time helping her
see how special she is and developing her sense of what value
she brings to the world. Assertiveness, communication skills
generally and the ability to manage conflict are three areas
you might decide to prioritise. Working around those with
you should increase her confidence.

**Q:** *My son is home educated so we spend a great deal of time*
*together. I now find, however, that if I ask a friend over, he*
*tends to treat any friends of mine as his, and expects to be*
*included in the conversation. Although I am pleased to find*
*he is confident and able to speak to my friends, I want him*
*to be considerate and let me have time alone with them.*
**A:** Congratulate yourself on teaching your child to be so
confident that he can talk to adults in this way; however, it is
easy to understand where the problem now lies. We all need
time with our friends, so you might approach this through a
social skills lesson for him, where you talk about boundaries
and appropriate behaviour in different settings. How you deal
with this depends on how old he is.

You need to work with him around boundaries and ask
whether he likes you to be there when he is with his friends.
He might like it to start with, but later wish you had gone
away. Once he has this sort of understanding, you can talk
about it being great for him to meet your friends but it's lovely
if you have time to spend with them on your own.

You could also turn the conversation into a game, for
further discussion. Situations on cards that pose questions

around 'What do we do if?' can extend his learning. This can help prevent him feeling his behaviour is being singled out and is particularly helpful if he is sensitive. Once you have talked about boundaries and choices in this way, ask him to think about how he will occupy himself and reward the changed behaviour. If he is eight or younger, think about providing an activity box that's only used for special occasions. It might contain special grown-up style colouring books, or Lego that's not available all the time – what is sometimes called a 'rainy-day box'. This could be something you give him when you want to reward him, and you only let him play with when he has been particularly good or when you have a visitor. If he is older, you could consider allowing him to watch a video you approve of on the television (naturally, it's not something you normally do, it's meant to be a treat) or encouraging him to get on with his homework or scheduled work, so that he can have less to do tomorrow.

Alternatively, you could let him spend a limited amount of social time on a gadget, read a book or magazine, to give you time to spend with your friend. He should go away until you call him back – this way gaining credit for leaving you alone. The wider point is both for him to like leaving you alone and for you to acknowledge his effort and say thank you. But you have to make sure that next time he is with his friends, you return the compliment.

**11**

# Creating Community – the Importance of a Wider Network For You and Your Home educated Child

This is the third chapter within the section of our book devoted to the social development of the home-educated child. It's entitled 'creating community' because it's very important that we think about how to build a wider support structure to which home-educated children and their parents/carers can both belong and contribute.

## Why does it matter?

It matters to your child, because creating a community offers the possibility of a home-educated peer group that can support and encourage their social development, which matters just as much as their academic progress. It matters to the parent(s) because home educating a child is an intense experience, which will draw on every part of you, so it's very important to be topping up your batteries through external contacts and support rather than being in 'give' mode all the time.

Although it's possible to home educate a child in many different ways, and for a variety of different reasons, the need to create a community around those involved is always important.

## How to find or establish a community network

It's possible to encounter community in various ways – and a straightforward google of 'networks for home educating parents' in your local area will yield organisations and individuals that are geographically close, and which could be your starting point.

Finding other parents of children who are being home educated offers you the opportunity of creating a study group that can meet weekly or fortnightly and work together on something together so that everyone has the experience of co-working and collaborating. What you work on does not have to be produced jointly. It could be done together or separately, but the planning does need to be shared: who does what, and establishing working methods for how you are going to communicate thereafter.

Another alternative is to educate home-educated children with other children of the same age, perhaps in a small collective; for example, children of ages seven to 11 (Key Stage 2). In this case it might be possible to variously locate classes so that they are not always in the same place at the same time, and the responsibility for hosting the learning can be shared. This enables the parents to share taking responsibility and to contribute their own particular interests and enthusiasms. A parent who is good at creative ideas might host the messy play, another take responsibility for maths or music, and in this way a curriculum can be designed that accesses the particular skills of competencies of the parents, inspires the children and helps them learn in different ways. Parents can meet for planning sessions together and, in the process, deliver an individual learning experience without being personally responsible for delivering all of it.

## A COMMUNITY PROJECT

**Purpose** To enable pupils to recognise and participate in a range of 'communities'.

**Rationale** A strong sense of community, both in terms of belonging and participation, are seen as desirable outcomes for children of all ages and their families, and are known to contribute to:

- Self-esteem
- Resilience
- Social interaction
- Personal responsibility
- Emotional literacy

This project encourages children and young people, as well as their parents, friends and wider family, to reflect upon how they engage with individuals and the wider community, and how those currently 'outside' the systems of friendship and support might feel and behave.

**Outcomes** Student(s) will know and understand:

- What a community is

- How individuals work together and play together effectively
- How we can be part of different communities and what the communities that surround us are
- What we get and what we take from being part of a community

Student(s) will be able to:

- Evaluate their own contributions to the communities they are part of (family, friendship groups, wider community)
- Empathise with others living different lives within a community
- Work/play with others
- Plan, research and deliver their own contributions
- Share their work with others

**Organisation** This project would work best if a few children work on it at home with their parents or tutors. They can be of different ages but should all be able to complete the tasks with support. All the participating children don't have to be home educated but all should be able to allocate a good amount of time to the work.

If there is a lot of interest when you post the idea to your support site or social networks, organise the children into pods with six participants in each, and have a big meet-up event for the pods to come together and everyone to share their work at the end.

Ideally, the children in a group or pod should meet up once a week to share their progress and ideas. If this is not geographically or physically possible, a virtual meeting via the Internet is the next best thing. Meeting up at the end, however, would be wonderful for the participating children, as it provides an opportunity to celebrate the new community they have created with each other through the project.

If you don't have a network of like-minded families, this could be the start of one. Google your nearest home-school network and get in touch. Invite families who are interested to participate.

The project consists of a half-day initial exercise followed by four weekly tasks that can be completed a little at a time. The child or young person should have the lead in organising their week's tasks and making things happen. At the end of the week they can meet with or communicate with their group to share what they have done and how it went.

The Community Project is all about the groups we are part of:

- Our family
- Our friends
- Our peer group
- Our wider community

Community starts with us and moves out into the outside world through our family to our friends, from our friends to our wider peer group and those we interact with, and finally to complete strangers who share our local environment or a part of it.

Create a booklet for simply recording results at the end of the week – a simpler one for younger children and a more detailed version for older young people.

## Introduction

Let your child know that they are going to be involved with some others working on a set of challenges that are all about helping people in the community. A community is any group of people who live together or work together and can be as small as two or three people or as large as a huge city, or even a country.

For the first activity to get your child or young person thinking about a community, you are going to ask them to draw their idea of a new city. They are going to draw it as a plan, not as a picture, as if they were looking down on it from above. To make this city self-sufficient, it is on an island surrounded by the sea and a long way from any other country.

First, we need to decide what the island/city needs to have. This can be recorded as a list or diagram, such as a spider diagram.

Once they have compiled a carefully thought-through list, they can begin to draw. They might prefer to sketch their island first or they may prefer to just do one drawing. They will need a large sheet of paper or several taped together.

Ask them questions to help them identify new aspects of their community, such as supporting the health needs of the people, supporting the transport of the people – from trains and stations, airports and bus stops, to car showrooms and repair shops.

- Ask them to think about electricity and where it comes from.
- Ask them where water comes from.
- Ask them where the clothes in the shops come from.
- Ask them where the food in the shops comes from.

- Ask them where the furniture in the houses come from.
- Ask them where the Internet service comes from.
- Ask them about phone services and how these work.

If they don't know the answers, look them up together online. Don't just tell them – they learn nothing when you do the work for them.

They may tire before this drawing is complete, so it might be best to work on it for two or three sessions over successive days.

**The first community task – the family**

Ask the student who they consider to be part of their family – perhaps drawing a genogram (a graphic representation of a family tree) or family tree, which provides a great opportunity to dig out some old photos and share some family stories.

The task is simply to choose five things in consultation with the family that will help and support them. These might be individualised actions to help one person, such as clearing up Grandma's garden, or tasks to assist the family well-being as a whole, such as keeping the bathroom super-clean and tidy for a week.

The student needs to decide:

- Who is included in the project? Is it members of their wider family or just the family they live with?
- How will they talk to everyone about what would be helpful? They might hold a family meeting or send round a family email, for example.
- How do you know when something is helpful?

- What is too little and what is too much?

At the end of the week they complete the task 1 sheet in their record booklet, which should contain all their notes and copies of emails, and so on, to share with their group.

### The second community task – friends

Ask the student to identify all the people they consider to be their friends. Are they all the same or are there different kinds of friends? If so, try to categorise or sort these friends into groups.

This task involves being a better friend – a more helpful friend – and it requires the student to talk to their friends to find out what they can do. As before, they need to decide how they will consult their friends, perhaps by having a Saturday afternoon get-together or perhaps by email. They should not agree to do anything they do not want to do or that they would consider unpleasant. They are simply trying to be a better friend and asking for information to help them do this. Younger children may need supervision during this activity if they don't have a group of friends they see regularly.

At the end of the week (or longer if their friendships are long-distance) they complete a brief record in their booklet as well as keeping all their notes, plans and emails, and so on, to share with their work group.

### The third community task – the wider peer group

Ask the student to think about all the other children who live in their town/area that are as yet unknown to them.

The challenge is to set up a simple but fun event and to

invite at least two people they have never spent free time with before. They can invite friends, too, and they will need at least one adult participating.

How could they meet some new children of roughly the same age as themselves who would be glad to have an invitation to a simple but fun event? Perhaps they could invite children with few friends or who don't get to go out very often to do new things? Perhaps they already know some young people like this or have some idea of how to reach them? Perhaps there is a local school or youth centre for young people with disabilities? Perhaps there are young people from the local home education network that they have met but not yet spent any time with?

Firstly, the student will need to plan their event. This might be something happening at their home like a film and pizza afternoon or something happening elsewhere like a game of football in the park. Then they will need to think of some people they already know to invite to help run the event and finally to think of a way of finding some new children or young people to invite.

Create a list of jobs to do, things to find out and how to find them out, and perhaps a budget. A budget is not essential, as there are many things that could be organised for (almost) free, such as a video-game tournament at home, trampolining sessions in the back garden, a 'bake-off' afternoon or a five-a-side football game. If there is a budget, it should be minimal and the student will be expected to work and plan within it.

The hardest part of the challenge will be to identify some new people from their wider peer group and invite them to the event.

As always, at the end of the task they fill in the details in their booklet but keep photographs, notes, planning sheets and to-do lists, and so on, to share with their group.

**The fourth community task – your community**

Ask the student to think about all the people in their town or local area who sometimes need help from others. Create a list and identify what a child or group of young people could do to help. The final task involves helping people they have never met in a meaningful way. It might involve raising money for a local charity, providing clothing or toys for refugee children, collecting food for a food bank, putting together bags of essential items to be given to homeless people, or any number of innovative ideas they may have themselves. A little research online will show any number of projects that children have set up to provide support for some of the more vulnerable people in society and in the world – work with your child to look for as many different ideas as possible before starting to plan.

The student can involve as many other young people as they like in this task, including friends, family or people they have worked with throughout the project. Ideas can be simple or complicated to match the age and capability of the students involved. The simplest idea would be just to empty out their toy cupboard of all unwanted toys to donate to a local charity shop. A slightly more involved project might require encouraging neighbours and friends to also clear out their toy cupboards to make a larger donation, or even having a front-garden toy sale or a stall at a local car-boot sale.

A more involved project might be cooking a large batch

of bacon and egg rolls, wrapping each in greaseproof paper and setting off for the town centre on a Saturday or Sunday to give a treat to all the homeless people gathered there.

For this project, they will have to make their own budget – if they want to cook bacon rolls, they will need to cost the raw materials and find a way to raise that money themselves. Perhaps sponsorship or doing chores for neighbours, friends and family members could raise the cash they need.

At the end of the task they complete their booklet and put together a presentation about the task. This might be a PowerPoint presentation, a slideshow of photographs with captions or a display on boards of planning sheets and photos. These can be taken to the final meet-up with their group so that everyone can see what they did and how they went about it.

Don't forget to ask the student how they feel.

## The role of online social networks

It's important that children feel they have both a peer group and a community, and virtual experiences can be great stop-gaps if you can't be in real ones all the time. There might be very good reasons why meeting in person is difficult – perhaps through illness or geographical isolation – and online contact might be a way of working around the physical difficulties.

Although online social networks have many advantages, they do also carry risks, and younger children are not necessarily resilient enough to deal with negative feedback that might come their way through involvement. Most social networks have an age limit. This is there for a reason and should be respected, so if you do decide to let your child have access below the specified age (for Facebook it's 13), you need to be sitting with your child while they use it, until they reach the required age. Along similar lines, they may want to WhatsApp their friends, but you should discuss boundaries over timing (for example, not during 'school' hours) and reserve the right to look at their phone at any time. You should also exercise control over where they use and leave their device; for example, it's never a good idea for a child to have access to their phone at night, and it should not be with them in their bedroom (even if only for charging).

The art of getting young people to accept and follow rules or behavioural expectations is to not impose them, thus exerting power over them, but to negotiate acceptable boundaries with them. Young children do not have the ability to make choices other than those that they want – so negotiation about anything important is not helpful. By all means negotiate bedtime, work to be done or chores, but don't expect them to keep to any agreement. For young children (under eight years) boundaries should be kind but firm and consistently applied – or they simply won't work. Lots of rewards in the form of well done or thank you, or a high five here and there, will also serve to help them keep to the boundaries.

As the child's brain matures, they become better at doing things they have said they will do, even when they don't want to. This maturation is physical as well as developmental. Your child will not learn to do it at five with lots of practice – they simply can't and don't operate that way. Children expected to keep to agreements made at a young age might well learn that they don't have to keep to any agreements, as nothing happens when they don't comply, so save negotiation until later.

Something like gadgets in bedrooms will always be a sticking point. 'All my friends do', 'You are mean' or sneaking their phone upstairs in their bag, are all common responses. The time to make agreements is before giving them a phone/tablet/laptop for the first time, when they will agree to just about anything in order to get the prized item. When upgrading, this might be another key point for negotiation. Be aware that a negotiation in which all they get at the end of it is more rules and restrictions is never going to work; there needs to be a trade-off of wants and rules to balance things.

There are some fairly alarming pictures on the Internet of plants grown in the proximity of a charging phone, showing no growth or considerable deformity and damage. This was originally a piece of research done as a science project by some students in the US. You might try replicating it as a way of showing good reasons for keeping gadgets out of sleeping areas, as sleep is when the brain does its growing in the young.

Generally speaking, for a home-educated child, social networking is even more important than it is for a child who is at school. They need to maintain relationships with friends and maintain their friendship groups – and social confidence can be built through developing online relationships. For children with specific learning difficulties or socialising issues, online networks targeted to their particular needs can be especially helpful; for example, there are networks for children with ASD where the children can be in touch with each other and communicate in the way they find easiest – without the painful issue of being required to sit together and the difficulty of making small talk. Online networks for such children can be a valuable tool in avoiding feelings of isolation.

Although online networking is valuable, it should not be to the exclusion of maintaining networks in the real world.

It's important for home-educated children not to become 'shut-ins'. Libraries, cafes, clubs and special-interest groups are good, but so are opportunities to mix with people of all ages, perhaps through visiting centres for the elderly or homeless. Such experiences can give children a perspective on the wider world that is important to them and enables them to be more socially aware of the real world than those in school all the time.

## Establishing a community for the parents and carers

The other issue to be considered under the heading of community is the importance of maintaining social networks for the parents of home-educated children.

Assuming responsibility for home educating your child can be a big pressure for parents. In the process, the few hours of the school day, when most parents know their children are safe and well looked after, and which may be the basis of their own working lives, times with other children – or just some down-time from parenting – are missing. Even if tutors are mainly responsible for the home educating, they still have to be managed by the parents/carers, and in the process both parties lack the 'secret life' of being an individual in an institution and where your behaviour is not interpreted, explained or condoned by those biologically or legally closest to you. Home educating offers much more visibility of the participants of the parent–child relationship and this needs thinking about, from your point of view as well as theirs. How are you going to have some wider social variety, to enable you both to explore and experiment with new social relationships, see the consequences, and learn in the process – without you both falling back on the much greater familiarity of each other all the time?

This is particularly so if you are a single parent. Being able to get out of the house is a luxury for any parent, but if funds are tight, this can be hard to achieve. It might be a good idea to set up a reciprocal arrangement if it's hard to afford babysitters, to make arrangements with parents in the same situation and organise a swap. Whereas it's tempting to involve your children in activities that mean something to you – and relate to interests you would like to share with them – it's a good idea to value time spent without your children; either through spending it with others of your own age or just going out on your own.

Parents who are home educating are 'on call' all the time, and you can't run on empty. You need to feed who you are and nourish your sense of self. Being everything to your child is not enough; you need to grow yourself in order to be able to bring new ideas to your relationship with them. As examples of what kind of activities to organise, book and film groups can be valuable, as can loose networks of friends getting together to talk, or perhaps evening classes where you learn something new – and in the process are moving through a series of shared experiences that provide something to talk about afterwards. Whatever you choose, the discussion of issues at an adult level can give you the time and space to return to both home educating and your wider parenting role with a renewed energy.

You will also find that such experiences use different parts of your brain and enable you to change the tone of your voice so that you are not always in parent child mode. Life is about learning and growing all the time, whatever your age, and being around children can block a parent's own development; usually because it's tempting to limit your understanding to their level of comprehension rather than your own. While learning with them can be liberating, enabling you to learn new skills and grow, and having to research how to deliver learning can be very developmental for all involved, you also need to be learning things that interest you, and that are at your own level. Always being in delivery mode can risk you over-involving yourself in your child. Looking ahead, there will inevitably be a need for your child to separate from you, so maintaining your own life in the meantime is very important.

## Questions and answers

**Q:** *One of the reasons we decided to home educate is that our home is very geographically isolated, and it was taking me a ridiculous amount of time to get to and from my son's secondary school. At certain times of the year the weather made it really difficult. But how do we manage to give him a sense of community that he can contribute to?*

**A:** Try to maintain as many of his friendships and relationships from his former school as possible, encouraging them to visit or perhaps come to stay overnight if short trips are difficult. This would ensure that he spends time with friends at weekends. You could also encourage him to try to create a virtual community with other home-educated children. To get started, you could use Facebook or google local availability. You can create a group online using WhatsApp[17] and install a programme such as Booyah, which, working through WhatsApp, allows you both to interact with a group of people at the same time.

You could also schedule several meetings with your home education network members during the week in which you arrange to meet up – online or in person – in order to talk to each other, perhaps to discuss a fantasy football team or a research project on another country. Establishing meetings three or four times a week can be a useful opportunity for the group to talk to each other or work out who is going to do what. Using Dropbox or iCloud can offer opportunities for them to share their work and have real-time interaction using computers.

**Q:** *I recently moved to West London with my Services husband and our two daughters, aged eight and six. The nearest school only had a place for the elder, and as no other vacancy was available locally, we decided to home school the younger child until a place becomes available at the same school as her sister's. At first she was thrilled to stay at home every day, and her sister was quite jealous, but now the older one has started making friends, she is beginning to feel quite left out and isolated. What can we do?*

**A:** If you are living in West London, it should be relatively easy to find other home educated children with whom you can form links so that they can have get-togethers and do some project work together a couple of times a week. This would give her her own mini school group, and it could be a good idea to establish more than one group; for example, one for maths and one for history. She doesn't have to be always working alone.

Assuming your older daughter is happy with this, consider inviting her school friends for play dates and asking them to bring along their siblings, so that your younger daughter gets to meet other children in the new school. Explore options for after-school clubs – even if the school does not have room for her yet, she might be able to join in their after-school activities – and, again, this would get her to meet other children in the school. Find out about local clubs such as Rainbows (for ages five to seven – or four to seven in Northern Ireland), Brownies (for ages seven plus) and Girls Brigade (for ages four plus). Google clubs and activities for her age group in the area, and she will find options. Choose two to three for her to select from only, as offering her too many choices might be overloading her. Ideally only one or two classes or groups a week is best. Hopefully she will be in school soon.

**Q:** *My 14-year-old son is the youngest in the family by several years. His older brothers and sister are away at university, so although he's proud to be part of a big family, over the years he has spent a lot of time on his own. He's a lovely boy but does not always think about others. He's very interested in his own pursuits, and we think he can be quite selfish. He's home educated because he's very musical and we really wanted to focus on his music to give him the best chance of getting into a conservatoire. While the decision we made to support his music education still seems to be a good one, we feel it's vital to support his wider socialisation. He is already polite, but does have the tendency to only think about himself and his own world. How can we encourage him to be part of the world a bit more?*
**A:** If he is happy interacting with others, and developing his talents, you are obviously doing a great job. It's quite common for children who have one area at which they excel to be quite blinkered about anything else, so you are right to want him to be more involved in other aspects of life. This will add to him as an individual rather than taking anything away.

It would be a good idea to encourage him to use his gift to interact with others; perhaps to busk for money in the street for a charity, play for an old people's home or go into schools to demonstrate his skill. It would be good to encourage him to establish a regular commitment with an establishment, so that he feels obliged to continue. He could perhaps talk about his love of music and how it began, and explain the pieces he has chosen to play. Along similar lines, he could offer a masterclass at a local centre, or to tutor someone younger at a local school – his involvement could be really inspiring. He will probably need some support in arranging this. You can go with him – or his tutors could do so (does he need an accompanist?). In addition to supporting him in making the visits, it would be a good idea to talk to him about the experiences, helping him to see the impact he is having, as well as what he is getting, from these interactions with groups.

Having a particular skill can either set you apart from everyone else or be your gift to the wider community. Encourage him to share his enthusiasm and passion – and everyone will benefit, not least him.

## 12

# The Importance of Maintaining Your Child's Self-esteem

Where does self-esteem come from? Essentially, self-esteem comes from feeling that we are successful, that we are people who achieve, that we are both useful and valued. It also comes from ourselves rather than from other people, so it relies on the individual recognising themselves as someone who succeeds rather than relying on others to point it out. If we don't feel good about ourselves, no matter how much others tell us we are marvellous, it will make no difference. On the other hand, if we do feel good about ourselves, someone pointing out our various defects won't make us feel too bad, although it might be upsetting to hear negative opinions from people we value.

For the home-educated child it is important to feel capable and successful, even if there are no others to compare themselves to. This involves introducing honest reflection into every aspect of their learning day. Collecting 'evidence' of change and success is also helpful; looking at their work from a year ago will usually amuse them when they see how much they have progressed.

Our core sense of ourselves is put in place when we are very young, long before we can speak or understand words, and it comes from feeling loved and cared for. The baby who knows that they can influence the world around them to get their needs met experiences themselves as an individual who matters, a feeling they take with them as they grow and learn more about the world. There is some evidence that whether we are glass half-empty or glass half-full people might relate to character traits we are born with, but it is undoubtedly our interactions with others that give us the strongest view of who we are.

It doesn't matter what we succeed in; it can be making people laugh, having friends that care for us, getting to bed on time or staying calm in a busy office. It is recognising ourselves as the source of these achievements both big and small that contributes to our feelings of self-worth and value.

As a child learns to recognise themselves as an achiever by observing and experiencing the reactions of others, their view might become distorted, particularly in our modern success-driven world, into 'How good am I compared to others?': how many friends they have (both online and in person); how good they are at sport; what they look like and how good they are at their various school subjects – criteria that have a lot to do with age and may change with environment and culture. Many children have never learnt to see themselves as achievers except by comparing themselves with others, which can lead to aggressive competition on one hand or feelings of worthlessness or unimportance on the other. After all, in a group of people only one can be the best at any particular activity or at meeting a particular standard. In a world where only the best are considered worthy, most of us don't make the grade; even the exceptional among us might only be top within a very limited range, so we need children to understand that simply being human and alive makes us worthy of as much love, care and consideration as anyone else. On a day-to-day basis each one of us strives for and achieves many things, big and small, and it is all those many achievements along with the things we work towards that make us unique and valuable to ourselves and those around us.

The most important aspect of self-esteem is the ability to believe in oneself, particularly when times are tough, or when we have messed up. Some children are devastated by mistakes or dismissive comments from peers, others shrug their shoulders and try again.

Home educated children, at home all the time, lack the day-to-day stimulation of comparing themselves, and being compared, with others. For many, this is a blessing and may even be one of the contributory factors for the decision to home educate. For some, having no one to compete with or compare progress with can be disempowering and demotivating. Whereas true self-esteem depends on how we feel about ourselves, for those who have not developed a strong and independent sense of self-worth, the feedback and validation we gain from people around us can be crucial to the process, and without such feedback such a home-educated child might be in a difficult position. They have no one to compare themselves with and so cannot gain a sense of how they are developing and learning within a group. Being part of a group can also keep an individual grounded or motivated through observing the achievements and reactions worthy of praise in peers; being on your own can support a false view of who you are in the world, and how your performance compares with that of others.

One of the most helpful ways in which we can learn to recognise ourselves as achievers without comparing ourselves to others is to have time and space to reflect on our actions and choices, and to have a clear vision of what matters and what doesn't. Here the home-educated child has an advantage over their more conventionally educated peers, as they are not constantly bombarded by youth-culture memes and the power of group identity. In primary schools a lack of coordination and a disinterest in sport are probably two of the most notable areas cited for boys 'not fitting in', whereas for girls an inability to read social cues, form alliances and manage disputes can leave them isolated. In secondary schools how you look matters a great deal, and working hard at any area of school work can lead to name-calling and bullying, as there is often a negative association to being a good student. For teenagers, the coolest feedback a pupil can gain may be 'high performance, low effort'. For the home-educated child of any age what matters and where the success criteria lie is managed on an individual basis. Of course, no child is oblivious to cultural influences aimed at their age range, and whether it is Disney princesses or footballers' hairdos, they will still know and understand what the important features of youth culture are.

Helping children understand what matters and what doesn't is reflected in many ways through the relationships within the family. What is discussed at mealtimes, what manners are expected, what viewpoints are expressed and where value and approval are given, all help a child understand their personhood and provide guidance and aspiration for the future. In terms of education, it is important for all children to have clear, attainable targets that stretch them in different ways and which reflect who they are, how they operate and what they know and understand. Setting targets on knowledge alone is simply not enough to produce well-rounded students. Reflecting on process and areas of challenge is just as important as assessing an end result.

These targets need to be measurable and attainable but also challenging, and to reflect the full range of the child's achievement, relating to their behaviour, concentration and dexterity as well as academic standards. If your child is following a syllabus, you may have targets already established. If you are putting together your own learning programme, you may find it helpful to establish developmental capabilities and build the child's understanding of the need to practise from there. Helping them to chart their own progress by encouraging them to decide when they have reached a target will help them progress and improve and consolidate their sense of themselves as someone who achieves – their self-esteem.

Of course, adult feedback is also important as a learning tool for helping them to improve or to identify a target, but how children respond to feedback is influenced by their age, and it is important to know what is helpful; for example, for children up to the age of nine, rewarding them for what they have done right is far more powerful than pointing out what they have done wrong. For a very young child, pointing out all the perfectly formed letters in a sentence or the correct examples of 'line sitting' will encourage greater effort next time. Tying in with a simple target, like 'Well done, there are ten perfectly written letters in that sentence – let's see if you can do 12 in the next sentence', will offer both reward and challenge in equal measure. At about the age of eight to nine a change begins, and for children of this age a degree of constructive criticism frequently works best. For a ten-year-old you could say, 'The paragraph is well constructed and you have used some excellent adjectives to bring your writing to life, but there are some problems with spelling. I can see eight words that are incorrectly spelled – can you find them? Let's make having a whole paragraph without any spelling mistakes one of your targets for next week.'

Teenagers, on the other hand, might find it helpful to reflect on challenges and triumphs and how they can improve, without this being adult led. In general, although they won't like constructive criticism, you can make requests to attend to specific things: 'Please ensure you do this.' Whereas critiquing the whole thing won't be appreciated, asking questions to make them reflect may have more impact. Some adolescents can react aggressively, or out of all proportion to criticism, even to the point of making errors repeatedly and defiantly to prove that they are not going to listen to anyone else's opinion. In such cases, supported target setting, self-assessment and some form of recognition and reward for meeting milestones will work best.

## Children with low or damaged self-esteem

In a competitive value situation, most children will not feel very good about themselves and some may feel very badly about themselves. Children with disabilities can often be made self-conscious or left feeling not good enough in mainstream schooling, and gender, race and ethnicity also have a bearing on how accepted and valued a child might feel in school.

Many children are being home educated because they were bullied at school or were unable to deal with the behaviour of others, or because they were taken out of school due to a particular situation that they might never have resolved. In the short term such a child might feel a great deal of relief to be away from the situation they found themselves in, but in the longer term this might result in them feeling that they can't get along with others and that other people don't like them. Such a feeling can be hard to change and may lead to problems as they get older. A child may have learnt that the only way to deal with other people is to keep away from them. A child who has been taken out of school in these circumstances may view themselves as, in effect, failing at school, and this might sit heavily on their feelings about themselves, and hence their self-esteem in relation to anything they view as school-like.

An effective approach to such issues might be to ask them to identify strategies to deal with the kinds of problems that arose in the past; for example, how to get friends or what to do if people are not nice to you. Such topics are of great interest to young people, so rather than asking them to think about their own situation, ask them to think about how they can help and support other children going through similar experiences. Perhaps they could create a website or blog containing help and advice? Perhaps they could produce leaflets made available for children at the local library? Researching online, reading books or exploring stories and just being able to think about the problems away from the stress of school life can help them create all manner of strategies for managing the behaviour of others without feeling shame or inadequacy.

## Using child-identified target setting to raise self-esteem

It's important for children to take ownership of the process of target setting and achievement: developing targets from the inside out and not the outside in. This helps them to commit to their 'work' and to feel suitably proud of themselves when a target has been reached.

This may, however, be particularly problematic with the child who has poor self-esteem, and who might avoid any form of self-review or target setting by changing the subject, fidgeting or creating a distraction, or even by throwing a tantrum or getting angry – even teenagers! In such circumstances 'baby steps' are required, starting with very simple and clearly measurable targets, such as writing three lines, completing two exercises in a textbook, reading five pages from a book and so on. Such targets do not require any judgements to be made, as success is clear-cut: they either do it or they don't. Make sure that the targets are reasonably attainable in the first instance, and gradually work up to more challenging targets and those that require more thought or quality judgements, such as writing a piece of descriptive prose, completing two pages of work that are neat and tidy, or staying focused on a task for 15 minutes. By mixing absolute targets with quality targets, academic with behavioural, physical with emotional, a parent can begin to stretch the child by ensuring that they have plenty of success to boost their sense of self-worth.

When it comes to setting targets for learning activities, it's important to ensure that they are working towards something that they are interested in and around which they can feel a passion and involvement. There will be times when they have to work on areas of the curriculum for which they have little enthusiasm, but if you involve them in planning when to do these sessions, it will encourage them to feel responsible for themselves and further empowered.

Here is a weekly target sheet for Rashid, aged nine.

## Figure 16: Weekly target sheet for Rashid

| Target | Yes or no? | Comments |
|---|---|---|
| To complete 3 pages in my maths workbook | | |
| To finish reading *A Wrinkle in Time*[21] and write a book review in neat handwriting. <br><br> To stick the review into my book review album. | | |
| To let my brother disagree with me more than 4 times without having an argument. | | |

| Target | Yes or no? | Comments |
|---|---|---|
| To work on my model robot design and to list all the things I need to do next week in order to make it work.<br><br>To provide a list for Dad and Mum of things that need to be found, bought or made by Saturday. | | |
| To make my bed every day.<br><br>To make my own lunch 3 times. | | |

One of Rashid's targets, to use neat handwriting, is supported by a clear understanding of what neat handwriting consists of. There are many examples of neat handwriting checklists to download free from the Internet. A good one is one which details and illustrates the expected criteria.

Targets are not the same as the child's timetable, as they include goals for their work not just the amount of time to be spent on them. Rashid may well have plenty of time in his programme for literacy, but finishing his book is something he has set for himself as a target – something he wants to do in the week ahead as well as any timetabled work.

Fourteen-year-old Natalya has a mixed programme in her week which includes four one-hour sessions working with different subject tutors, each of whom also set her one-and-a-half hour's 'self-study' to be completed by the next week's tutorials. Her targets cover her other learning and exploration work as well as her formalised curriculum. She has had problems in the past with not doing her work, even when she has self-directed it. In order to keep her to her targets she has set up a 'checked by' system – where someone signs her target sheet to 'prove' she has met them. Her targets are about attending and meeting her expectations rather than the quality of her work at this time. These are the targets she has set for herself, with the exception of the cooking target, which was set by the family at a family meeting – they get to choose one target for her every week that benefits the family.

Figure 17: Weekly target sheet for Natalya

| Week beginning 9 October | | | |
|---|---|---|---|
| Target | To be checked and signed off by: | Comments | Personal reflection |
| Complete all set work: Maths English History French | Rufus Emma David Laura | | |
| Spend 2 hours in the library researching suffragettes for project folder. | Librarian David | | |
| Plan, shop for and cook a meal for the family. | Mum Dad Viktor | | |
| Choose 3 novels to read for November – research online reviews to make a choice. | Mum | | |
| Go to the gym 3 times. | Gym attendance record – Dad | | |
| Attend art class. | Mrs Radford | | |

For Natalya, just doing all the things she has said she will do helps her to feel good about herself. She has been labelled lazy and underachieving all her life at school.

Asking a child to identify a reward for meeting all their targets might be helpful, although rewards should be non-material (something like choosing a movie for the family to watch on Saturday afternoon, a trip to the local town with friends, choosing a favourite meal for the family to share and so on) offer a prolonged feeling of achievement and a chance to get some kudos from family members or friends.

Another really valuable strategy for supporting the home-educated child's self-esteem is to ensure that there is something to show for their learning. Pre-packaged syllabuses often include certificates and stickers which can be completed at required stages, but there is still a real value in collecting work completed over a period and packaging it into a document that can be referred to in future.

For younger children, home-made certificates, stickers or 'well-done' cards to stick on the wall, on the fridge or on display elsewhere, give the child an opportunity to show their achievements to visitors and family members as well as having reminders of how well they have done.

## Widening the scope for boosting self-esteem

Some other strategies to support the child's self-esteem include:

- Self-publishing packages offer the chance to make a book out of material that is uploaded to a website. These can be photos or text, and offer a beautiful and lasting record of a child's work at a very low cost.
- A travel log for the season or a journey can be a very valuable way of recording a significant experience.
- Alternatively, buy a nice folder for a completed module or topic work, label it and ensure that it's securely stored for the future. Seeing that an adult values their work and wants to keep it can be a big

boost to a child's self-esteem. For the child, just knowing that a bank of their work is being kept will develop their own sense of personal value, and being able to look back at a their work in the future, and being able to see instantly how improved handwriting and more intricate sentences make progress clear, can support the development of self-worth.

- From there on you could think about how to share this with the wider world; for example, should additional copies be produced and shared with relatives? Could a picture be turned into a family Christmas card or a series of images used for a family calendar?

- Consider producing a yearbook. The process of looking back through a year's work and picking out what best depicts the progress that has been made can be very pleasurable (ask anyone who has put together a 21st birthday book for their child). Information stuck in a scrapbook can be given captions, and you can upload them if your compilation is being made online. You may end up with a better record than in school.

- Might some parts of the work be made available online? This could range from a simple book review to an article or opinion piece. Educational publishers or organisations supporting home education might be interested in sample work for their resource bank, and your child might, as a result, end up contributing to the body of work that is seen by others – this is particularly valuable if it relates to a specific area of the curriculum.

- Feeling proud is very good for self-esteem – and this can apply to the parent as well as the home-educated child. Offer yourself and your child the chance to look back at what has been achieved: the bank of stuff that can be compared with last month, last term or a year ago. Your child is the person who made that happen; you are the person who helped it happen. Help them reflect on what has been achieved, look at the body of work, see how they have grown – and feel proud.

## Questions and answers

**Q:** *I am a home educating parent with a nine-year-old son. We have been home educating him for two years, because he didn't do well being in large classes and we could not afford a private school, but I am now finding that whenever I correct a spelling or a piece of number work he withdraws and won't try again. Of course, I do it kindly, but he tends to disengage when I give him feedback and just gives up. How can I encourage him to have a more open attitude to learning?*

**A:** It's important to take away the notion of right and wrong, so instead of giving him corrections on the work he completes, could you move to more experience-based learning that he can verbally report back? Perhaps you can use different media; for example, could 'answers' to assignments be delivered via photographs, or maths problems explored through building models or drawing pictures? It might be a good idea to take away the notion that answers can only be given using a paper and pencil, and that they have to be marked as either right or wrong. Trying to get him to learn how numbers interact with each other doesn't have to be recorded; it can be spoken and then discussed. Alternatively, you could write down the answers he gives and encourage him to copy what you have written.

If problems with spelling and writing persist, you could use a voice recorder that converts words into text, and encourage him to use the spellchecker as a separate process.

You might also find it helpful to think deeply about how you provide feedback; for example, what are the words you use when discussing accuracy and inaccuracy, and are these words that are associated with failure? Children learn from an early age to feel successful or unsuccessful. Your child, possibly through negative experiences associated with schooling, has learnt that he doesn't learn in the same way as his peers – and it seems that this has been translated to the experience of receiving feedback at home, too. He may have transferred the role of critic from teacher to you, so now you need to take that away. You need to find a way of talking to him that is about recognising his achievements and not his failures.

As an example of such a positive approach in action, when shown a new piece of work, before you consider what is wrong with it, can you both find five things that you love about it? Leave what's not so good to one side, and let him gain confidence from noting what he got right, not wrong. Notice his pleasure as you do it, too. Then, rather than pointing out the errors, ask him if he can see anything he feels might be improved (if there are specific answers to questions, give him the answers to check first). Ask him how he can improve things, and if you can help in any way. By doing this, his self-worth will grow with every mistake spotted and worked on rather than him shrivelling and feeling a failure. It won't be easy straightaway; most changes in approach take time, and you might need him to support you in doing it differently.

**Q:** *We have two home educated children, a 14-year-old girl and a 13-year-old boy. We took a decision to home educate our daughter because of her particular abilities and our desire to stretch her, and her brother naturally did not want to go to school if she did not have to.*

*Our daughter is very academically gifted, and although she gets on with her work, my son is constantly trying to outdo her in little things. He probably feels she is smarter than he is (while this is true, she is also 18 months older) but he constantly provokes silly arguments, puts her down, seeks to score points and turns every day into a competition. He does it to us too, but his sister bears the brunt. It's tiring and unnecessary.*

**A:** Acknowledging that you've got a brilliant sibling is difficult, however old you are, and particularly difficult if the behaviour of those that surround you place an emphasis on a person's value being related to how smart and capable they are.

An individual's value lies in everything they are, not just one aspect. For whatever reason, your son has not got that message. He has probably grown up with a sister who is often praised, and receives a lot of attention and rewards, and so is now trying to prove a point. It's always hard when you believe that someone you know is perfect and you are not. An individual's response might take different paths: it may make you want to copy that person or bring that person down in other people's eyes. In this case, it's not necessarily unkindly meant – he's just reacting. He needs reassurance that he is an individual who has value, even if he might not be as smart as her. He needs to know that you love him just the way he is, and for all sorts of other things rather than how quick he is at academic work. Start encouraging him in things he does well: how well he gets on with his friends, how he copes with the ups and downs of life, how good his manners are, how helpful he can be. These are valuable qualities too. Encourage him to follow his own interests, and all (including his sister) take an interest in them, and he may start to see himself as equally valuable as her.

**Q:** *My daughter is seven and has always been home educated except for a couple of months in reception. I'm a single mum, and she is my only child, so the bond between us is exceptionally strong. That first couple of months in reception were a nightmare for both of us: she would scream and cling on to me every morning when I tried to drop her off, which would end with both of us in tears. On a couple of occasions, when I did get her into school, the school rang me to come and take her home again because she was making herself ill, so in the end I made the decision to keep her at home until she was more independent.*

*Not only is she not more independent, but if anything she's more obsessed with me than she was before, and she can't do anything if I'm not with her. She constantly sits on my lap or even climbs on me and wraps her legs around me when I'm standing up and talking to someone, and she moves my face with her hand so that I'm looking at her. I can't go out alone or even shower alone. She has to be with me, and we even share a bed. I try to boost her self-esteem and tell her that she can do all sorts of things if she would only try, like dressing herself or reading by herself, but she just won't try. I know that her behaviour isn't normal, because I see other children of her age running about playing with each other, which she would never do, but I don't know how to help her.*
**A:** Parents often ask about 'separation anxiety', because it is a phrase that has become popular in parenting circles, but it is actually quite rare in a child as old as yours; however, your description of the way you and your daughter live makes me

think that this could possibly be exactly that, and if it is, the best course of action is to get professional help. The idea that your daughter will just grow out of this is unrealistic – that's not how humans work most of the time. She has known no other way of being, and will only change with carefully structured and supported behaviour modification that should be done with a specialist. You may also need to speak to someone yourself, as some of the things you say would seem to indicate that you, too, have a degree of anxiety about letting your daughter be independent and free. No matter how many times you say you want her to be like every other child, it would seem that you still get a great deal of comfort from how much she adores and needs you, and you have built your life around this relationship.

It is hard to have a true sense of self-esteem when the notion of self is so tied up in another person. Both you and your daughter need to learn to separate and be individuals, and that takes time and practice. The first step might be to book an appointment with your local CAMHS (Child and Adolescent Mental Health Services) who are there to help in all kinds of issues relating to well-being. If you don't want to make the referral yourself, ask your GP to do it for you – they frequently make referrals so will be happy to help. You might have to wait a while for an appointment, but you will get one. There is no quick fix for the situation you are in and it will take time and effort, and possibly a lot of upset along the way. In order to create change, it will be necessary to start taking more steps apart from each other, and while this will be difficult at times for both of you; in the long run it offers the possibility of more freedom and independence as well as greater self-worth for both of you.

# Conclusion

In writing this book we have been helped by many people who shared their successes and setbacks with us, and a few things have become abundantly clear.

Anyone can home educate their child or children. That is, of course, the law, but we also passionately believe that every child deserves to grow into a person able to make their own choices in life and to follow their own path while having a connection to the world around them, and both empathy and compassion for everyone else who shares the planet. For some children this happens at school, for others it happens through the tireless commitment of a parent or parents – or their wider community.

In our lifetime we have seen changes taking place that have altered the environment, human life and social interactions, and possibly even threatened the future survival of our planet, so how the young of today face and embrace those challenges matters more than ever before. Schools alone cannot necessarily provide all the support and individualised learning each child needs in order to become all they can be, so for every parent an element of home education is necessary now. We have been enormously impressed by how dedicated and willing to be challenged so many parents have shown themselves to be, and our aim has been to provide some support for their journey.

Home education is often misunderstood. It is considered to be of less academic value than school education, to provide less social development than school does and to be a breeding ground for extremist thought and minority beliefs. The truth is that it is neither better nor worse, neither more nor less successful; it is just 'otherwise'. There are great schools out there, and there are great home educators too.

Some of the key themes that have emerged during the research and writing of this book include:

1. That with enough commitment and application, surely anyone can home educate effectively. As a parent, managing an effective home education for a child or children is not dependent on qualifications or having achieved a specific educational level. It is rather about commitment and a willingness to facilitate the most amount of learning out of every opportunity that arises and to create as many opportunities as possible.

2. The experience of home education as either learner or educator is often remembered long after it took place – and is often highlighted as enabling a particular closeness between parents and their children.

3. Keeping home-educated children involved in both contemporary culture and their wider community are important issues of which to be aware at all times. With the rapid growth of virtual connections this has never been easier, nor more necessary.

4. Effective resources of every kind are available to support those seeking to home educate. Among the most valuable of those resources are the networks and groups all over this country and other parts

of the world that provide ideas, suggestions and support for each other.

5. The habit of reading for pleasure sustains all forms of education and personal development, and a love of reading is one of the greatest gifts any parent can pass on to their child – for entertainment, information or developing new ideas. It is sometimes one of the things that gets squashed in schools when children are introduced to it too early or in ways that encourage them to feel a failure. No other country in the developed world pushes children from such a young age as we do in the UK. So many learn that they are failures before they are developed enough to perform all the actions and tasks required in reading, writing and maths – the core subjects promoted in schools – before they are even at an age when most children in continental Europe are starting their formal schooling. Home education offers the most natural way of learning these key skills by observing, counting and being read to. A good foundation that inspires children to want to learn these key skills is invaluable.

# Postscript 1

# Maintaining Your Life as a Home Educating Parent

There are many challenging aspects of home educating, but one that doesn't always make it to the websites and blogs is taking care of yourself and your wider network, so that on a day-to-day basis you are not the only person involved in your child's learning journey – and your own life.

## Getting or creating support

To home educate effectively you, your partner (if you have one) and your child(ren) need to network with others to provide support, opportunities for socialisation and shared working for all – as well as the chance for some time to yourself. Becoming part of a local network offers the possibility of sharing responsibility for certain elements of the curriculum, as you can discuss strengths and interests with other home-educating parents. Once you have built your trust in each other you will be able to add variety to the delivery and supplement the educational experience with individuals who can offer a different set of skills: perhaps you could take the children once a week for an extended maths session, they take them for reading or craftwork or football – so you both gain some time on your own. Or perhaps you could contribute to a general pooling of time and talents, organised within a network? Sharing with others means that you are not ultimately responsible for every little bit of their education and their time; you can use the skills, strengths and enthusiasms of other parents in the network for outings and project work, or for managing the other aspects of your life that still need to be attended to – such as shopping, laundry and preparing food. Home educating does not need to have such rigid boundaries as the conventional school experience; the division between 'learning time' and 'non-learning time' is not so firmly established. For many home-educated children everything is part of their learning time.

If you are in a relationship, it is rewarding to share the role of educator with your partner, and with today's more flexible working conditions, parents might find that they are able to work from home on certain days of the week or work extended hours on some days and have more time at home on others. Some parents are managing a full-time job and home education, using flexible working arrangements to juggle home education and paid employment. Even in split families, where parents are no longer living together, it can still be possible to share the education of the child(ren) if you are able to maintain a sufficiently 'professional' or amicable relationship. Co-educating takes a lot of honest discussion, and probably shared planning, too.

It might also be a good idea to see what parts of your wider life you can delegate in order to create time for home educating. Can you recruit someone to help with the cleaning, or draw in grandparents living nearby to feed you a few days a week? Involving the wider family in the whole experience of educating at home can offer benefits to others who might be feeling lonely. You may find that if you ask for wider support you will receive offers that help make the home education part of your life more possible. For parents home educating a child with physical challenges or special needs there may be local volunteers willing and able to give help that might be accessed through your local council volunteer agency or through a local or national charity. There might also be specific grants available to pay for equipment, carer time or resources through a range of charities. There are websites offering compilations of charities and what they offer, such as www.disability-grants. org, which might help you support your child more easily.

Grandparents and other older people from the community might like to be involved in wider activities: reading stories, playing with your children, taking them on trips. Of course, if they are unknown to you, having an up-to-date DBS check is important, but as many older people enjoy spending time reading, playing or sharing skills and educating children, don't be afraid to ask on community noticeboards online or in community spaces where you live. There is no need for them to become part of the whole experience, but rather spend time thinking about who else might like to be involved, reviewing on a regular basis to find out how it is working for everyone, including the adults.

## Creating personal space

The home educated child needs physical boundaries at home just as you do, because learning at home is a 24-hour-a-day process. It's important that both child and parents have spaces within the family home that they identify as theirs and times in which they can pursue quiet and individual thoughts and interests; we all need to isolate ourselves and regroup from time to time.

Other ways of separating the day into home education and wider time could include:

- Having special clothes that you wear during the learning day, both for parent(s) and child(ren).
- Signals/rituals that mark the beginning and end of the day. It's very good practice to get into the habit of filling in (or letting them complete once they are older) your child's journal and both reviewing progress for today and identifying priorities for the morning. This is an ideal end-of-day routine; putting it off until tomorrow means that you have to start by remembering what was done yesterday. It can be a physical book or on the computer. End-of-day rituals for parents you might try include having a shower, changing clothes – or a cup of tea in front of *Countdown*.
- Timetabling so that all parties know when the day ends.
- Wearing a virtual hat – 'I've got my teacher hat on now'.
- Switching the phone off so that it can't ring.
- Being in a specific space.
- Clearing away the books used and putting them out of sight at the end of the day.
- Turning on the television – having 'no more work' or rules such as 'everything neat and tidied away' before you switch it on.
- Turning off the router – so that there are no gadgets in bedrooms.
- Eating – in order to mark the end of the daytime and then fit in evening activities.

## How to avoid burnout

It really helps to have a pre-decided list of fun things to do, for yourself and also for you and your family – a list of pleasant future plans. Some home-educating families we have talked to have formalised the process, writing out things they would like to do on pieces of paper and putting them in a box from which they make an occasional withdrawal. Items for inclusion might be a trip to the park to feed the ducks, a board-game night, making personalised pizzas together, cycling along a beautiful cycle path together to a nice cafe or putting on a workout video and having a go all together, going swimming together, window-shopping or a trip to IKEA to plan a fantasy make-over, spending an hour watching cartoons or making your own, or doing something you've never done before – perhaps ice skating, rollerblading or bungee jumping.

Rewards work on a personal level, too. Have a list of 'feel-good' treats that come without any guilt or agenda to choose from in times of stress or relaxation. Some items to include on your list could be buying yourself a book or a magazine, making a cake, going to the cinema, going for a walk, lighting scented candles, having an aromatherapy bath, going for a cycle ride, sorting out a drawer or mending something. Pick a treat whenever you want some quality time – then, even if it's difficult, or the wrong season, go ahead and do it!

Being at home you have uninterrupted access to the biscuit tin, as well as other treats, so learn to ration yourself with things you generally do to console yourself, particularly confectionary and alcohol. Writing the list of consoling pastimes while you are feeling strong and happy should ensure that when you need a pick-me-up your list of choices will not include items that have a negative echo later on.

You can also help to avoid burnout by having a set of beliefs about your own thought processes. Over-observation of the 'should' in every situation is bad for both our sense of self and our stress levels, so learning to be kinder to yourself, and asking those in your life to remind you of the things that don't matter and the 'shoulds' that can be let go of or worked around will be enormously helpful. The 'shoulds' don't have to run your life for you. It might be a good idea to find yourself a coach/counsellor/wise friend who will listen and help you highlight what is really important.

## Making the most of life in a family

Family time promotes resilience for all of you, making you all feel part of an identifiable group. Knowing your family and being in touch with it can be like the roots of a tree, holding you firmly to the earth with a sense of history and permanence. A family can be a wider, extensive place where we feel a sense of belonging even when relationships are fraught or upsets get blown out of proportion. In a family we learn tolerance and forgiveness – eventually everything blows over. Families don't always get on, but they can learn to value the contributions of different age groups and varying levels of social skills, no matter how often we fall out with them. The poet Lemn Sissay, who lived with a foster family until he was 12, before he was then taken into the care system, commented[22]:

A family is a group of people proving that each other exist over a long period of time. Dysfunction is at the heart of all functioning families, but at the same time a family is also a PR company for itself – and they tend not to like external involvement. Lacking a family from the age of 12 I had no one to dispute the memory of me.

Not getting on can be as big a learning experience in a family as togetherness. Social resilience is developed through being around people who don't always do what we want them to. Today a family does not have to be biological – it might be friends rather than relatives; stepsiblings or stepchildren, who are going to be there through thick and thin, people who become the families that we create for ourselves.

How we keep in touch with them can be digital or real time – via Facetime, video conferencing, Skype – the mechanism doesn't matter. What does matter is making sure that these important relationships are part of a family's life, providing a sense of community within and without to rely on. Families also give children a different experience of what does and does not matter in life; even when family members seem to hate each other at times, the relationship continues and eventually moments of caring and happiness take place. Noticing the good moments is important for you as a parent and for them too – knowing that a family is both a trial and a joy matters, and learning that relationships take effort is a valuable life lesson.

We have recommended the importance of regular family meetings in our other writing on parenting, and for the home-educated child the family meeting is every bit as important. A family meeting should not be about the home education but rather about family life, and whose responsibility it is to do what. Essentially, it is about recognising problems without blaming anyone and coming up with a range of solutions to try. At the next meeting we reassess: did the solution work? If yes, we adopt it from now on; if no, let's look at another from the list of options we created to try.

A family meeting enables everyone to review different roles, consider how the unit operates as a group and discuss issues that are common to all. Our book on parenting teenagers, *Whatever!*[23] offers a list of ten principles – of which you might only discuss two at a single meeting to decide how things need to be. The greatest strength of regular family meetings is discussing as equals the issues that come up on a daily basis that affect everyone. The most important feature is that the family is open and honest – even about the difficult things – and that everyone has an equal voice.

## Privacy

Finally, have your own boundaries for the home educated child. The tendency today is for children to have access to everything, and for parents to have relatively little time or space of their own. Insist on it – your room, your space, your bed. Children should not have access to your sleeping space, which for some parents is the only private space they have. Obviously, if your young child is unwell or frightened in the night they might get to snuggle in bed with you for comfort once in a while, but this is a rare and limited occurrence. Your room and bed are not shared family space. Too often the rights offered to children are not echoed in the way parents manage their own time and space.

As children grow older they often want parents to leave their rooms alone and to respect their privacy in the same way that they respect that of their parents; however, this agreement over 'private' space is one that has to be earned. If they want their room to be private, they need to take responsibility for it – which includes cleaning it and keeping it tidy, putting washing in the basket and changing sheets, and so on. They don't get to have a private room with maid service. It is either a room you go into or it is a room you don't go into – but one that is always maintained to a certain level of cleanliness and order. An important part of childhood is growing towards privacy and personal responsibility.

It is important to mention that too much responsibility being given to young children can cause anxiety; most children need to feel held. The offering of too much choice – leaving everything 'up to you' – can be bewildering and worrying. Although children's views and opinions should be listened to, they need to feel that the ultimate responsibility for making most decisions rests with adults until they reach an age where they are neurologically capable of complex reasoning and decision making. It is worth noting that the ability to make a choice based solely on consequences, when you would rather do something else, is among the last skills to be formed and is not in place before the early twenties.

Children often need to share their bedrooms with siblings, in which case deciding on private space can be difficult. In such circumstances, the issue of private actions is more important than private places. When lying on their bed, perhaps reading or listening to music using their headphones, a sibling has the right to be private – and to be left alone. Deciding what and when privacy is allowed, and how this can be managed, might take up several discussions at family meetings. Siblings might choose to create a contract with each other or post their own set of rules on their side of the room. Ideally, respect should be something that is understood and valued rather than demanded and written down, but sometimes clear lines and boundaries can help as a starting point to a greater understanding. Gill has seen personal privacy created in one family of several children, living in a small house with a long garden, where each family member had their own garden shed.

Similarly, you are entitled to property of your own, such as your laptop, and your clothes and toiletries, so that children become aware of boundaries; however, for the child, we would maintain that no gadget is fully private until they reach around the age of 16, and a child's awareness that their phone might be monitored can make them more careful about what they do, who they contact and how they 'speak' in texts and apps. Their personal diaries, if they have them, should, however, be strictly private. Gadgets can be seen by you because they potentially carry the risk of unwanted behaviour from others or contact by people unknown to you – a paper diary does not. If they want to keep a personal diary it can be kept on a computer – obviously not online so that it is not shared with others, or they can use a more traditional paper one. It can even have a lock and key, if they like, or it could be kept in a lockable box.

Finally, remember to have fun, with your child(ren), your partner (if you have one) and your friends. Education is not always a serious business, and it is often the things we enjoy the most that not only make life good but also help us to learn.

## Questions and answers

**Q:** *My home educated child does not understand that I sometimes want to go to the cinema with a friend rather than taking him along, too. He is so used to being with me all the time that I can understand his reaction, but his protests are hard to deal with.*

**A:** You are doing the right thing, and need to help him understand the importance of a variety of relationships being important to all of us. You need to point out to him that there are times when we all enjoy the company of one friend over another, and no one (not even him) wants to be with the same person all the time. Spending some time with a friend is not a negative reflection on your love for your child, or the importance of their love to you, just part of understanding that we all need to be with people of our own age or peer group from time to time. Whatever you do, don't let what your child says stop you, even if they don't understand. You are not giving him a good role model if you give into his demands all the time.

**Q:** *I gave up work to stay at home with my children all the time and manage their education at home, but to be honest I now miss the intellectual stimulation of work, and am finding that being with my children full-time is not as engaging and satisfying as I hoped it would be. I find myself getting bad-tempered with the children and need to improve my attitude.*
**A:** We need to introduce you to the parent asking the previous question. You need to build up your network, and use it to provide you with both stimulation and free time. Try to be proactive, to find new ways to recognise your achievements in managing the situation at home. One of the key differences between working at home and in the workplace is the lack of feedback; there is usually no one to tell you have done a good job or to acknowledge your effort.

You therefore need to find your own criteria for success. Aim for these on a daily, weekly or monthly basis, as befits the complexity of what you are setting up and the goals you are seeking to achieve, then check off your own performance against them. Many people pay more attention to what they are getting wrong rather than what they are achieving, so if that's you, make a point of writing down five things you did right each day. When you feel right about yourself, you will be a better encourager of your child. You could also, funds permitting, get access to a life coach or a counselling friend, who can help you get a better perspective. Whether it's a paid role or a sympathetic friend, it is really important to have someone to offload to. Let them listen, but then do a swap back, so that you share the positives with each other. Taking care of yourself and your self-esteem is very important to the process of supporting your children.

**Q:** *How early in a relationship should we introduce the idea of home education? Being a home educator is something I am very proud of, but it tends to attract negative attention from those I meet. I want to build sympathy towards home educators. Can you advise on what I should say?*
**A:** As your network gradually builds with other home-educating parents, you will find you need less explanation – after a while those you meet who are doing the same thing will be looking for reinforcement from you.

In explaining to the unconvinced, think about a wording you are happy with – such as 'We decided to home educate our child as we thought it the best option for him' – you could add 'at the moment' but don't feel you have to justify your choice. If there's a silence, then don't feel you have to fill it. It might be that those who have made other choices see a decision to home educate as an attack on the choices they made, in which case it might be helpful to stress that this was your family's decision in response to particular challenges you faced. You could also stress that research has shown that home-educated children tend to achieve well both academically and in the workplace.

Sometimes the most difficult responses can come from your

own family, who might be particularly critical if your choices differ from those they have made. But sharing some of your processes might help them understand the choices you made. You could also consider blogging about what you are doing, and sharing your findings, so that others can see the progress your children are making.

Finally, be a little patient. The more you share who you are and what matters to you – the more you will find that sympathetic or open-minded people are drawn to you. In general, if we want intimacy, we have to share something of who we really are.

The bottom line is that you cannot get everyone to agree with your choices, but you don't need them to. If they want to have a go, let them. Listen kindly and point out that they cannot change your belief any more than it appears you can change theirs, so why not talk about something else.

If you do lose some friends or acquaintances along the way, good riddance; you'll soon find plenty of like-minded others with whom to share your ups and downs.

## Postscript 2

## Getting the Terminology Right: Is Educating Children at Home 'Home Schooling' or 'Home Educating'?

When we were asked to write a book about home educating we were full of interest and enthusiasm – but we soon became aware that the topic sometimes divides opinion within parents and groups that support them, not least over the terminology used. Although the UK Government website, and other official bodies, refer to 'home schooling' we were quickly made aware by many of the parents we spoke to that these committed and dedicated people have strong feelings about the term, choosing instead to refer to themselves as 'home educators' and their children as 'home educated.' We gathered the views of those involved.

### A PARENT'S VIEW

Commenting on the terms 'home educated' and 'home schooled', a parent remarked: 'There is no absolute legal use of either term in the UK. The only term used to describe what we do is in section 7 of the Education Act 1996, which talks about parents' obligation to provide an education to their children either at school or "otherwise", which is where the organisation Education Otherwise gets its name from.'

The term home schooling was popular in the early days of our movement (the 1980s through to the late 1990s) largely because the home schooling movement in the US took off a decade before the UK movement (the mid-1970s), mainly as a result of the Equal Rights amendment which put black children in formerly white schools in the south of the US. Many white families objected to this, which led to them withdrawing children to home school them instead, and the term that was used in the US was simply adopted in the UK, as it was already established in much of the literature.

Up until the mid-1990s what we do was described by most people as 'home schooling', although a few people used the term 'home education'. From the mid to late 1990s, however, there were discussions about whether the name should be changed to 'home education', discussions that largely centred on the association UK-Home-Ed, and its mailing list – which has since become www.homeeducation.org.uk.

For those who embarked on home schooling, visits to inspect what was going on were the norm, and a refusal to allow them could easily result in social workers turning up at the house with police in tow. Those doing the inspecting were often retired head teachers, many with no experience of home education, so would arrive at the home with the expectation of seeing 'school at home', or some experience that related to their time working in schools. There were at that time very few home educators, perhaps only 2,000–3,000 in the UK as a whole.

Online discussion became very engaged in the issue of whether those involved in 'home schooling' were rather organising 'school at home'. A group of us therefore set about calling it 'home education' and writing to all local authorities trying to change the term they used away from 'home school'. There were other terms we objected to as well, particularly EOTAS (Education Other Than at School, see page 91), as in the 1996 act this referred to children enrolled at a school but receiving an education at home paid for by the local authority, usually due to illness, disability, long-term exclusions or pregnancy. EOTAS had specific laws relating to it, and some local authorities, who didn't train or even inform their staff, were applying the wrong legislation to those home schooling. We worked very hard to change the perceptions of local authorities to enable people to be able to home educate in whatever style they wanted by getting all parties to use the term 'home education'.

By around 2000 most local authorities were referring to us as 'home educators', or elective 'home educators' or even 'elective, home-based educators' – or some other version of those words.

As the community has grown, from a couple of thousand to perhaps as many as 100,000 home-educated children in the UK (including Scotland, Wales and Northern Ireland), the message has, however, been diluted. Many of those new to the community do not know about the history of the term and why it was regarded as so important. Local authorities have, on the whole, changed their attitude. Although some families still have problems with them, fewer local authorities expect to see 'school at home' as the standard approach.

While some people continue to feel strongly about the issue, and there are Facebook groups where persisting in calling yourself a home schooler can lead to your removal from the group, many now involved routinely refer to themselves as home schoolers.

## ANOTHER PARENT COMMENTED:

In December 2015 Liz Truss, then Secretary of State for Education, put out a press release damning 'home schooling' (sic) as a means to radicalise children. Truss's comments were followed by remarks from Neil Basu, a senior officer in the Metropolitan Police, who claimed that home schoolers were a hotbed of radicalisation. The home educators thought it significant that Truss, a professional politician, had used the term 'home schoolers', thus separating from inclusion in her remarks those who are 'home educating'.

Since then, the media, legitimately exploring the issue of children being radicalised, has, however, increasingly used the term 'home school' for all those educating at home; failing to distinguish between those educating at home for individual, ideological or practical reasons, and those keeping children at home for intentional isolation/suspected radicalisation and those who are excluded from school (such as for behavioural problems or pregnancy) and are therefore being home educated by default. The issue of illegal schools, usually established without permission or inspection to educate children within particular ideologies, has also confused the issue – and led to blurring of boundaries and intentions.

Home educators remain resentful that isolated examples of those convicted of the abuse or incarceration of children are represented as a representative sample of the community involved with home educating in general; for example, on 18 February 2018, *The Sunday Times* made no distinction between children being educated at home with those who are being radicalised and encouraged to join ISIS[24]:

> tens of thousands of home schooled children in Britain, many of whom are completely 'missing' from official records. Either their parents never enrolled them in school or, if they did, councils were not notified when they were withdrawn.
>
> No one knows how many have disappeared. Councils put the number of home-schooled children in England alone at 45,000; home education groups say it is closer to 80,000.
>
> Last November the peer Baroness Cavendish told the House of Lords that it was 'an outrage' that the government did not know the exact figure. It is amid fears that growing numbers of such children are at risk of being radicalised, trafficked, abused – or simply growing up ignorant – that peers will next month be asked to back a new law setting out plans for a compulsory register of children once they reach school age.

Similarly, Sally Weale, Education Correspondent of the *Guardian* reporting the rise in pupils being educated through 'alternative provision' in October 2017 conflated the story with those being home educated in general.[25]

Toby Harnden, reporting for *The Sunday Times* on the plight of the 13 Turpin siblings, found them to be at home, malnourished and cruelly treated, and was swift to make the link between their situation and their manner of education:

> Like almost 1.8m youngsters – more than 3 per cent of America's school age population – the Turpin children were taught at home. David Turpin, a university-educated computer engineer who worked as a defence contractor, registered his house as Sandcastle Day School, at one point classifying it as a private religious institution. California law dictated that no oversight was needed beyond a fire safety inspection, and even this was not carried out.[26]

It is worth noting, however, that it can be very difficult to find out about home educating unless you are part of the community already doing so. Presumably fearing negative feedback, most user groups are not open to the public. Home educators in general prefer to give statements to investigating journalists rather than interviews, and there are concerns that the trends quoted by those supporting home education (for example, that children do better being educated by their parents) are largely unproven given that many home educated children do not take part in formal testing.

Rachel Coleman, founder of the US organisation the Coalition for Responsible Home Education[27] (CRHE), believes that physical and verbal abuse, and educational neglect, are easier to hide in this context:

> It's not that we would argue that home-schooling parents are worse because they home-school, or that home-schooling itself is abusive. It's just that when there are already risk factors for abuse, home-schooling can further isolate a child already in crisis,' said Coleman. 'There are no safeguards in place to protect the children in home-schooled families.[28]

Home educators would argue that to assume all home-educated children are being mistreated or radicalised overlooks the completely valid educational and social reasons why some parents choose to educate their own children rather than assume that the state should take control of the process. They would also point out that in the UK, if children are not registered for a school place they are not required to inform the local council. It is perhaps surprising, given the amount of data held about us all today, that the details of children of school age are not already held as part of the wider documentation of society. And issues of child mistreatment regrettably occur regularly amongst those being schooled through state systems, with post-tragedy enquiries just as regularly asking how the signs could have been missed.

# Resources

**Further information and useful websites:**

**BBC** Information from the BBC on home education and access to relevant resources. www.bbc.co.uk/schools/parents/home_education.

**The Home Office** The Home Office website – very clearly written. www.gov.uk/home education. You can find out more about safeguarding issues here: www.gov.uk/government/publications/safeguarding-children-and-young-people/safeguarding-children-and-young-people.

**The National Association for Special Educational Needs** www.nasen.org.uk/about.

**Other websites and organisations**

Home education information, support, resources and networking:

**Education Otherwise** A UK charitable organisation supporting home education through community, information and promotion. Provides information on local groups. www.educationotherwise.org.

**Elective Home Education Service** An excellent free platform for finding what you want in terms of resources, events and general information. The site does not review or recommend, but simply offers a portal where you can easily browse appropriate materials and providers by age of child. www.electivehomeeducationservice.co.uk.

**Home Education in the UK** Information, local networks by area, resources and descriptions for teaching specific elements. http://home-ed.info.

## Organisations/websites offering specific support.

### ASD (Autistic Spectrum Disorder)

**Express** is a non-profit charity that offers a community cafe and hub in the heart of the community in Kingston upon Thames with an autism-friendly environment that includes quiet areas and sensory areas, fully accessible facilities and opportunities for people on the autistic spectrum to express themselves through art and social media. There is drop-in advice and support as well as opportunities for volunteers and work opportunities for carers. The website gives details of groups and activities running at the centre, including dads' groups and girls' groups, as well as others. www.expresscic.org.uk.

**The National Autistic Society** National charity solely concerned with supporting people with ASD and their families. Information, advice and a helpline. Not specific to home education, however. www.autism.org.uk.

**PPUK Potential Plus UK** Address: Challenge House, Sherwood Drive, Bletchley, Milton Keynes, MK3 6DP. www. potentialplusuk.org.

READING AND LITERACY DIFFICULTIES

**British Dyslexia Association** A range of support information, resources for free or to buy, and information on events, webinars and services. www.bdadyslexia.org.uk.

**The Driver Youth Trust** is a national charity dedicated to improving the life chances of children and young people, with a focus on those with literacy difficulties and who may have SEND (Special Education Needs and Disability), particularly children with dyslexia. 'We focus our resources on specific areas where we believe we can make a sizeable and sustainable difference with a view to creating systemic change in how young people who face literacy difficulties are supported in education.' The website provides excellent resources for supporting children and young people at all levels. www.driveryouthtrust.com.

## Tutoring

There are many online and 'in-person' tutors and tutoring services – we cannot include them all; however, if you find a local service that seems to suit your needs, check that it is registered with the Tutors Association, which takes individual and corporate members.

**The Tutors Association** This is the professional body for tutors and the tutoring profession in the UK. All members are DBS checked. The website allows members of the public to find tutors or check that tutors are members, as well as access to some interesting blogs. http://thetutorsassociation.org.uk.

## National Curriculum sites

**Council for the Curriculum, Examinations and Assessment**
This is the Northern Ireland review and advisory body. The website offers resources and information. http://ccea.org.uk.

**Curriculum for Excellence** Education Scotland's site, which provides information on its Curriculum for Excellence, including areas not given much time or space in the general UK Curriculum such as experiences and outcomes. Useful for all. Curriculum downloads and learning benchmarks are available to download in Gaelic or English. Useful Parent-zone with a 'learning at home' section. Designed for all parents, and not specific to home-educating families but includes excellent downloadable activities. https://education.gov.scot.

**Gov.Uk** Information on the National Curriculum for England, with programmes of study by subject. Also includes a link to find local advice on 'Elective home education' from your council. www.gov.uk.

**Learning Wales** General curriculum information, but also a downloadable database of learning resources available in the Welsh language. http://ccea.org.uk.

## Learning resources

Free or low-cost resources (under £5 per month):

**BBC Bitesize** Huge range of small clips to enhance any topic, arranged by age and subject for all four UK countries. Free sign-up. www.bbc.co.uk/education/clips.

**Quizlet** A website that allows you to make online teaching materials and lessons – perfect for home learning. Sophisticated tools for students to make their own learning sets or for 'teachers' to make them to use with students, student tracking so that you can see what they have done and what needs further attention, lots of excellent diagrams to use and other ready-made materials – although some are very specific to particular elements of a curriculum. Range of packages available giving greater access to tools and resources from free to £2.92 per month. https://quizlet.com.

**TES Teaching resources** (*Times Education Supplement*) Over 700,000 resources, from diagrams to lesson and topic plans. Some free, some paid for by item; all created and posted by teachers or other professionals. PowerPoint presentations, videos and paper activities or plans to download. Also available, materials produced by organisations concerned with health and well-being or broader education concerns such as the British Nutrition Foundation or Oxfam's excellent world issues and ecology materials. Registration is free. www.tes.com/teaching-resources.

**Commercial resource/education sites with costs** (2018) – these are intended as samples only; there are many more online. These have not been vetted by us, so make sure you look at user feedback, results and the small print before purchasing. Home-education networks are a great place to find out about resources and agencies.

**EdPlace** Online support or teaching materials and lessons aligned with UK National Curriculum maths, science and English from year 1 to GCSE. Can be a top-up or a full course. Prices vary from parent to teacher, as the services are different. Offers a £1 trial. Packages start from £99 a year for a three-subject single-student package. www.edplace.com.

**InterHigh** An online secondary school providing a full Key Stage 3 and 4 education at home. It also works to exams and has impressive exam results. Students learn at home using Cloud-based lessons, which can be accessed at any time to suit. Enrolment is online and is like any school. There are open days. 'InterHigh school offers families a special home-educator's package. Families are able to choose any 3 subjects from all the current subjects on offer, including core and additional subjects, and study these subjects for a year's course for a total of £2,100 a year. (Key Stage 3 only – years 7, 8 and 9) The commitment is for a minimum of a year and there is an option to pay in 10 monthly instalments by direct debit of £210 a month . . . In year 10, families can choose any 3 subjects from all the current subjects on offer, including core and additional subjects, and study these subjects as a 2-year course for a total of £4,200 (year 10 only) The commitment is for the duration of the iGCSE course, i.e. years 10 and 11, and there is an option to pay in 20 monthly instalments by direct debit of £210 a month.' www.interhigh.co.uk.

**Reading eggs** Online platform for teaching children to read with interactive books and games. Also offers an online maths programme. 'Our 12 month subscription will give your child access to all parts of the Reading Eggs and Reading Eggspress programmes for children aged 2–13, including 120 reading lessons, 96 spelling lessons, over 200 comprehension lessons and over 2500 e-books in our online library. The cost of the subscription is £39.95 – that's less than £3.40 per month! Our 12 month subscription to Mathseeds will give your child access to all parts of our growing numeracy programme for children aged 3–6. The cost of the subscription is £29.95.' Combined subscription also available. www.readingeggs.co.uk.

# Appendix

# Tips for Storage and Equipment

A former reception teacher has provided some useful tips for creating a stimulating home learning environment for a primary- or nursery-aged child (to use alongside the suggestions in Chapter 5).

When a school sets up a new nursery or primary classroom it costs thousands of pounds in storage equipment and resources. For a home educating parent the same can be true – but it doesn't have to be. There are lots of places that sell 'educational' resources on the high street or online at considerable cost, but almost all toys and activities they sell can be purchased elsewhere, bought/received pre-used – or made yourself for a fraction of the cost.

With younger children, you need to have a lot of different objects to sort, count, sequence or use for experimenting with in water, with weights or balances or for using within artwork and collage.

Buying these in the kinds of quantities required can be expensive, so try instead to collect shells, clean pebbles, buttons, marbles, small plastic cars, plain plastic counters, bottle tops and so on. Ask your friends and family to save things for you, too, as well as sharing ideas with your home education network.

There is a lot of debate about glitter at the moment, as it is virtually indestructible and finds its way into the oceans eventually, where it is harmful to marine life. Most children love it, but most children also love animals and the sea – so think carefully about using it.

A lot of schools and parents use food items for artwork such as pasta and pulses. Personally, I feel that this is not teaching children to respect food and to understand that food is a valuable commodity that some people can only dream of having in any quantity. Teaching children respect for those without the advantages most of us routinely experience can take many forms, and I believe that not using foodstuffs for decoration and art is one of them. Try instead using things from the natural world that you collect together, such as pressed flowers or leaves, conkers and acorns, if you can find them, feathers (but not bought ones), stones and shells, and so on. You could make collecting found items part of every walk or outing.

Storing all these items can be cheaply done using plastic takeaway containers with lids. Again, these can be collected free from people you know or bought online or from a shop, brand-new for as little as a few pence each. The more you buy, the cheaper they are, so think about buying a generous quantity and selling on those you don't need. As they won't last forever, having a good supply is useful. They can also be used for storing mixed paint or glue so that it won't dry out, and any number of small items. The boxes come in different sizes and stack neatly on top of each other.

One of the other items that every classroom has in abundance is the plastic tray. These come in bright colours and are used for storing books, paper, children's work and larger items. The cheapest versions are advertised as litter trays for pets and, again, these can be bought very cheaply online.

Some other items that you can buy (all available new on eBay) to use for storage or for activities include:

- Rigid plastic seed trays. The best ones are those with holes in the bottom, as these are easy to clean and wash out. They tend not to come in attractive colours, but they are a really useful resource for great table-top storage to prevent everything ending up on the floor while the child is engaged in an activity.
- Inflatable paddling pools for babies make excellent cheap alternatives to water-, messy- and sand-play trays. These are small and can easily be used on the table. There are inflatable sand and water trays for sale costing a few pounds, which are also useful, but the sides are quite low so they can be messy.
- Compartment dinner plates – the sort used for school dinners – make great sorting trays. These come in different shapes and sizes including some that look like big flowers. They can be used for the buttons, beads and other items that you keep for sorting practice – or for generally keeping a neat-and-tidy workspace.
- Wooden flowerpot trays are large trays divided into five or 10 equal compartments, which are great for storing pens, pencils or chalks, or for the general storage of small items.
- Plastic bottles make great paint pots, although the best was the old-fashioned straight-sided bottle which is rarely found these days. One-and-a-half litre water bottles work well. Cutting each plastic

bottle in half and smoothing any rough edges will give you a disposable or reusable paintpot. If you can find a straight-sided one, carefully cut it and invert the top into the base to make an excellent paint/water/gluepot that won't topple with a brush left in it.

• Kitchen-cleaning caddies – plastic boxes with a handle in the middle – make great storage for anything that might spill, such as paint and water pots and messy brushes.

Storing trays can be a problem, and the bespoke chests designed to take them can be quite expensive. An old chest of drawers with the drawers removed and a cheerful coat of paint makes a great tray holder. One can often be picked up for nothing on your local Freeshare network – easily managed through the Trash Nothing app.

Buying items such as paint and glue is cheapest in bulk, so try to find some other people from your home education network to buy with, or sell on any unused quantity.

Rolls of lining paper can be a cheap alternative to sheet paper. Thread a heavy string through the middle and hang it high on a wall for a great alternative to an easel. Just pull down a new, clean length whenever you need to. You might first want to make sure that there is either a plastic sheet covering the wall or that you have painted the wall with washable gloss paint – and that there are plastic sheets or wipeable tiles on the floor surfaces beneath.

Blackboard paint can transform an old cupboard door into a fun chalking area, and you can buy reusable whiteboard sheets on a roll that stick to the wall by static alone and therefore leave no marks. These can be drawn or written on using washable felt pens or dry-wipe markers.

# Notes

1 For example, Price Waterhouse Cooper https://www.pwc.com/gx/en/services/people-organisation/workforce-of-the-future/workforce-of-the-future-the-competing-forces-shaping-2030-pwc.pdf

2 www.potentialplusuk.org

3 Lin Bian, Sarah-Jane Leslie, Andrei Cimpian, *Science*, 27 Jan 2017: vol. 355 (6323): 389–91

4 Damon E. Jones, Mark Greenberg, Max Crowley, 'Early social-emotional functioning and public health: The relationship between kindergarten social competence and future wellness', *American Journal of Public Health*, 1 Nov. 2015, vol. 105 (11): 2283–90

5 www.nytimes.com/2018/01/16/us/california-captive-family.html

6 For example, Lab in a lorry: http://www.kingston.ac.uk/schools-and-colleges/book-activities/lab-in-a-lorry

7 www.theguardian.com/education/2011/dec/05/rise-of-flexi-schooling

8 http://hollinsclough.staffs.sch.uk/Flexi.htm

9 www.oxfordshire.gov.uk/cms/sites/default/files/folders/documents/childreneducationandfamilies/educationandlearning/schools/atschool/absence/EducationSupervisionOrder.pdf

10 www.legislation.gov.uk/ukpga/1996/56/part/VI/chapter/II/crossheading/school-attendance-orders

11 Department for Education. Research evidence on reading for pleasure, May 2012. www.gov.uk/government/publications/research-evidence-on-reading-for-pleasure

12  Chris and Ellyn Davis, Elijah Company (2004), Double Portion Publishing Inc.

13  'The link between pupil health and well-being and attainment: A briefing for head teachers, governors and staff in education settings', PHE, 2014

14  *Habits of Mind*, Arthur L. Costa and Bena Kallick, 2009, artcostacentre.com

15  Stacia Garland, 2014, www.exquisite-minds.com, quoted with permission

16  Carrie Clark, Speech and Language Kids www.speechand languagekids.com

17  As of May 2018 users of WhatsApp must be over 16

18  One of the earliest systems of writing

19  Creator of the first English dictionary 1604, 149 years before Dr Johnson

20  Personal, Social, Health Education

21  *A Wrinkle in Time*, Quintet (Volume 1), Madeleine L'Engle, Square Fish

22  Talk at Kingston University, 21 February 2018

23  Hines and Baverstock, *Whatever! A Down-to-Earth Guide to Parenting Teenagers*, see the appendix, Piatkus, 2nds edition 2017

24  'Hunt begins for the legions of missing children being educated at home', *The Sunday Times*, Sian Griffiths and Iram Ramzan, 18 February 2018, p. 9

25  'National figures for excluded pupils "tip of the iceberg"', *Guardian*, Sally Weale, 10 October 2017, p. 8

26  'Tortured and starved', *The Sunday Times News Review*, Toby Harnden, 21 January 2018, pp. 26–27

27  www.responsiblehomeschooling.org/

28  www.theguardian.com/us-news/2015/oct/19/raashanai-coley-dark-side-home-schooling

# Index

reports and feedback 64, 108, 110

safeguarding issues 111

selection 110–11, 139–40, 194

small-group tuition 64, 65, 131

structuring the experience 64

Tutors Association 325

university 51, 52–3, 65, 84

unruly children 195–8

video games 197

tournament 272

vulnerable people in the community, helping 273–4

Wales 80, 90

Washington, George 14

Watson, Emma 14

well-being, promoting 162

'What do we do if ... ?' game 262

'What would you say if ... ?' game 234–5

WhatsApp 275, 279

whiteboard sheets 334

whole-family projects 97

Williams, Serena and Venus 14

workbooks 138

working in groups

behaviour guidelines 242–3

helpful and unhelpful behaviours 244–5

marking performance 243–4

reflection sessions 245

social skills 241–5

time limits 243

very young children 243

*see also* collaboration and co-operation; home-educators networks

worksheets 138, 158

writing skills

creative writing/storytelling 127–8

difficulties 176–7

four- to seven-year-olds 123

handwriting practice 126–7, 156–7, 291

multi-faceted 156

'muscle memory' 127

narrative progression 156

reluctant learners 155–8

seven- to 11-year-olds 126–7

writing for purpose 127

Yahoo Answers 212, 248

yearbooks 294